Rebel Girls

Rebel Girls

Youth Activism and
Social Change across the Americas

Jessica K. Taft

NEW YORK UNIVERSITY PRESS
New York and London

NEW YORK UNIVERSITY PRESS
New York and London
www.nyupress.org

Library of Congress Cataloging-in-Publication Data

Taft, Jessica K.
Rebel girls : youth activism and social change across the Americas /
Jessica K. Taft.
p. cm.
Includes bibliographical references and index.
ISBN 978-0-8147-8324-5 (cl : alk. paper) —
ISBN 978-0-8147-8325-2 (pb : alk. paper) —
ISBN 978-0-8147-8337-5 (ebook)
1. Teenage girls—Political activity—America. 2. Youth—Political
activity—America. 3. Social action—America. I. Title.
HQ799.2.P6T35   2010
305.235'2097—dc22   2010024128

New York University Press books are printed on acid-free paper,
and their binding materials are chosen for strength and durability.
We strive to use environmentally responsible suppliers and materials
to the greatest extent possible in publishing our books.

Manufactured in the United States of America
c   10 9 8 7 6 5 4 3 2 1
p   10 9 8 7 6 5 4 3 2

*For all the girls fighting the good fight
in their schools and communities.*

Contents

Acknowledgments

Several amazing political and intellectual communities have sustained and inspired me throughout the process of research and writing this book. These communities of activists, radicals, dreamers, rebels, and dissidents have been the source of countless late-night discussions on many of the broader themes that I write about in this book. To all of the members of these groups, both formal and informal, I am incredibly grateful. I have learned so much from each and every one of you. Particularly, I want to thank Ginny Browne, Brian Helmle, Diane Fujino, Matef Harmachis, Anthony Francoso, Xuan Santos, Ofelia Delgado, Lashaune Johnson, Amory Starr, Chris Bickel, Sheila Katz, and Hagar Kotef. Each of you has been a source of both support and insight. My parents, Mark and Susan, encouraged my intellectual curiosity from an early age, and I thank them for helping me to become someone who would keep on asking questions. My partner Gabe was always supportive, accepting my long absences for field research, my incredibly messy office, and my distracted book-filled brain without flinching or complaining.

John Munro and Sandi Nenga deserve special thanks for giving the entire manuscript detailed, thoughtful, and careful readings, and offering me so much wonderfully specific feedback. Jordan Camp also read several chapters and provided some invaluable ideas. Finding Hava Gordon and having the chance to talk youth activism with another sociologist has also been very helpful to my thinking. Many thanks also go to my faculty mentors at the University of California at Santa Barbara all of whom supported my research from the beginning, giving me the freedom to roam the region and seek out these stories. Their trust in me and my work was a real gift. As a scholar of previous generations of young activists, Dick Flacks was excited about my ideas, enthusiastic about my writing style, and appreciative of the girls I've studied. Verta Taylor taught me a great deal about professional sociology and social movements scholarship. Finally, Avery Gordon was a constant inspiration to me as an example of a rigorous and radical scholar-activist. Her feedback has, from the start of my graduate school career, always been the type that moves me forward.

Thanks are also due to Ilene Kalish at NYU Press. From our first meeting, I've appreciated both her encouragement and the obvious fact that she understands the importance of research on youth and is someone who, as my teens would say, "gets it." I've also benefited greatly from the anonymous reviewers for the press, finding their comments to be thought-provoking and useful for pushing the work in new and productive directions. Additionally, I want to acknowledge that this material is based upon work supported under a National Science Foundation Graduate Research Fellowship. Any opinions, findings, conclusions, or recommendations are my own and do not necessarily reflect the views of the National Science Foundation.

This book also would not have been possible without the many friends, activist comrades, and strangers who heard about my project, were excited about it, and helped me to find girl activists. There are far too many of these individuals to name, but I want them all to know that I am deeply grateful for their assistance whether it was forwarding an email about the project to a group of teens they knew, spending hours over coffee discussing the local political terrain, or introducing me to girl activists. Finally, I owe so much to the seventy-five teenage girl activists who took the time to tell me about their lives and politics and who welcomed me into their communities. The generosity of these young women is something I will never forget. You've enriched my life personally, politically, and professionally. From the bottom of my heart, I thank you all. *Mil gracias chicas.*

Introduction

Growing Up and Rising Up

Nenetzin stands in the center of the plaza, her arms painted white, wearing a skeleton mask and a bridal veil. Along with a dozen other young activists all dressed as skeletons, she sings a song about remembering those who have died due to poverty, domestic violence, state repression, and other social and political injustices. It is "El Dia de los Muertos," the Day of the Dead, and Nenetzin's Mexican youth activist collective is interweaving tradition with political theater to educate others and build oppositional consciousness. At the end of the singing and dancing, another young skeleton steps forward to inform the audience that this performance was part of the construction of La Otra Campaña, a Zapatista-initiated campaign for building an alternative progressive politics in Mexico.

* * * *

Emma reports on labor issues for an independent, public access television show in Vancouver. She has presented stories on a speech given by anti-war activist Cindy Sheehan, a day of mourning for workers who have died on the job, and other "progressive, or working things that are going on around the city." In addition to being a media activist, Emma also played a key role in the organization of a student rally in support of striking teachers. Emma and some of her pro-labor friends convinced a citywide student organization to take a stand on the issue and coordinated an exuberant display of student solidarity. Taking over a major intersection, the teens played music, danced, had fun, and demonstrated to the city that they wanted the district administration to return to contract negotiations with the teachers' union.

* * * *

Manuela and I sit at her kitchen table, making pins out of foam, ribbon, and printed logos for tomorrow's Communist Youth of Venezuela (Juventud Comunista de Venezuela or JCV) concert and cultural event. We talk about Presidents Chavez and Bush, and discuss the future of social movements in Venezuela and the United States. As members of the JCV, Manuela and her comrades see themselves as having an important role in Venezuela's revolutionary Bolivarian process. They spend most of their time and energy doing political education work with the many young people who are excited about Chavez and the possibilities of his government, but, according to Manuela, do not yet understand all of the economic and social problems and their potential solutions. Chavez speaks openly about socialism, and the JCV is trying to work with youth to mobilize for substantial, "real" socialism, not just a few minor reforms. To do this, they hold study groups, discussing global political economy and reading Marx, Lenin, and Che. And they organize community events, like the upcoming concert, trying to bring youth together to talk about the problems they see around them and to develop their collective knowledge.

* * * *

Pitu, a tiny seventeen-year-old with a pixie haircut and wearing a fluffy pink sweater, takes my hand and leads me around one of Buenos Aires' most well-known *comedores,* a new set of social institutions that can be loosely translated as soup kitchens. A cooperative, self-governing, and democratic enterprise that includes a pasta workshop, soup kitchen, photo shop, textile factory, screen-printing operation, and bakery, this *comedor* provides prepared and raw foods, employment opportunities, and political and social community for its members. Pitu is the youngest member of the center's youth group, a subsection of the organization where youth participants gather together to talk and learn from each other, and to work on their own projects or assist in the various facets of the organization's operation.

* * * *

Lisette's dedication to fighting against environmental racism and for community health and safety finally paid off in the summer of 2001 when a San Francisco Bay Area toxic waste disposal facility, which her youth organization had been trying to shut down for more than eight years, was forced to close. Motivated by her anger at the health problems her community has experienced because of the facility's lack of concern for the well-being of neighborhoods of poor people of color, Lisette spent countless hours planning and implementing educational events, rallies, and press conferences. She and her peers also documented the company's violations, went to planning meetings, confronted the regulating agency, and lobbied politicians. As an activist, Lisette has been focused primarily on this one campaign for several years because, she said, "I know everything is connected and messed up, but let me try to just focus on this one thing because, if not, then I just feel like it's too much." Now, with the facility closed, she and her group are moving on to new projects, and Lisette is hopeful that she'll see some major "systemic changes" in her lifetime.

*   *   *   *

These brief stories about five teenage girl activists provide just a glimpse of their vibrant political identities and practices. From the young Zapatistas with the braids and bandanas who climbed the fence at the WTO protests in Cancun to throw flowers at the police to the U.S. high school students designing curriculums to educate their peers about child labor and sweatshops, teenage girls in the Americas are participating in a variety of struggles for social justice. Radical cheerleaders at a high school in Los Angeles, wearing red shirts with black stars, chant against the U.S. war in Iraq and in support of striking workers while doing splits and pyramids.[1] Forty-four juveniles were arrested at the 2004 American Indian Movement march against the celebration of the Columbus Day Parade in Denver, Colorado.[2] Girls and queer youth are increasingly visible in the boisterous pink blocs that have mobilized at numerous large-scale protests since the initial pink and silver column at the IMF/World Bank protests in Prague in 2000. The MST land occupations in Brazil include whole families, not just adults.[3] The YouthPower! program of Desis Rising Up and Moving in New York, Khmer Girls in Action, in Long Beach, California, and other community-based youth groups organize for immigrant rights and against the detention and deportation of community members. Philadelphia students have resisted the privatization of their schools. Teenage women working in export processing zones are forming workers' organizations. Young sex workers are organizing for their rights to health and safety. Anti-capitalist urban youth are reclaiming buildings, setting up squats, and creating autonomous spaces. Across the United States, youth are fighting for increased spending on education and against the development of more juvenile justice facilities and youth jails.[4] Teenagers are actively participating in indymedia centers and youth media projects, producing a variety of alternative media and challenging the corporate concentration of television, radio, and print news. And, on March 6, 2003, hundreds of thousands of students walked out of classes around the world to protest the impending U.S. bombing of Iraq.[5]

Within academic and activist circles in the United States, we sometimes get a fleeting impression of the teenage girls who participate in these and other struggles. Before beginning to seek them out for this book, I would see them in a photo of the workers' meeting outside the export-processing zone, in an independently produced video about a protest at a trade summit, in a brief mention by an older activist of some "cool youth" they know, across the circle at a meeting, or chanting and dancing in the streets. But finding documentation of their stories, their organizations, and their words is not easy; they are rarely considered and written about as significant political actors. They appear, but they do not speak. This book aims to address this silence and to illuminate the experiences and perspectives of these uniquely positioned agents of social change through the analysis of in-depth interviews and participant observation with progressive and Left-leaning girl activists in five different cities in the Americas.[6]

Girls' activism is an extremely underexplored scholarly topic, largely invisible in the academic literatures on girlhood and on social movements. Research in the growing field of girls' studies has focused primarily on girls' self-esteem and psychology, sexuality and sexual behavior, friendships, school and peer relationships, media consumption, production and cultural practices, and issues of growing up and constructing identities in various contexts.[7] These works often describe girls' acts of resistance to dominant gender norms, or address girls' consumption of commodified versions of feminism, but very few have made girls' politics or political identities the central focus of study.[8] Additionally, the volumes on feminist generations and the relationship between young women and feminism have largely ignored the specific experiences of teenage girls, focusing more on college-aged women.[9] Indeed, the invoking of "girl" in these writings generally occurs in comments upon how young women do or do not embrace this identity and how this either empowers or diminishes them.[10] Thus, actual teenage girls are virtually erased from the discussion as talk about "girls" in this context refers primarily to a debate about young women and their "girly" feminism (or post-feminism). This means that the stories of girls like those in this study, girls who are involved in a multitude of political struggles, are left out of these debates due to the elision of the terms "girl" and "young woman."

A similar situation exists in the literature on youth movements. Studies of the student and youth activism of the 1960s and beyond have not often addressed the specific experiences of high school and middle school students, focusing primarily on college and university-based movements.[11] In studies of white student movements, youth has been collapsed into one category, with college students representing all young people, a situation that contains both age and class biases. Studies of the Chicano movement and the African American civil rights movement more frequently acknowledge the presence of younger activists, but the consciousness and experiences of these younger activists has not often been the focus of study and analysis.[12] Social movement scholars, despite having noted the impact of race, class, gender, and generation on the activist experience,[13] have generally not studied teenagers. The dynamics of age and ageism, the impact of being below the age of legal majority, the role of teens in social movements, and the characteristics of young people's activism are all not yet a substantial part of the literature in this field.[14] Girl activists' ideas, stories, and theoretical contributions thus remain largely hidden from view. They continue to appear in both the public and academic domain only as occasional images—as visual objects rather than as intelligent and intelligible political subjects.

In contrast to girls' absence from the literature on social movements in the Americas, they are figures of central importance to contemporary processes and discourses of globalization and global citizenship. Teenage girls and young women in the Global South are a major source of labor for the global economy. As structural adjustment programs and the shift to export-oriented economies erode subsistence economies and thus displace small farmers and producers, families are forced into greater participation in market economies, either formal or informal, and children and youth play an important role in this income generation.[15] Young women and girls frequently leave the rural areas for work in the cities or export processing zones (EPZs) so that they can send money to support their families.[16] Hired for their supposedly "nimble fingers" and assumed passivity, they make up a significant portion of the labor force in most of these zones, in maquiladoras, and in agro-business greenhouses.[17] According to the AFL-CIO, 90 percent of the 27 million workers in EPZs are women, most of them between the ages of sixteen and twenty-five.[18] An International Labor Organization document reports that nearly 2 million girls in Latin America work as domestic laborers.[19] Teenage girls also labor for the global tourist industry in a variety of locations. They sell trinkets and souvenirs in the informal economy,[20] are sex workers,[21] and work as maids and servers in hotels and restaurants.

Meanwhile, in the Global North, business magazines identify the importance of teenage and "tween" girl consumption.[22] Teenage girls represent the most highly sought after market segment in the United States,[23] and a major marketing research company reports that "the current generation of teenage girls has tremendous buying power."[24] Teenage and young women's clothing has more fashion seasons than any other category of clothing, with stores aimed at this market changing their inventory for as many as eighteen fashion seasons. Girls' studies scholar Anita Harris has persuasively argued that "it is primarily as consumer citizens that youth are offered a place in contemporary social life, and it is girls above all who are held up as the exemplars of this new citizenship."[25] Consumption and participation in the global marketplace are central features of contemporary images of idealized girlhood.[26] The image of the girl is frequently deployed as a model for the "appropriate ways to embrace and manage the political, economic, and social conditions of contemporary societies," and an indicator of the supposed potential benefits of global capitalism.[27]

In addition to being central to the economic processes of globalization, girls—and youth in general—are also being targeted by a wide variety of social programs designed to encourage particular forms of global citizenship. Receiving significant money from governments and numerous private foundations including the Ford Foundation, the Carnegie Corporation, the Kellogg Foundation, Pew Charitable Trusts, and the William T. Grant Foundation, youth civic engagement programs are a widespread and growing part of civil society and the field of nonprofit organizations. The heavy investment in such programs indicates the political, and not just the economic, importance of teenagers, both male and female. Although most civic engagement programs are not gender specific, there are some significant indicators of widespread interest in *girls'* empowerment and civic identities, a theme developed in the following chapter. Empowered girls are not just an ideal for other girls to model themselves after but are also models for contemporary citizenship more broadly. Girlhood is not an irrelevant social category, but one that is important to global capital and global citizenship, and, therefore, to our understandings of political resistance and social movements in the Americas. According to the transnational theorist Chandra Mohanty, "it is especially on the bodies and lives of women and girls from the Third World/South—the Two-Thirds World—that global capitalism writes its script, and it is by paying attention to and theorizing the experiences of these communities of women and girls that we demystify capitalism as a system of debilitating sexism and racism and envision anti-capitalist resistance."[28] The centrality of girlhood to the global economy and to global civil society provides a theoretically rich reason for looking at the political identities and practices of teenage girl activists.

Identities, Cultures, and Strategies

Progressive teenage girl activists in the Americas, despite their numerous differences of national and local context, of ideology, and of biography, have far more in common with one another than we might expect. They make surprisingly similar identity claims, asserting many shared understandings of what it means to be a girl, to be a youth, and to be an activist. They also make quite similar strategic choices in their movement groups, continually committing their organizational and individual time and energy to ongoing political education, to building egalitarian activist communities, and to the construction of "positive" and hopeful feelings, messages, and projects. These three strategic clusters—the politics of learning, of participation, and of hope—emerged in all of my research sites.

Intrigued by the surprising pattern of strategic tendencies within girls' activism, I follow the suggestion of prominent social movement scholar James Jasper that movement researchers study how and why movements make the strategic choices they do.[29] Jasper suggests that strategic choices are not merely rational decisions made to further interests, but are deeply embedded in cultural and institutional contexts. Symbolic meanings permeate strategic action, and Jasper therefore calls on cultural sociologists to "specify concretely where they saw meanings and what effects those meanings had."[30] Preceding Jasper's cultural approach to strategic action in movements by nearly twenty years, Ann Swidler has also suggested a theoretical model for understanding the messy relationship between culture and strategic action. Swidler treats culture as a "tool kit of symbols, stories, rituals, and worldviews, which people may use in varying configurations to solve different kinds of problems."[31] And, like Jasper, Swidler views strategy not as a necessarily conscious plan, but as "a general way of organizing action." Swidler also notes that in the context of explicitly ideological spaces, such as social movements, a group's symbols, narratives, and doctrines have a much more direct influence on action than in other parts of more "settled" social life. Guided by this approach, I ask what, then, are the shared (and divergent) cultural toolkits and symbolic meanings that girl activists draw upon and reproduce as they formulate their political practices and develop their strategies for social movement activity?

In addition to enacting similar strategic approaches to politics, girl activists also express many shared understandings of their collective identities as girls, as youth, and as activists. These identity claims are some of the key symbolic and discursive resources that girl activists reference as they develop their strategic political practices. In constructing their activist identities, girl activists weave together a variety of discourses on gender, age, and generation. They draw upon widespread popular narratives about what it means to be a girl, to be a teenager, and to be growing up in this particular historical moment. Gender, age, and generation are each important aspects of girls' identity talk and will all be recurring themes throughout this book.

Mary Bernstein has outlined three levels of analysis for identity processes within social movements: identity for empowerment, identity deployment, and identity as a goal. Bernstein notes that identity, at all three levels, can "help to explain the goals that a movement pursues, the strategies employed, who is mobilized, and what types of outcomes are achieved."[32] In my analysis, I am particularly interested in the relationship between activists' identity narratives, or their stories about who they are, and their choices around strategy. It is important to note here that I am not working with an essentialist notion of identity. It is not the case that girls take up shared strategies simply because they are girls. Rather, they take up these strategies because of how they have come to understand, negotiate, and redefine the meaning of girlhood, of youth, or of activist. What I propose is an active, engaged, culturally embedded process of the construction of identity narratives, which then guides choices for strategic action, not a simple linear relationship between identity as a fixed essence and strategy as a direct outcome. The relationship between identity and strategy is not determinate.

As girl activists construct and claim their political identities, they explicitly define themselves partly in and through sets of traits that support the political strategies explored in the second half of my analysis. For example, being open-minded and "still learning" are characteristics frequently attached to adolescent and student identities, while enthusiasm and optimism are things that girls themselves associate with their youthful energy and girlish hopefulness. The linking of these specific characteristics with various aspects of their own identities thus enables and encourages girls' tendencies to make certain choices in their political groups and organizations. The relationship between identity and strategy is also not entirely unidirectional. Although I focus on how identity claims shape strategic choices, girls' strategic choices and their approaches to practicing politics also play a role in their identity narratives. In what Bernstein refers to as a "feedback loop,"[33] identity narratives may guide and support particular strategic choices, but these strategic choices also continue to reinforce various aspects of girls' identities. Their strategic actions become part of their stories of themselves as particular kinds of people.

Identity claims and narratives of the self are not, of course, the only component of girl activists' shared cultural toolkits. The girl activists in this study take part in situated versions of transnational and cosmopolitan youth cultures, or what Sunaina Maira and Elisabeth Soep refer to as "youthscapes."[34] They are also all somewhat loosely connected to another transnational culture: the diffuse cultural and political formation that has been variously named the "movement of movements," the "alternative globalization movement," or the "global justice movement."[35] Although they organize around a wide variety of issues, the girls I chose to include in this research were, for the most part, involved in organizations that have some kind of direct or indirect relationship to this transnational network of movements against neoliberalism, corporate power, and empire. Even when they are not directly connected to this network, this highly visible movement culture provides an important backdrop and resource for their activism. This context figures importantly in girls' generational identities. Girls' political subjectivities and practices therefore reflect many ideas, narratives, images, tactics, and strategies from within this expansive social movement field. And this transnational political culture and its evolving profusion of open-ended, horizontal, and hopeful ideologies and practices is a key part of girl activists' shared cultural toolkit. Therefore, in analyzing girls' use of these strategies, this book also contributes to broader conversations about contemporary social movements and the possibilities for radical political practice in the era of neoliberalism.

Girl activists also share a structural location. As minors, they are excluded political subjects, marginalized within formal politics and within social movements. This marginalization, of course, plays a role in their choices for strategic action. The inability to vote or to run for office, the difficulty of setting up long-term institutions and organizations without financial resources, the importance of schooling and educational institutions to their lives, and the fact of parental power and authority all shape teenagers' political choices in important and often unexpected ways. Girl activists also have some common social needs that can be connected to their experiences as adolescents and to the dynamics of this particular social category. Some of their strategies are not only political choices supported by self-definitions and transnational movement cultures, but are also actions that meet and fulfill their some of these social needs. For example, spending energy on "building community" is not merely a strategic choice rooted in girls' understanding of themselves as "relational" and good at socializing with others, but it also provides them with necessary social networks and peer support as they struggle with the challenges of adolescence and growing up.

The similarities of teenage girls' gendered, age-specific, and generational identity narratives, their shared social location as adolescents, as well as the contemporary transnational movement context, help to explain some of the consistent patterns in girl activists' strategic choices. Within these patterns of action, however, there are also many important differences in girls' political practices. Girls' strategies for political contention are not homogenous or universal but are located in divergent national, racialized, and class-specific communities, histories, and social movement cultures. Localized political cultures and contexts lead to a diversity of forms of political action and strategy. As I discuss each strategic configuration, I also illuminate how it operates differently for girls in different settings, scenarios, and local political-cultural contexts.

Local Political Cultures and Contexts

Girls' activism is both transnational and locally situated, a phenomenon well suited for a multi-site ethnography. Throughout this book, I aim to uncover transnational commonalities, connections, and patterns, but to also keep my analysis grounded in the divergent specificities of five unique urban areas, each one a significant social movement center within the Americas. These five sites, in the order in which I studied them, are: the San Francisco Bay Area, the United States; Mexico City, Mexico; Caracas, Venezuela; Vancouver, Canada; and Buenos Aires, Argentina. Each of these metropolitan areas has a well-known and well-documented social movement history, each continues to be a site of heightened political activism, and each has a particularly strong youth movement sector. They are, in short, "hotspots" for activism in general and youth activism in particular. Limiting my study to the Americas enables me to focus on some of the distinctive dynamics of the social movements and politics of this region,[36] but each site is also a vastly different political context, therefore presenting me with a diverse array of windows into teenage girls' activism. In order to introduce readers to these five local contexts, I provide very brief descriptions of a few key features of each location's youth movement sector. Readers who are familiar with the movements and politics of these cities will find my descriptions here to be cursory and simplified. They are not intended to be comprehensive, but rather to introduce readers who are unfamiliar with these contexts to a few of the most immediately relevant particularities and literatures.

SAN FRANCISCO BAY AREA. The San Francisco Bay Area has long been an important center of progressive and radical social movement activity within the United States. Its more recent history includes the founding of the Black Panther Party in Oakland, the emergence of a vibrant gay and lesbian movement, the American Indian occupation of the island of Alcatraz, a sizable and shifting set of countercultures including beats and hippies, and a new model of community-based organizing led by communities of color, developed by activists at the Center for Third World Organizing (CTWO).[37] Furthermore, the Bay Area's social movement history has been shaped by the enduring strength and legacy of student activism in the area. The Berkeley Free Speech Movement is often described as the beginning of the waves of college student activism that spread throughout the United States in the 1960s.[38] Additionally, in 1968 San Francisco State University was the site of the first student strike for an ethnic studies department.[39] Narratives about the importance of the Bay Area to progressive politics in the United States and to youth movements, whether accurate or not, continue to color the region's perceptions of activists of all ages and generations.

Today, youth activism in the Bay Area is highly institutionalized. A multitude of community organizations either work entirely on "youth organizing" or include programs for youth within their broader work. Compared to much of the rest of the United States, California has a particularly extensive network of formalized opportunities for youth involvement in progressive social change. Furthermore, according to Ryan Pintado-Vertner, "the San Francisco Bay Area, due to its strong activist history, more liberal political climate, long-standing and developed philanthropic sector, and strong web of youth service agencies has the strongest infrastructure and most youth organizing projects, members, and funding."[40] This is partly due to the work of some CTWO graduates who introduced youth organizing to the Bay Area by involving youth in a campaign against lead poisoning. Once a few projects had been developed, many activists began to see these as models, and the number of youth activist organizations multiplied quickly throughout the 1990s and early 2000s. These nonprofit youth activist organizations were, by the time of my research, generally well established, with their own institutionalized patterns, curricula, and political practices.[41] Although modeled after community-based organizations, they incorporate and develop elements of youth cultures, drawing particularly heavily on hip-hop culture.[42] In the period during which I conducted interviews and observation in the San Francisco Bay Area (fall 2005–fall 2006), these groups were variously focused on educational justice, environmental racism, juvenile justice, gentrification, community development, immigrant rights, and challenging the INS raids and deportations, or some combination of these issues.[43] Although not all of the girls I interviewed in the Bay Area participate in structured youth organizations of this type, their presence certainly has a very important impact on the area's youth activist community.

MEXICO CITY. With an estimated population of nearly 30 million people, the metropolitan area of Mexico City is one of the largest in the world. As such, its social movements are also large, varied, and not necessarily integrated or connected to one another. Like the other cities in this study, Mexico City has a well-known history of student and youth activism. The young activists there often spoke of themselves as the political descendents of the student activists of the 1960s, several hundred of whom died in the 1968 Tlatelolco massacre.[44] An annual commemorative march organized by young activists memorializes the 1968 movement and the ensuing repression and massacre of protestors. Another significant moment in the history of student and youth activism in Mexico City was the 1999 student strike against the institution of fees and the increasing privatization of the Universidad Nacional Autonoma de Mexico (UNAM).[45] Lasting nearly a year, the 1999 strike continues to loom large in the imaginations and political consciousness of young Mexican activists.

The centrality of UNAM and student politics to the Mexican youth activists can be better understood in the context of the particularities of the relationship between the various public high schools and the university. Many of the Mexico City activists who are discussed in this study were students at one of several high schools that are formally part of the administrative and institutional structure of UNAM. Some of these schools are *preparatorias* (called *prepas*), which follow a traditional curriculum and method of instruction. Others are Colegios de Ciencias y Humanidades, or CCHs, schools founded by student and faculty activists from UNAM in 1971 and which were intended to be more experimental and, in some cases, oppositional, in their approach to education. The students who attend both of these types of schools are, in part, governed by the UNAM administration and, until recently, could largely expect guaranteed entrance to UNAM upon completion of their high school educations. Because of these ties, high school activism in Mexico City is most closely aligned with college activism, rather than the more community-based organizations, as is the case in the San Francisco Bay Area.

I arrived in Mexico to conduct interviews and participant observation in the fall of 2005, a particularly interesting moment in Mexican social movements. Within the domain of student activism, there had been a recent upsurge in the levels of repression experienced by student activists. In response to the escalating violence, several high school activist groups had begun sit-ins and takeovers of school administrative offices. In the broader landscape of Mexican politics, the presidential elections were only a few months away, and the Zapatistas, probably one of the most visible social movements in Mexico and in the Americas, had recently initiated a new phase in their struggle, a project they called La Otra Campaña, or the other campaign.[46] Re-emerging on the national scene after a period of some quiet, the Zapatistas had called for a series of *encuentros*, or encounters, to discuss the project of consolidating and building connections between various struggles. A few of the girls in this study traveled to Chiapas to participate in the *encuentros*, and several others were actively involved in local conversations about La Otra. These two concerns, of increased repression and of the possibilities for a new Zapatista-style national politics, dominated the youth activist scene during my time in Mexico.

CARACAS. Recent Venezuelan political and social movement history has been dominated by the powerful presence of Hugo Chavez Frias, the controversial president first elected in 1998. Since his election, Chavez has been engaging the population in an ongoing social and political revolution.[47] Chavez and his various supporters have written a new constitution, re-nationalized the oil industry, and devoted oil money to a variety of social projects, called missions, including literacy, health care, and job-training programs. The economist Mark Weisbrot recently noted: "In Venezuela, the economy (real GDP) has grown by 87 percent since the government got control of the national oil industry in early 2003; poverty has been cut by half, most of the country has access to free health care, and educational enrollment has risen sharply."[48]

The opposition to Chavez comes largely from the middle and upper-middle class and the economic elite. The opposition parties have been well supported by the U.S. government, which continues to attempt to undermine the major changes being made in Venezuela by naming Chavez "a dictator" despite the fact that he has been elected in internationally certified elections.[49] Since the opposition's 2002 coup attempt and the ensuing protests that demanded Chavez's return to power, many Venezuelan activists have argued that social movements and activism have been and continue to be vital to the survival of the Chavez government. In their view, it is not just a government that has been elected, but a government that has been defended by popular social movements and that must continue to be defended. This sense of democratic ownership over their government shapes the activist experiences, identities, and practices of the girls I interviewed, all of whom are at least nominally part of pro-government groups.

The ongoing political changes happening in Venezuelan, called the "Bolivarian process," have brought many previously excluded and marginalized Venezuelans into social movements, political parties, and community organizations. Venezuelan social movements, then, are often very closely tied to the state, working alongside the Chavez government, the pro-Chavez parties, and the various missions. This is also the case for youth activism: many of the girl activists I interviewed were part of youth wings of political parties, particularly the Communist Party, or active in some of the different missions and state-sponsored programs for civic engagement or youth voice. I arrived in Venezuela in January 2006, starting my research there at the Americas meeting of the World Social Forum. It was only a few months after the World Youth Festival, an event that brought together fifteen thousand young people from around the world for political discussions, cultural events, and organizing. Thus, there was a decidedly internationalist tone to Venezuelan youth activism. Energized both by their own highly politicized national context and the spirit of hopefulness that seems to surround Venezuelan activists, and by their interactions with young people from other countries, the Venezuelan girls were an intensely positive group.

VANCOUVER. With its sparkling luxury high-rise condominiums towering above a neighborhood often referred to as "the poorest zip-code in Canada," Vancouver is full of political, social, and economic tensions.[50] In recent years, the British Columbia provincial government's cuts to social spending have combined with the forces of gentrification and development, angering many and giving rise to substantial social movements, including youth movements. One of the most notable of these recent movements has been the Secwepemc community's resistance to the expansion of the Sun Peaks resort onto unceded tribal lands. I went to Vancouver in spring 2006 after hearing about the vibrancy of the Native Youth Movement. When I arrived, however, I found that the movement had largely gone underground. Furthermore, gaining access to the groups that remained active proved to be very difficult.[51]

Adult Vancouver activists frequently told me that I was there during an especially quiet period in the ebb and flow of the city's social movements. After my departure, Vancouver movement politics have once again revitalized as the community organizes in resistance to the 2010 Olympics. This, of course, is one of the major challenges for scholars of social movements—it is difficult to always be in the right place at exactly the right time. Despite the "quiet," however, there were several major movement organizations that provided an important backdrop to the struggles and practices of youth activists, including Vancouver's Bus Riders' Union, modeled after the Los Angeles BRU, the Vancouver chapter of No One Is Illegal, a grassroots anti-colonial immigrant and refugee rights collective, and www.stopwar.ca, Vancouver's anti-war coalition. While a few of the girl activists I interviewed had connections to some of these organizations and movements, many others were more heavily tied into school-based humanitarian organizations, a tendency discussed throughout this book.

BUENOS AIRES. Like Mexican youth activists, teenage participants in social movements in Buenos Aires see themselves as part of a long history of student activism. As in Mexico, this history also includes substantial repression. From roughly 1976 through 1983 Argentina's military dictatorship abducted, tortured, and caused the disappearance of tens of thousands of activists, many of them very young. For today's high school students, this period represents the youth of their own parents and plays a substantial role in how their families see their newfound activism. Unlike other recent cohorts of youth activists in Buenos Aires, the teens I interviewed were born after, rather than during, the era of this Dirty War. And, instead of coming of age during the years of Argentina's supposed neoliberal economic success, they were reaching adolescence and becoming politically aware during the 2001 economic crash and the ensuing popular rebellions. In December 2001, when the government froze people's bank accounts in an effort to use these resources to manage their foreign debt, millions of Argentines took to the streets and forced the government to resign, then proceeded to refuse four more governments in just a few weeks.[52] This rebellion, as a powerful and liberating opening of collective political space, plays an important role in the memories and identities of today's teenage activists.

In the years since 2001, Argentine social movements have continued to explore some of the innovations that were developed during the rebellion, including participatory democracy, horizontalism, and organization outside the traditional political party structure. In addition to the divides between the autonomous movements and the Left political parties, the movements of unemployed workers (the *piquetero* movements) have also split into pro- and anti-government factions. In the 2006 Argentine winter, girl activists could be found on all sides of these divisions. They were especially visible within the *piquetero* organizations, the youth wings of various Left political parties, and, most importantly, the activist-oriented student centers within their high schools.

* * * *

Each of these five cities was a rich and exciting field site for my research on girls' activism. Beginning in fall 2005, I spent between one and two months in each city, conducting participant observation and in-depth interviews with seventy-five girl activists, approximately fifteen per location. For reasons of confidentiality all of the girls' names, and many of the organization names, have been changed. The girls selected their own pseudonyms, a practice I've implemented in order to allow girls to contribute to the construction of their textual personas.[53] I continue to stay in contact with many of these girls, sending updates on the progress toward publication of their stories, and receiving replies from them about their political and personal lives. In reading their messages, I have been struck by how committed to the project many of these girls continue to be. They nearly always remember their pseudonyms and remind me of them in their emails to make sure that I'm connecting their words to the right persona. The research experience was clearly not irrelevant or unimportant to them. My ongoing relationships with these girls not only remind me of their generosity, warmth, and spirit, but also of my responsibility to them and my commitment to producing a book that they will appreciate and that respectfully shares their insights and stories.

Of course, wanting to write a book girls appreciate and can recognize themselves in does not mean writing only what they want to hear. While I am generally very complimentary of their political practices, there are also many implicit and explicit criticisms scattered throughout the text. Such criticisms are intellectually and politically important, and they are meant constructively, but there is certainly a chance that some of my girl readers will disagree with my assessments of the problems, silences, and failures of their groups. I offer my critiques with a great deal of respect and affection for these girls, and I hope that they learn from them, rather than feel betrayed or hurt by my portrayal of them.

In addition to the issues of betrayal and what Lorraine Kenny refers to as "writing behind girls' backs,"[54] representing girls also raises other important methodological concerns around voice. My ongoing relationships with the girls and their occasional involvement in the research process do not negate the very substantial interpretive and representative power I have as the author of this text. That authorial power feels especially intense when considered in relationship to the translating process. My interviews took place in both English (in the United States and Canada) and Spanish (in Mexico, Venezuela, and Argentina), and all were transcribed in the language in which they were conducted. I worked with and coded the interviews and quotes in the original language, only translating a quote from Spanish into English near the end of the writing process. The translations are my own and far from perfect. Translators make countless small choices about how to select the "best" words and phrases to capture a given statement. The words people use to describe their political beliefs are quite complicated, and some of the particular and nuanced meanings of what the Spanish-speaking girls had to say has probably been lost in this process.[55] The translation process has been further complicated by the challenge of trying to maintain girls' own distinctive teenage voices. As I translated the voices of girl activists from Latin America, I struggled to keep them from sliding into the sounds, words, and rhythms of their peers from the United States and Canada, on the one hand, or into a flat and dry "adult" language on the other. I have made a good faith effort in these translations and hope that the girls themselves would still recognize themselves and their words. But, each translation is also a rewriting, a retelling. This means that I have not only authored the analysis around these girls' voices but have also had a role in writing their voices. This is also partly the case for English speakers as well. While the words are much more their own, in some cases girls have asked me to remove some of the ums, uhs, likes, sorta, ya know, and other teenage filler words from their transcripts. I've tried to keep the flavor of their voices present in the quotes I use but have also occasionally removed some of these extra words in order to make a quote more comprehensible. (Re)presenting girls' voices, particularly those that needed translation, has required some authorial choices on my part. Such choices are always part of the writing process for any qualitative study.

The challenge of writing about five different locations, each with its own internal diversity of experiences and perspectives, was often daunting. I have tried to identify themes and patterns in girls' activist lives and practices without, I hope, flattening differences. In regards to terminology, I often distinguish between "North American" and "Latin American" girls and their organizations. This designation is a little awkward given that Mexico normally falls into both of these categories. However, I find that the Mexican teens have far more in common with their Argentinean and Venezuelan peers than with the girls from the United States and Canada. Therefore, lacking a better phrase, I use "North American" to refer to the shared characteristics of the United States and Canadian contexts and "Latin American" to refer to Mexico, Venezuela, and Argentina. In the analysis that follows, I've tried to remain attentive to the most significant and substantial differences in girls' practices, particularly as they are tied to their national contexts and, at times, their racial and class identities, however, not all of the many differences can be discussed at all times, and there is certainly much more that could be said about each of these domains.

Located in their own struggles against and within the global flows of power, girls' activism illuminates a set of radical political practices that aim to "counter the scattered hegemonies that affect their lives."[56] By tracing out these practices, this book challenges and responds to girls' absences from scholarly and public discussions of social movements and to highly prevalent images of girls as either passive victims or empowered consumer citizens.

The first half of the book explores how teenage girls negotiate these dynamics of invisibility and exclusion as they construct their activist identities. In chapter 2, I address girls' conceptions of what it means to be an activist and situate their activist identities in relation to more widespread discourses about girls' empowerment, civic engagement, and youth apathy. Chapter 3 then turns to an analysis of how girls' emergent activist identities are built upon rhetorical strategies that claim social movement standing and political authority for youth. Finally, my exploration of their identities addresses girl activists' complex relationship to girlhood, arguing that they view girlhood as diametrically opposing activist identity yet simultaneously supporting it. Rejecting particular elements of girlhood and trying to escape the limits of the category itself, they redefine what it means to be a girl.

The second half of the book then examines girl activists' social movement strategies and collective political practices. Each chapter in this section takes up one of their shared strategic tendencies, looking at how it is understood and enacted by girl activists in various locations and organizations. First, I address girls' commitment to learning and the ongoing process of political education, and analyze some of the major differences between girls in North America and Latin America in terms of the creation of spaces for intensive and theoretical political conversations. I then turn to girl activists' interest in building participatory activist communities, highlighting their contributions to our understandings of horizontalist political engagement. Finally, a discussion of girls' spirit of hopefulness explores the ways that political optimism shapes political action. Taken together, these three strategic clusters reflect girls' affinity for some of the most fruitful and dynamic elements of contemporary adult radicalism, elements frequently discussed in numerous theoretical and philosophical texts on social movements and social change in the Americas.[57] Resonating with these conversations on prefigurative, open-ended, autonomous, and horizontal political practices, this book provides an ethnographic accounting of how such practices are developed and worked out, on the ground, in various social movement contexts, from the perspective of girl activists, a group that, due partly to their identity narratives, seems to have a particular affinity for these modes of doing politics. Throughout my discussion, I aim to not only provide an empirical accounting of the shape of teenage girls' activism, and to elaborate the complex relationship between identity, culture, and political strategy, but also to suggest how girls' political practices can provide adult scholars and activists with some intriguing models for effective social movements and social change.

Part 1

Building the Activist Identity

2

We Are Not Ophelia

Empowerment and Activist Identities

In January 2004, in a speech to the International Women's Health Coalition, the then secretary-general of the United Nations Kofi Annan told the assembled group "when it comes to solving many of the problems of this world, I believe in girl power."[1] Girls, according to Annan, need to be educated to take up the mantle of civic responsibility and humanitarian leadership. Meanwhile, the Nike Foundation, a charity wing of the giant athletic gear corporation, focuses all of its funding on adolescent girls in the "developing world" in order to "empower impoverished girls by expanding their opportunities, capabilities, and choices."[2] Countless organizations, books, Web sites, and after-school programs around the world state that their mission is to "empower girls." Furthermore, an additional panoply of programs and initiatives focus on enhancing the civic engagement of all youth, both girls and boys. Taken together, these programs and statements suggest the high levels of transnational corporate, non-governmental, and philanthropic interest in girls' empowerment and girls' civic identities. Whether it be expressed in concerns about boosting girls' self-esteem or the potential for reducing poverty through girls' education, the figure of the empowered girl and the notion of girls' empowerment are powerful and pervasive features in our current discourses of girlhood.

But what, exactly, does it mean to empower girls? What kind of power do empowered girls possess and demonstrate in these imaginings? And what are the implications of this version of empowerment for teenage girls' critical political participation? In this chapter, I briefly deconstruct and analyze the current institutionalized models of girls' empowerment and civic engagement, contrasting them with the activist practices, strategies, and social change visions of the girls who are featured in this book. I'll argue that empowerment, as it is currently articulated, is quite distinct from activism. Girls' empowerment is all too often focused on incorporating girls into the social order as it stands, rather than empowering them to make any meaningful changes to it. The girls in this book, on the other hand, are interested in substantial social change, they are "empowered," but they are critical of the narrow versions of empowerment usually offered to them. They are not the kind of empowered girls usually celebrated by the media. They are not likely to turn up on Oprah, nor to be featured in popular teen magazines for their "positive social contributions." Their empowerment is too rebellious, too critical, too political. Girl activists embody an alternative kind of empowered girl citizen and a different understanding of empowerment, both of which will be made visible throughout this book.

This chapter also explores how girl activists construct and define their identities as *activists*, as opposed to empowered individuals. Responding to Chris Bobel's call for further research into the ongoing construction of activist identities within social movements,[3] I ask what is activism and who is an activist? Definitions of activism can be drawn from people's explicit commentary on the subject and extrapolated from their political practices. Therefore, I pair girls' statements about the meaning of activism with concise descriptions of the activism I encountered in my research in order to offer an overall picture of these young women's social movement activity. This chapter thus provides an ethnographic introduction to these girls and an analysis of their conceptions of activism and activist identity and situates both of these within and against popular and academic discourses on girls' empowerment, civic engagement, and political agency. I begin by contrasting the social change goals of activism with the individual goals of empowerment, then turn to the different kinds of practices embodied in activism and in programs for youth engagement, and, finally, address how girls' discussion of their collective activist identities responds to adult discourses of youth apathy and the idea that any youth who engages in politics must, therefore, be a truly exceptional individual.

Activism and Empowerment

My account of girls' activist identities is, of course, shaped by my own research practices and criteria for inclusion in this project. Consequently, it is also worth addressing some of those choices here. I conducted preliminary research before my arrival in each metropolitan area, gathering information about local social movement organizations and youth activist groups. I contacted as many of these adult and youth groups as possible before and during my time in each city, asking for their assistance in locating teenage girl activists. Then, I followed the suggestions and leads of these local movement participants, seeking out girl activists by visiting the recommended locations, organizations, and events. When choosing which leads to follow and which groups or organizations to contact, I focused only on those that could be considered part of left and/or progressive social movements, broadly conceived. I did not include organizations and events that primarily emphasized individual growth and personal development, government-centered political participation, or community service. Instead, following agreed-upon sociological definitions of social movements,[4] I looked to spaces and groups engaged in collective, non-governmental, and change-oriented political activities. Once I had made contact with some girl activists in these locations, I used a snowball sampling approach, asking the girls themselves for their help finding other activist teens. This means that for each city there are a few tendencies and groupings of girls, each branching out from an original set of contacts.

Unlike much social movement research that narrows its focus by selecting a single movement for analysis, my research is not movement-specific. David Meyer notes that a great deal of research on social movements has found that "protesting and organizing for a variety of related social change goals over several decades is the rule rather than the exception for individual activists."[5] Therefore, he continues, instead of always centering our scholarship on a particular movement, we could look at activists as a distinctive group of people who participate in many movements and struggles over time. It was this approach that guided my research: I sought out girl activists across progressive movements and, in doing so, found that a majority of the girls that I met in one movement context were also often involved in one or more other political activities and organizations.

When I encountered teenage girls in these social movement spaces, I would ask them if they were interested in participating in the study and if they would self-identify as activists. Only those girls who acknowledged and claimed an activist identity or who said that they were somewhere on the route to becoming activists were then interviewed. Girls who replied that they were not really active, were just stopping by this single event to see a friend, or who were not regular or frequent participants in any kind of collective political project were not interviewed. Thus, both ongoing involvement in social movement activities and/or organizations and an activist self-identification (including as someone "becoming an activist") were necessary conditions in my own determination of who was or was not a girl activist.

Rather than simply relying on my own criteria to create a definition of girl activist identity, I wanted to know how the girls themselves understood and constructed activist identities both through their narratives and their political practices.[6] Central to their understandings is the claim that activism, first and foremost, is about a desire to create change, to make the world into a different and better place.[7] According to one interviewee from Mexico, Sicaru, activism is "the interest in trying to change things, not just staying like this." Ixtab, another Mexican teen, stated that activism is "doing something to change the situation." Ella, from the San Francisco Bay Area, described an activist as "someone who spends time trying to make the world a better place." Of course, people have conflicting ideas about what would make the world a better place. Changes are not neutral, and they are assessed based on particular values and beliefs about what makes a good community or society. Girl activists have a variety of visions and hopes for the world, many of which will emerge and be discussed throughout this book.

A unifying theme in these visions, however, was girls' expression of what Paul Lichterman has called "public-spirited commitment," or "a dedication to some public good partaken of in common by members of a community or society."[8] Activists concern themselves not only with their own well-being but also with that of others and of communities. Lucia, from Mexico City, argued that "an activist is someone who . . . struggles for people—someone who is involved and who wants things to get better, not just for themselves, but for people who they know and people who they don't know." In this view, activists are people who act for the good of communities, not just the good of individuals. Activists view entrenched social structures and systemic problems as presenting barriers to community well-being, a view which then necessitates collective action. Ana, from Buenos Aires, argued, therefore, that an activist is "someone who sees what is really happening and who has a critical vision about this. . . . An activist is someone who can do many things. . . . and who doesn't just have the capacity (because everyone has the capacity), but who also has the desire, who wants to change what they see." It is worth noting here that this public-spirited commitment is something that girls think anyone can develop. By emphasizing community well-being and a critical understanding of the social, political, and economic problems facing communities, these girls draw links between activism and a particular way of seeing and understanding the world—a sociological, rather than individualized, understanding. The changes they imagine are about creating a world that is better for many people, not just improving their own abilities to deal with and overcome the problems they see in the world.

Girl activists, located within different communities, political contexts, and struggles, address a breathtaking range of social problems and contemporary political issues in their activism. Because schools and education are particularly powerful forces in girls' lives, many of their organizations focus on improving these institutions. In all five locations I encountered girls organizing and agitating for more decision-making authority in their schools and more influence over educational policy and curriculum. They also work toward racial equity in education, for safer schools, for low-cost student transportation, and against the privatization of public education. In addition to student rights and student issues, girl activists engage in projects focused on the well-being and rights of children and youth. Several of the young activists were involved in campaigns that address teenagers' reproductive rights and access to quality health care and health information. Several others were active in labor organizing and worker's rights campaigns, including those oriented toward the needs and rights of child and youth workers.

Girl activists participate in numerous local campaigns around issues of community development, including struggles against gentrification, unemployment and hunger, challenges to destructive building proposals (shopping malls and highways that would disrupt important ecosystems and community spaces), demands for corporate accountability and solutions to ongoing corporate environmental health and safety violations, and projects that aim to build alternative, community-controlled social service institutions. These local campaigns, particularly in Latin America, are complemented by activism aimed toward the global institutions that structure local problems. This includes mobilization against free trade agreements and the institutions of neoliberal globalization including the World Trade Organization, the International Monetary Fund and the World Bank, anti-corporate campaigns, resistance to privatization, to structural adjustment and other neoliberal economic policies, struggles for immigrant and refugee rights and against displacement, and other related goals that could be identified as part of a global justice or alter-globalization agenda.

Girl activists are also specifically concerned with the problem of violence, both state-based and individual. Many of the girls I interviewed are active in a loosely structured anti-war movement and speak out about U.S. imperialism, the war in Iraq, land mines, and/or militarized violence. A few are also involved in trying to address the Israeli occupation of Palestine. Other girls engage in activism around prison issues and the rights of imprisoned people, making improvements to the California juvenile justice system, against police brutality and racial profiling, and against torture. Still others are part of campaigns that address political repression and violence against activists or that mobilize for the freedom of political prisoners. Finally, some of the young women organize against hate crimes, violence against GLBTQ (gay, lesbian, bisexual, transgendered, queer) individuals, and gender-based violence.

Alongside this almost dizzying array of specific concerns, most girl activists expressed their desires for widespread and systemic social change. Many of them have big dreams and expansive hopes for an entirely different world. This was the case for Celia, a seventeen-year-old who was so interested in the political struggles happening in Latin America that she decided to leave her native Italy to spend a year as an exchange student in Venezuela. An activist in both countries, she sees herself as part of "a movement of youth who imagine something better for the world. Or, of youth who haven't lost the hope of changing the future of the world, who want to make a world with equality, with justice." Girls in all five locations spoke out and acted against inequality and oppression in its multiple forms: racism, sexism, homophobia, ableism, ageism, economic inequality, and international or global inequalities. They want "a world where all of us are equal, where there is no discrimination" (Victoria, Caracas). In addition to the ideals of justice and equality, young women spoke about working to create a world based on the values of ecological sustainability, solidarity, community, democracy, love, liberty, human rights, peace, and indigenous people's rights to land and sovereignty.

Many of the Venezuelan girls associated their social change goals with socialism and Chavez's Bolivarian project. I also met and interviewed girls who were part of Communist or Socialist youth organizations in all three Latin American countries and who framed discussions of their visions in terms of anti-capitalism and a proletarian revolution. Young activists like Aura, from Mexico, emphasized how their objectives are "to overthrow capitalism and create a society without classes, where workers have power." Whether they are Marxists or unaffiliated "revolutionaries," "radicals," or "progressives," girl activists have hopes for deep and systemic social change. They are not just interested in addressing the immediate problems they see in front of them, but in creating a world that is very different from the one they are currently living in.

A defining feature of activism is its emphasis on social change. In striking contrast, programs for girls' empowerment tend to focus primarily on personal change. Girls' empowerment is frequently presented by globalized media institutions and a variety of girls' organizations as a process by which girls learn to develop their own personal power, in particular, the power to make choices and construct their own individual identities. According to one source, contemporary discourses of girlhood "emphasize young female subjectivities as projects that can be shaped by the individual. [They] encourage young women to work on themselves, either through the DIY self-invention and the 'girls can do anything' rhetoric of girl power, or through the self-help books and programs that are available to transform girls in crisis."[9] Empowerment here is limited to building girls' individual strengths, psychological well-being, and personal efficacy. The empowered girl, in this view, is the girl who is able to have power over herself, the power to be whoever she wants to be, a figure that Anita Harris refers to as the "can-do girl."[10]

This emphasis on changing the self can be seen in some of the mission statements of key organizations for girls around the world. These organizations regularly identify a variety of social problems that produce barriers to the happiness and success of girls (unequal education, sexualized media cultures, inadequate access to contraception, etc.), but their solutions are primarily oriented toward improving girls' individual ability to cope with these problems, rather than removing or changing the problems themselves. According to these groups, girls have specific needs that these organizations can meet by helping them to be "strong, smart, and bold" (Girls Inc), "build character and skills for success in the real world" (Girl Scouts), or providing "the opportunity to build their capacities through skills, resources, and knowledge, so they can act upon their decisions and maximize their potential" (Nike Foundation).[11] Countless programs for girls' empowerment in North America and Latin America participate in this discourse, emphasizing how individual girls can be helped to overcome the various challenges of girlhood, develop new skills, and become empowered.

Girls' empowerment as a discourse of self-change and individual growth is not, however, identical for all girls. Rather, it is a discourse that takes on a variety of racialized and located forms. Programs for more privileged, middle-class North American girls tend to focus on helping these girls to navigate the treacherous waters of falling self-esteem and aggressive peers in order to become empowered.[12] Low-income or "at risk" girls in North America are instead told that they must overcome the supposed dangers of their upbringing and make "healthy choices."[13] Meanwhile, according to a variety of the development organizations and policy makers, girls in the Global South (including but not limited to Latin American girls) need to be empowered in order to free themselves from the constraints of their patriarchal national cultures and excessive machismo. This version of the empowerment discourse not only replicates heavily criticized ideas about third-world women as victims of "local" patriarchies whose potential contributions are stifled by "traditional" ideas, but also provides discursive support for the idea that Latin America's young women experience substantial benefits from the "opportunity" to work.[14] According to a recent *New York Times Magazine* article, girls and young women in the Global South are an "unexploited resource" who should be "tapped" for greater economic contributions, which will, in time, empower them.[15] Empowered girls, are, in the words of the Nike Foundation, "ambitious entrepreneurs" and "prepared employees."[16] Although narratives of girls' empowerment are clearly race, class, and location specific, they are also consistently about changing girls, rather than changing the social world.

"Empowering girls" has very positive connotations, invoking ideas of gender equity, community improvement, and a brighter future. But, when examined more closely, it can also be simply another way to present meritocratic notions of personal growth and individual opportunity. As an entirely individualized project of self-creation and transformation, this version of girls' empowerment weaves together the language of liberal feminism and gender equity, colonialist images of third-world women who need to be saved, and neoliberal ideologies of individual responsibilities and self-production. Individual empowerment makes no references to social and political rights, to economic justice, to equality, or to changing the overall contexts and conditions of girls' lives, but only discusses girls' individual strength and resilience. Any girl then who does not "succeed" is just not empowered enough.

This does not mean that the idea of individualized empowerment for girls should be dismissed completely. The organizations in both North America and Latin America that are concerned with the well-being of girls are, of course, engaged in valuable work. Acknowledging the importance of girls and expressing an interest in empowering them is certainly much better than simply ignoring girls and the very real challenges that they face in their lives. By focusing on psychology, self-reliance, healthy choices, and individual achievements, however, this approach to girls' empowerment encourages girls to think of their lives in these terms, often at the expense of a more sociological or political analysis. As girls learn to assess their lives through the language of self-esteem, healthy decision making, and individual opportunities, they are more likely to see their problems as personal troubles, rather than as issues of public concern. If their problems are not seen as publicly relevant, they are also much less likely to engage in social action to remedy them. By only teaching skills for facing barriers as self-made individuals, not removing them, this model of empowerment implies that society, the public, and the community are unchanging arenas. The empowered girl, in this model, thus has the power to remake herself, to define and reconstruct her own individual identity, but not to make social change. The young women who are a part of this study, on the other hand, do not want to merely overcome the problems they see around them, but to change the conditions of their lives and the lives of those around them. These young women are motivated not to simply remake themselves as "successful individuals," but to remake the world as a more just and equitable place. Girls' activism and girls' empowerment have very different goals.

Activism and Civic Engagement

Being an activist requires more than just a desire for change, a collective vision, or a hope that life could be better for more people. It requires action or "actually doing something," as some girls phrased it. In their view, if you aren't doing anything to make the changes you want, then you aren't really an activist. Lolita, a fast-talking, upper-middle-class Argentine involved in the youth wing of a leftist political party, described this distinction between those who just think and talk and those who also take action: "an activist is someone who fights for their political ideas and who actively demonstrates them. They are different than an intellectual, or an *intelectualoide,* as we sometimes call them, because those people tend to sit and discuss Marx, Trotsky or Hobbes in a cafe for 500,000 hours. On the other hand, an activist approaches things more practically and not only theoretically. They demonstrate, they struggle constantly." Estrella, an environmental activist from Mexico, made a somewhat different point about the relationship between theory and action but also suggested that the key to an activist identity is the action: "I know a lot of youth who in reality, all they do, I called them youth, but you could call them intellectuals, because they continue to be very, very interested in these issues and in politics. But in reality they don't do anything. So, I feel like a true intellectual isn't only theoretical, but is also activist. You have to act and not just be observing everything that happens and that's it. . . . Because one form of activism is being involved with others and sharing what you know, and other people sharing what they know." For Estrella, activist identity is not necessarily opposed to an intellectual identity but makes important contributions to knowledge and intellectualism. Activism, and being involved in collective struggle with others, enhances knowledge. Being an activist isn't in opposition to being an intellectual, but, according to these young women, activism requires more than just talk and ideas—it demands concrete engagement to change the world. Girls' sense of activism here is compatible with research on adult activists, which has found that activist identity is "built on a high valuation of doing something." [17] While goals and visions for the world are certainly an important part of being an activist, activists are people who try to create changes, not just people who want change to happen.

The specifics of this concrete action for social change can vary a great deal. Activism, girls argued, includes many more political activities than just going to marches and public protests. This is not to say that they don't participate in these kinds of activities; approximately 90 percent of the girl activists I interviewed had been part of at least one march or rally. But marching and rallying is not, according to many girl activists, the only way to enact your politics. Emerging as activists in the context of the ongoing but unsuccessful attempts to prevent a U.S. war on Iraq by holding marches, marches, and more marches, San Francisco Bay Area teens had a particularly negative response to definitions of activism that overemphasize this specific form of social movement participation. Girls like Clare and Emily described their shifting relationships to marches as the core of an activist practice. Clare "used to assume that activism was going to a march. . . and then as I grew up a bit, I see myself doing more community-building and less of, I guess, the marching, really." She still goes to marches sometimes, but she is engaged in a variety of other social change activities that focus on education, mutual support, and the creation of a more equitable and inclusive school community. This wider understanding of activism, she says, has helped her to feel stronger and more confident in claiming an activist identity. I asked her, "Is activist a word you would identify with?" She replied, "Yes, I think so. I think especially after I've been able to redefine the word for myself. . . . It's an interesting thing, like I think you have to widen your definition of it before you can really connect with it." Going to marches was, for Clare, not a satisfying or sufficiently effective form of activism, but at first she thought it was the only form of activism. For her to really feel like an activist, she needed to rethink the meaning of activism and discover other kinds of political practices. Emily had a similar story. The main thing she remembers about her eighth grade year is the anti-war protests. She went to every possible rally, student walk-out and march she could. But, "when the war broke out, I was home alone and I started crying. It was like, everything that I had been like dedicating all my time to, was just like worth nothing and it was so frustrating." Now a graduating high school senior, Emily coordinates an organization for women's rights at her high school. She still tries to get out to protests and rallies every now and then, but says that her faith in them has been shattered. She doesn't believe that the government pays attention. She says that they don't care about what people think. This was a hard truth for the idealistic San Francisco teen. But she has kept on organizing, focusing her attention on other kinds of change, on building young women's strength and solidarity. Responding to her frustrations with the limits of marching at a young age, Emily has moved to a new kind of activist terrain, one that includes other kinds of political practices.

Definitions of activism that identify protesting as the essential and necessary element of activist political practice, are, in the view of many young women across the Americas, very limited.[18] They suggest that activism can, and should, include other activities aimed at social change and community improvement. Girls' views on the multiplicity of forms of political action coincide with the findings of many feminist sociologists of social movements who have argued for the necessity of expanded conceptions of social movement activism. By keeping definitions of "the political" open, these researchers have identified a multitude of spaces beyond the state as fields where activism occurs,[19] and contend that changes in discourse, ideas, meanings, consciousness, and gender regimes should all be considered as significant political "outcomes" or goals.[20] Furthermore, Taylor and Van Dyke emphasize the value of viewing a wider "repertoire of tactics" as political actions; they critique the definition of tactical repertoires found in protest event research for overemphasizing public and highly visible tactics at the expense of less obvious forms of political action. Their own definition, which emphasizes contestation, intentionality, and collective identity, expands the concept of tactics to include cultural and discursive political acts and acknowledges that "a movement's particular forms of protest are not only directed to external targets, but they also have an internal movement-building dimension."[21] The case of teenage girl activists indicates that such an expansive definition is sociologically useful for seeing the varied terrain of gendered social movement activity, *and* it is a definition that resonates with movement participants' own conceptions of their activism.

Girls' understanding of activism as involving a multiplicity of tactics beyond protest also reflects the contexts in which they are emerging as political actors. According to one collective of activist writers, "Reinventing tactics of resistance has become a central preoccupation for the movement of movements. How do we make rebellion enjoyable, effective, and irresistible? Who wants the tedium of traditional demonstrations and protests—the ritual marches from point A to B, the permits and police escorts, the staged acts of civil disobedience, the verbose rallies and dull speeches by leaders?"[22] In Argentina, the autonomous social movements have "begun to articulate a new and revolutionary politics, embodied in various new practices."[23] In Mexico, the Zapatistas speak of "another campaign" and propose new ways of doing politics.[24] And in Venezuela, the dynamics of Chavez's Bolivarian government and the broader revolutionary process have led activists to develop novel forms of engagement in both state and non-state politics.[25] Girl activists in these locations, like many of the adult activists around them, use a mixture of "old" and "new" tactics. But unlike many adults, they have only been activists during this period of reinvention, expansion and reinterpretation of activist practices. It therefore seems obvious to many of them that activism involves far more than the tactic of protest. On the other hand, many North American girls like Clare and Emily are unaware of this shift in the meaning of activism in some movements and locations. Despite this lack of an explicit relationship, these girls are also redefining activism to include and incorporate a wider array of practices.

For girl activists, one of the most important and pervasive elements in their tactical repertoire is political education. The vast majority of their activities and practices have a strong educational component. They hold countless workshops, film screenings, study circles, and cultural events to educate themselves and their peers about the many problems they see in the world and about ways to contribute to social change. Several young women are also engaged in media work, constructing youth-run, democratic, and alternative media institutions including a radio station and a small handful of newspapers. The Las Voces collective outside Mexico City is one example of a group that uses both conventional and innovative political education tactics. The group publishes a regular newspaper, hosts film screenings and discussions, and attends many protests and direct action events together. When I met them, they were also working on a piece of political street theater for *el dia de los muertos,* a Mexican holiday to honor and remember the dead. I spent many hours with the group making masks, building coffins, cooking up wheat paste to construct bones, and talking about the script and messages for the event. On the day of the performance, I arrived at the *zocalo,* or central plaza, partway through their first run-through. The skeletons sang songs about death caused by injustice; there was a large crowd gathered around watching and applauding as the youth interwove tradition with political theater in order to educate others and build oppositional consciousness. In the week that followed, when I met up with each of the three teenage girls involved in Las Voces for interviews, they all told me how effective they felt the performance was because it captured people's attention and opened their minds to a new way of thinking about the world, "letting a message into their consciousness."

Although political education is a vital component of girls' activist practices beyond public protest, it is certainly not all that they do. Some teen activists make use of formalized channels of political intervention. This includes lobbying, petition drives, precinct walking, party building, and other legitimized forms of influencing public policy. Others use confrontational direct action to make immediate demands upon authorities: nearly one-third of the girl activists I interviewed had taken part in an action of this kind.[26] These direct actions included student strikes and walk-outs, school takeovers in which students occupied administration offices until certain demands were met, disruption of anti-immigrant vigilantes on the U.S./Mexico border, and an encampment to prevent the "development" of sacred indigenous land.

In addition to tactics that contest or challenge dominant knowledges, institutions, and policies, girl activists, like many adults, also engage in the creation of alternatives. Sometimes referred to as prefigurative politics,[27] this too is a direct form of political action. Instead of waiting for external authorities to take care of a community's needs, activists address the problems they see themselves, building alternative institutions and new community spaces in which they can enact their visions for change. In girls' activist practices, this includes not only the development of democratic youth media institutions but also workers' centers and organizations, and various cooperative, democratic, and community-run kitchens, health clinics, and childcare programs. Other girls focus on constructing and strengthening the alternative and democratic institutions within their schools including student centers in Buenos Aires, *cubiculos* in Mexico City (see the section on *cubiculos,* p.40), networks of students of color that provide each other with support and collectively intervene in educational equity issues in the San Francisco Bay Area, and the organization of *voceros,* or representatives, who represent students in important school decisions at local, regional, and national levels in Caracas.

Teen girl activists also participate in some social change activities that are less clearly "social movement" practices. This includes some tactics that are perhaps better understood as community service or even charity, such as shoreline clean-ups, visiting the elderly in nursing homes, U.S. and Canadian youth traveling to countries in the Global South to help build schools, volunteering at hospitals and soup kitchens, and raising money for international organizations that work on development, human rights, or poverty issues. A final set of social change practices used by the teenage girl activists I interviewed are individual, socially responsible, daily behaviors like recycling and green, local, or fair trade consumption choices. Despite the fact that these individual and service-oriented practices may seem outside the scope of social movements and therefore outside of many understandings of activism, I mention them here to draw a more complete picture of girls' social change practices. However, it is also important to note that even though such tactics were part of girls' larger repertoire of political practices, none of the girls I interviewed used only these more individualized tactics.

Supporting girls' tactics for change (protest, education, confrontational direct action, formal political pressure, alternative institution building, service, and responsible individual behaviors) is the practice of movement building and political organizing, or getting more people actively engaged in the process of trying to create social change. A great deal of the research on social movements discusses such practices primarily as "recruitment"[28] emphasizing organizations or movements seeking out new members as resources to be mobilized for other actions and tactics. In contrast, I want to re-frame these activities as "organizing," highlighting how engaging people in the process of creating social change is, for some activists and movements, not simply recruitment to do something else but is itself a substantial social movement tactic and an intentional strategy for action. Recruitment implies that people are being brought into something that already exists in order to add numbers, while organizing suggests the building of a collective project and a collective agenda together.

For teenage girl activists, other youth are not merely a "resource" to be mobilized for political ends. Rather, they see an inherent value in encouraging more young people to be part of political communities and collective struggle. Activists refer to a lot of what they do as "organizing work," but I use the term here specifically to refer to those political practices that directly aim to develop more active movement participants and increase the engagement of a larger community. For girl activists, this includes planning open forums to discuss and strategize about the future of their movements or groups, spending time talking with other youth (or other community members) about the problems they see and ways that they might want to affect change, or encouraging friends, classmates, or family to come to an event. The act of organizing is not a singular strategy, like political education, protest, or direct action, but is instead a foundational element within most movement strategies.

Girls' activism clearly involves taking action on social issues, being politically and civically engaged. In much the same way that activist goals exist outside of the discursive and institutional regime of girls' empowerment, activist practices also exist outside and beyond a more widespread public interest in girls' civic engagement. Although these girl activists are certainly engaged and active citizens, their practices are quite distinct from those commonly promoted in programs designed to empower girls as citizens and participants in their communities. Youth civic engagement programs, as they have developed since the late 1980s and early 1990s, primarily aim to involve young people in formal, state-based politics and/or conventional civil society activities, especially volunteering.[29] Empowered youth citizenship, as it is understood and produced in the world of contemporary youth civic engagement programs, does not generally include dissident social movement activity and "outsider" political strategies.

Community service and service-learning initiatives are extremely widespread throughout the Americas.[30] Many U.S. and Canadian high schools have implemented community service requirements; several Canadian provinces have official policies making service mandatory for graduation.[31] National youth service policies in Mexico and Venezuela also require a fixed number of hours of community service of either college or high school students.[32] Numerous programs for girls' empowerment also emphasize community service and "caring for others." For example, when the Girl Scouts address community participation and civic engagement directly, it is discussed and practiced only as "service," not "politics" or "social change." Girls are encouraged to conduct service projects, which are necessary for earning silver and gold awards. Service, according the Girl Scouts, is defined as "doing something helpful for others without expecting or asking for money or any other reward."[33] Although the Girl Scouts has had a government relations office since 1952, which aims to "inform and educate key representatives of the government . . . about issues important to girls and Girl Scouting and lobby for increased program resources," girls are rarely involved in this part of the organization.[34] The office and the adults involved lobby on behalf of girls, not with them.

Many scholars writing on the issue of youth and politics, while supportive of efforts to engage youth in community service, are more deeply concerned with a decline in young people's participation in governance and formal political institutions, rather than just in civil society per se.[35] Therefore, a sizable number of civic engagement initiatives are designed to bring young people into contact with local, state, and federal governments. Governments around the world have set up a variety of youth councils, assemblies, and other consulting bodies of young people.[36] Howard Williamson writes that there is "a massive groundswell of interest in the idea of youth participation and promotion of more active citizenship."[37] From a children's participatory budget council in Brazil[38] to a six-month, Europe-wide training program on participation and citizenship for minority youth,[39] young people's participation in government-sponsored bodies and programs for civic engagement is seen as an ideal expression of healthy civic engagement and as a sign of governments' newfound respect and appreciation for the voices of young people. Unfortunately, however, many critical scholars have found that such programs often give youth little real political power or authority.[40]

While some young people get involved in either community service or government-sponsored youth organizations, many of the girls I interviewed remain highly critical of these institutional attempts at including youth. Violet, a San Francisco Bay Area eighteen-year-old, said that "when I think about city youth councils and stuff my first response is that is not—that is for adults to say that they have youth input and it is not really coming from the youth at all. I'm very skeptical." Similarly, Lisette, also eighteen and from the Bay Area, pointed out that although her town has a youth council, "they don't have any power. . . . When I went to the city council, they were like 'well, don't we have a student council?' I was like 'you don't even know?'" She went on to say that when she went there "they were trying to organize like a basketball tournament to raise money for I don't know what, and I was like why are you here, and they were like well I'm just getting hours for my community service." Frustrated by her attempts to find space to make social change within conventional youth civic engagement programs, she got involved in another program that was about contributing to the community, designed not just for youth. But she quickly found that this was not a way to make change either. In one meeting, "somebody asked, well, once you develop [the downtown] what is going to happen to the homeless people and the answer that the city council member gave, he was like, well eventually with all the new buildings and everything is going to go up in price, so basically saying that the homeless people will just slowly go away by the themselves and it's like whoa, that's totally hypocritical to say at one time that you want to make this a community but yet you want to kick out the people that don't make it look good. So, that really turned me off." And, in my previous research with Washington, DC, teens who were working on developing a new sexual harassment policy, the girls expressed a great deal of anger over their treatment by school board members. They were particularly angry at being referred to as "policy sprouts" and were frustrated with the way board members were condescending to them.[41] Many girls' direct experience with government attempts at including them have not been particularly positive.

Activism, as a form of youth civic engagement, happens primarily outside of the boundaries of formal, institutionalized politics. Youth civic engagement discourse and programming, on the other hand, centers formal political participation, implicitly suggesting it is the ideal type of youth political action. As Anita Harris argues, "with the move toward enhancing youth participation, there has now emerged a preferred way of being politically engaged and of expressing social critique. Participating means displaying oneself and speaking out in particular ways in particular places, places that are on view to the authorities who grant this empowerment."[42] Thus, youth participation programs can act as a form of regulation, encouraging particular forms of civic engagement and particular kinds of political expression, all under the watchful eye of the state.

A variety of articles from the civic engagement perspective indicate the possibility that youth participation programs are a way to manage and contain youth dissent and more rebellious forms of political activity. In their recommendations to government, James Youniss and his co-authors encourage politicians to distinguish the "protest generation" and the historic connection of youth and social movements from the current generation of youth.[43] They imply that today's youth can still be successfully incorporated into the government, but that if they are not reached, they may become more like other, more troubling, activist-oriented groups of young people. Youth participation in social upheaval and revolution remains a present threat to governments and is thus a concern to civic engagement scholars.[44] Activism, as a set of dissident and extra-institutional political practices, is thus related to and yet quite distinct from the forms of civic engagement commonly promoted in the numerous programs aimed to incorporate young people into the mechanisms of governance and community service.

Activism, Apathy, and Exceptionalism

Activism is defined not only through social change goals and "outsider" political action, but also through participation in organizations, collectivities, and groups. Being and becoming an activist is not an individualized act, and girls' activist identities are closely linked to those organizations in which they participate. Many scholars have emphasized the centrality of political communities to social movements and highlighted the importance of activists' understandings of their collective identities.[45] Collective identity within social movements refers not only to the movement's negotiation of the meanings of broader identity categories like "youth," and "girls," but also what Jasper refers to as movement and organizational identities.[46] Some of the girls I interviewed were part of youth groups with ties to particular Communist and Socialist political parties. These young women saw themselves not just as

activists but as Communists, Socialists, Trotskyists, Leninists, and/or Marxists. A handful of girls in Mexico and in the United States described themselves as anarchists, and three of the girl activists I met in Mexico identified
themselves as Zapatistas. Most of the girl activists I interviewed, however,
did not associate themselves with a specific ideological grouping or theoretical tendency. Instead, many of them defined themselves more through their
affiliation with a particular movement or with multiple movements, describing themselves as being part of youth movements, ecological movements,
student movements, anti-poverty movements, anti-racist movements, and
global justice movements, to name a few.

In addition to these macrolevel ideological and movement affiliations,
nearly all of the interviewees were part of one or more specific, localized
organizations or groups. They did most of their activism and political organizing with these collectives. Many of these groups were school-based,
meaning girl activists' primary movement relationships and connections
were with other students in their high schools. In Buenos Aires, I interviewed girls from five different student centers. These centers are student-
run organizations within the high schools that organize social events, community service opportunities, and work for political and social change both
inside and outside their schools. Within some of these centers there are also
agrupaciones, or student political groupings, which are more tightly knit
activist collectives made up of teens who share similar political views. Some
of the agrupaciones are connected to political parties, but some are considered independent. In Mexico City the majority of the teens I interviewed
were part of *cubiculos*, or small activist clubs within their schools. Unlike
the Buenos Aires schools with their single student centers, the Mexico City
schools tended to have multiple *cubiculos*, organized largely by ideological tendency. One could walk down a hallway past two different Socialist
cubiculos, an anarchist *cubiculo*, a Zapatista *cubiculo*, an eco-*cubiculo* and a
PRD (Partido de la Revolución Democrática, the official left-center political party) *cubiculo*. Many of the Vancouver girls also organized primarily
with people from their own high schools as part of environmental clubs,
global issues clubs, or clubs focused on addressing problems in the schools.
Several of the Bay Area youth I interviewed were involved in school-based
organizations that focused on educational equity and justice, gender equality, or anti-racism.

In and around Caracas, as in the San Francisco Bay Area, most girls were
part of citywide or metropolitan areawide youth organizations. In Venezuela,
these citywide groups include not only a Communist youth organization but

also a youth rights organization and an organization for young workers. In the San Francisco Bay Area, one of the regional groups is actually made up of school-based chapters, and activists therefore work both in their school communities and with teens from other schools. I interviewed Bay Area girls from a Jewish youth organization, a girls' organization, a few peer health organizations, and a youth environmental racism group, all of which were formalized nonprofit organizations. I also conducted a few interviews with girls in Cuernavaca, a city two hours outside of Mexico City, who were all founding members of Las Voces, the citywide youth collective described earlier. Finally, a few girls, scattered across the five locations, were involved in community-based organizations made up primarily of adults.

These small groups and immediate social networks were a crucial part of how girl activists saw themselves. They were not just individuals who would go to an event every now and then; they actively engaged in collective planning, organizing, and political action with a group or organization. In our conversations, they partially described and defined their activist identities in and through their organizational ones: "an activist in the student center," "a member of the Zapatista collective at Prepa Z," "part of Students for Women's Rights," or "a global issues person." Being an activist meant they were part of something bigger than themselves—that they were part of a movement, part of an organization, or part of a collective that was trying to create social change together.

Girl activists are part of communities of activists, usually communities that include other youth activists. Speaking from within these communities of teenagers involved in social movement activity, girl activists regularly reject and respond to a third prominent discourse about girls' political identities: the widespread assumptions of youth apathy and the concomitant idea that any youth who is involved in activism must, in fact, be an extraordinary or exceptional individual. In doing so, they also construct a definition of activist identity that suggests that anyone, through participation and learning, can become an activist.

Throughout the Americas, there is a powerful perception that teenagers are apathetic and disengaged from politics. In the United States, a major report on the need for improved civic education in schools argued that such education is needed in order to "address disturbing trends related to youth civic engagement, including a decrease in young people's interest in political discussion and public issues; their tendency to be more cynical and alienated from formal politics, more materialistic, and less trusting; and a decline in their voter participation rates."[47] The United Nation's 2007 World Youth

Report's chapter on Latin American youth also argues that young people in that region are growing "increasingly apathetic" and are distrustful of and disinterested in politics.[48] Youth civic engagement scholars have also catalogued what they see as a waning civic spirit, lack of political knowledge, and general apathy of young people.[49]

Even many adult activists participate in this narrative. Veteran activists frequently complain of youth apathy, and feminist organizers worry about a decline in feminist identification and activism amongst a supposedly "post-feminist" generation. I have therefore found myself in countless social situations informing skeptical adults that high school activism, although not exactly commonplace, is actually a regular feature of youth culture in some cities, and that there are probably many more teenage activists in the world than most adults would expect.[50] Upon hearing about the struggles and achievements of teenage social movements, many adults then proclaim that the girls I study must be truly "exceptional" young women who are very different from their peers. They regularly suggest that activist youth must be "just incredible" and "very special."

As I traveled to each of my research locations, I sought out adult activists for their advice and assistance finding teenage girl activists. I began to track and document adult responses to the idea of teenage activism. North American adults (in both Canada and the United States) were the most likely to be convinced that girl activists are incredibly uncommon and therefore "very special" individuals. A woman in her twenties who has worked with several San Francisco Bay Area organizations that focus on youth activism described how, in her opinion, many adults view youth, particularly youth of color, as a hot commodity. She told me that "there is competition for youth. They are made to be figureheads and get tokenized by these adult organizations that keep saying, 'oh, we want you.'" Referring to this as young people being "vulturized," she suggested that the idea of the exceptionality of teenage activists leads to adults "using" any youth activist they encounter, trying to bring them in and make them a youth voice for their own organizations in order to appear more youth-friendly.

Despite the well-institutionalized activist organizations within many Mexico City high schools, some of the Mexican activist adults I encountered were quite cynical about the political engagement of youth. One middle-aged woman activist told me that "this generation is not really that active. There aren't many girls so don't expect too much." Her husband agreed, saying that "there aren't many youth under eighteen with political consciousness." They both suggested that instead of looking for the few activist girls, I should study why most teens are not active. A few days later, I met a woman in her twenties who works with youth on reproductive rights issues and asked her what she thought about this perception that there are not really very many teenage activists. She nodded and said that "they are active, they are just invisible." By emphasizing how rare and special young activists are, adults can unintentionally contribute to the ongoing invisibility of this group.

The invisibility of high school activism was also noticeable in Venezuela. Many of the major national youth organizations define youth as starting at age eighteen. The Instituto Nacional de la Juventud, for example, which coordinates elements of youth participation in the missions and government-led community development, defines youth as eighteen to twenty-eight years of age. Before that, according to one of their staff members, you are a child or an adolescent but not a youth. The Frente Francisco Miranda, another space of youth engagement in the Bolivarian revolutionary process defines youth as ages eighteen to thirty-five. High school students are thus more likely to be lumped together with children and therefore are not generally visible as activists. Despite this tendency to see teens more as children than youth, adult responses to my search for girl activists in Venezuela were fairly mixed. Some adults seemed to think that activists of this age were extremely rare, while others were sure that they were just as involved in social movements and community projects as everyone else.

Finally, the adult activists in Buenos Aires were generally confident that I would encounter plenty of high school girl activists to interview. Unlike many of the adults in my other four research locations, they did not seem to find high school activism any more extraordinary than the activism of adults. While many of them did not themselves know any teenage girls involved in social movements, they were sure that such girls existed and most even had some suggestions about where to find them. After my experiences searching for girl activists in my other four research locations, this adult confidence in the normality of high school activism was very striking.

The girl activists I have met are indeed wonderfully smart, dedicated, and passionate individuals, but they also adamantly and actively refute the idea that they are special. Instead, they understand activism as an ordinary practice that can be a part of the life of anyone who is so inclined, including young people. Josephine and Megan, two white, middle-class Vancouver teens, were quite vocal about their frustrations with adults who think they are "sooo incredible."

JOSEPHINE: Like, some people, like we were saying before, adults are so amazed, like, "wow, you are so young and you are doing all this stuff," and before I was like "thanks" and everything, but I just realized . . . that they are congratulating me because they don't—it is not even in their head that somebody so young could even accomplish something like this.

MEGAN: They don't think it is possible.

JOSEPHINE: So it's not like, "oh, good job."

MEGAN: It's actually not a compliment.

JOSEPHINE: It's more like, "what you are doing, I'm so impressed you could even have gotten that far. And you are the only youth, you are the only one who could do it. And all your other friends, they should all be like you." And I'm like, "no, everybody does that."

MEGAN: Yeah, they think we are special.

JOSEPHINE: Yeah, we hear stuff that you are so special.

MEGAN: And we're like "no, it is normal."

Josephine and Megan argue that statements about how youth activists are "amazing" assume that most youth are not capable of such involvement. By proclaiming youth activism and youth activists to be extraordinary, adults perpetuate an association of youthfulness with political inaction or inability. Normal youth, in this narrative, are apathetic and politically disengaged. It is only the talented and committed few who are seen as capable of becoming politically active. Instead of accepting this claim, girl activists regularly suggest that anyone, of any age, can be involved in activism.

In emphasizing activism as a collective, rather than individual, project and highlighting their organizational affiliations, girl activists reject the notion of activism as the act of heroic individuals. The discourse of activism as a form of exceptionalism is ultimately, as Josephine and Megan indicate, a discourse of individualism. Adults who are "wowed" by teenage girl activists are implying that they are achieving a great deal on their own and do not necessarily see that individual girl activists are part of whole political communities of activist youth. While it is not actually true that "everybody does this," as Josephine says, it *is* the case that she knows a lot of other people who are equally active. From her perspective, she really isn't extraordinary: she is just one of the many girls she knows who are involved in social movements and social change. In addition, everything she does is not really her own to claim—the accomplishments and achievements adults see as making her so special are collective. Girl activists see themselves not as isolated individual exceptions to the rule of youth apathy, but as just a few examples of a much more extensive group. From the perspective of girl activists involved in communities of struggle, their own activism is just one part of something larger. From where they stand, activists are not singular individuals who achieve a great deal, but ordinary people who are working in groups toward shared goals.

By imagining activist identity to be an ordinary rather an exceptional achievement, girl activists provide narrative support for their efforts to mobilize other youth. According to Lisette, "there are a lot of young people who really do care, who want to do something that is important but they're just not given a chance." If girls believed in their own exceptionality and their own "special" status, they would be much less likely to try and engage other youth. Alicia proposed that girl activists are not really all that special, but they do provide an example for other girls: "We demonstrate to people that it is not just men who are capable of doing this work that, until recently, was mostly directed by men. We are an example . . . and we show that to other girls." Instead of seeing youth activists as special and amazing individuals, they work to increase the number of youth engaged in activism, since, as Ixtab put it, "adults don't always realize that any youth, or adult, or just any person can become involved in politics." Because they believe that other youth can also be activists and that being an activist teen isn't really all that extraordinary, girl activists emphasize the importance of educating and organizing other youth to become activists as well, something they say adults don't often think is even possible.

In conclusion, teenage girl activists define activist identity around three key features: activists, in their view, are (1) people who want to make substantial changes to the social world, (2) are engaged in various kinds of action to make those changes, including extra-institutional political tactics, and (3) are part of political communities or collectivities taking such action. These activist identities exist outside and in contrast to three institutionalized discourses about girlhood, namely (1) the widespread articulations of individualized girls' empowerment, (2) formal civic engagement, and (3) youth apathy. These girls enact a different kind of empowerment, constructing themselves as particular kinds of empowered girl citizens. They claim political and social authority for girls and highlight girls' roles in creating meaningful social change. Furthermore, girls do not see this kind of political engagement as extraordinary; they consistently position activism as a normal activity, for youth as well as for adults. The girls in this study are engaged in a wide array of activist projects and utilize a variety of political tactics, but they do not want these activities to be seen as special. Instead, they choose to see their activism as an example other youth can follow. They suggest that all youth are capable of becoming activists. Being teenagers, they suggest, is no barrier to activism. In the next chapter, I'll show how they draw upon these youthful identities in order to construct social movement standing and claim political authority.

3

We Are Not the Future

Claiming Youth Authority

The outside walls of the school were covered in hastily lettered posters and photocopied lists of demands, and a red and black flag hung from the bright yellow fencing. Liliana, a graceful young woman with big dark eyes stood at the gate. Dressed all in black, her hood pulled close over her head, a black bandana tied around the lower half of her face, she was carefully watching who was entering and leaving school grounds. Walking up to the entrance, it was obvious to me that something was happening here: Liliana and her friends, students at a public high school in the trendy Mexico City neighborhood of Coyoacan, were involved in an intense struggle to remove the *porros,* or thugs, who had been violently harassing and beating up the teenage activists and other students. Despite numerous requests for the school and university administrations to take action for student safety, little had been done to stop these attacks. Therefore, the student activists, upon seeing that the adults who were supposed to look out for them had failed to do so, took over the administration offices, demanding a new principal and the implementation of a set of community-based procedures to deal with the *porros.* Teachers in support of the administration cancelled classes, attempting to push the students to back down on their demands. The students responded by organizing a parents' meeting, which led the parents to pressure the teachers back into the classroom. After several weeks, the administration began to dialogue with the students and eventually agreed to most of their demands. Without the impetus of the student activism, it seems likely that nothing would have been done to address the dangerous and repressive situation.

During the occupation, the teenage activists were focusing on a very specific problem in their own lives—a threat to their safety. The adults around them had neglected their needs, so they took action for themselves. They were not the only students occupying school offices in Mexico City in the fall of 2005; they were part of a larger high school and university movement against political repression. Young people around the city were frustrated with adult failures to address their concerns, and thus they were taking action. In doing so, they were claiming their rights, as youth, to be activists and social movement actors in the face of both direct repression and dangerously negligent inaction.

One of the key features of social movements is that they are spaces in which ordinary people claim political or social authority, the right to "make history."[1] Movements and their participants have to construct themselves as legitimate actors with political, social, or cultural rights to participation. Furthermore, one of the defining features of transgressive contentious politics is that "at least some parties to the conflict are newly self-identified political actors."[2] McAdam, Tarrow, and Tilly propose that scholars of social movements explore more fully the mechanisms by which such new actors are constituted. A great deal of social movement research has addressed the formation of these collective identities,[3] showing how such identities are constructed through the production of boundaries, group consciousness, and negotiation.[4] However, Karen Beckwith argues that the collective identity literature has not sufficiently considered the necessity of what she calls "political movement standing" in "linking identity with agency."[5] Using the example of women activists, Beckwith suggests that when a group is fundamentally seen as external to politics they have to make assertions "to both internal and external reference groups of their legitimate presence and involvement in a movement."[6] Legitimacy is not inevitable or guaranteed, but is socially constructed in the process of collective action as activists make assertions of standing and discursively infuse their identities with political authority. These articulations and claims of authority transform "collective identity into a political resource for collective action."[7] For groups who are marginal to, or excluded from, politics and social movements, authorizing their presence and agency is a vital aspect of their identity work.

Given the feminist scholarship on how women activists construct political legitimacy for themselves in part on the basis of their identities as women in both gender-based and non-gender-specific movements,[8] I expected that the young women in this study would also make being a girl an important part of their activist identities. However, this was not the case for those I interviewed. One of the reasons might be that many of the authority claims made by adult women are based on the symbolic power of motherhood, which, as a positive symbol of care and concern, is one that teenage girls have little access too. Teenage motherhood is not generally a symbol of moral authority but instead one of deviance and misbehavior.[9] Instead of authorizing themselves as girls, these young women claim social movement standing primarily as youth.

This is not to say that their other identities are unimportant to their political selves nor that these other identity categories are absent from girl activists' authorization claims. They sometimes make assertions to standing in more specific ways—as youth of color, as poor youth, and occasionally as girls. They also make claims of political authority that do not reference their youth at all, claiming that they take action as poor people, as Venezuelans, as blacks, or as bisexuals or lesbians, for example. My argument here is not that girl activists *only* authorize their political action as youth. Rather, remembering that most girl activists are primarily involved in youth-based groups and organizations, I suggest that "youth" is an especially significant aspect of their collective political identities and therefore the identity around which they *most often* focus their claims to political authority and legitimacy.

Developing political and social movement standing for youth requires substantial symbolic labor. For teenagers, the process of achieving political legitimacy is complicated by their distinctive relationship to the state and political citizenship. Youth activists are officially excluded from formal political participation; the girls interviewed in this study (with a very few exceptions) are not allowed to vote or run for office.[10] Youth do not have the full rights of voting citizens and therefore do not have access to or influence with political decision makers in the same way that voting adults do. Young people also continue to be seen by policy makers and other adults primarily as objects of public or civil policy, not as subjects to be engaged in its formation.[11] When young people engage in dissident and radical politics, their activism is frequently dismissed as generational rebellion, or "just a phase," rather than treated as substantive, meaningful political action.[12] Finally, as Hava Rachel Gordon writes, youth are seen as "citizens in the making," and are "socially constructed as citizen participants only in the future tense: ill-equipped to participate in social and political decision making as youth, only capable of this participation as adults."[13] Therefore, the girls in this study, despite the increasing public discourse around the value of "youth participation" still face substantial challenges in positioning themselves as fully engaged, active citizens who are taken seriously as equal participants in social movements and political decision making. This chapter explores key discursive tools girl activists use to authorize their politics and to construct social movement standing in the context of their political marginalization. Specifically, I address three narrative threads in their construction of youthful political authority: egalitarian democratic rights, difference, and youth responsibility.

Democracy and Equality

The vibrant student centers of Buenos Aires are the organizational home for student activists seeking democratic voice and authority in their schools. In contrast to U.S. and Canadian student councils (which, according to many of the girl activists from these countries, do little more than plan school dances), the Buenos Aires student centers are social movement spaces. Students in many of these centers are organized into *agrupaciones*, or political groups, each with its own ideology and platform. In most schools, there are several different left-wing *agrupaciones*, some of which are connected to formal political parties, and some of which are not. Most schools also have some representation from more moderate and conservative *agrupaciones* as well. The students elect delegates, coordinators, secretaries, and presidents of the centers who, in most cases, run as part of an *agrupacion*. The *agrupaciones* organize political education workshops, film screenings and study circles and meet regularly to discuss their strategies and direction. The centers themselves also organize educational events, community work, and solidarity actions, and act as a force for student influence in educational policy and school change at the national, local, and school levels. But their main task and foundational principle, according to many of the girls who participate, is to increase students' decision-making power in their schools. According to Milagros, a fourteen-year-old participant in her school's center, activists there organize their fellow students to "improve the lives of the secondary school students because many times . . . they are not consulted about things, even though they are the ones who will see, who will be changed by things, like the educational law." Throughout the city, the student centers' founding mandate is to claim political authority for youth on the basis of an assertion of students' democratic rights to decision-making power within their schools.

Even when they are working for minor concessions and changes, Buenos Aires student activists tend to frame their work in terms of democracy and the rights of students to have some authority in school decisions. At one school, I met a group of teens who were concerned about the rising costs of printing and photocopying. In response to the problem, they decided to create a copy center that would be affordable, provide some jobs to other students, and be student-run. In working to get student and administrative support for the center, according to Julia, they "explained it in a way that related it to the lack of democracy within the school so that we could call into question, or put on the table, the issue of power within the school." The copy center was one manifestation of the larger struggle for student-run, student-led spaces within the school.

Ana, a sixteen-year-old student center activist, like many of her peers, explicitly draws on the discourse of democracy in order to claim political authority and voice on educational issues.

> In the school, there is a rector who is the ultimate authority, who is the only one who can decide about everything. We believe that this is not democratic, if you like, because what we say is that the educational community, that is the teachers who give classes, the students who come to study, the other workers who maintain the school, we should be able to make our own decisions. One person can't come from a position from above, from a political position that can be manipulated as needed and then say to us, this "yes" and that "no" because it isn't him who will live the decisions that are made.

Ana, Milagros, and many other Buenos Aires teens consistently reference the ideal of democracy when struggling to claim authority in their schools. In particular, they argue that democracy means that those affected by a decision should have significant voice in the making of such decisions. According to these teens, it is partly because they are so obviously affected by educational policy that students have a right to political power in this arena. Thus, the language of democracy gives girl activists a useful discursive tool in their struggles to construct themselves as legitimate political actors, particularly in the arena of schooling and educational policy.

One of the benefits of the widespread contemporary interest in youth civic engagement and the health of democracy is that it provides another useful foundation upon which girl activists can build their claims of political authority. Despite the limitations of the civic engagement literature and its associated government-sponsored programs, the presence of this powerful social discourse on the importance of youth participation is certainly useful to girl activists as they work to demand more substantial, meaningful political power. Diana, a Bay Area teen, asks adults to encourage and support youth activism in order to strengthen and improve democracy:

> I feel like if we keep on, if we like give our young generations the tools to create a good democracy, then they are gonna create it. But if we just let them go through the first twenty-five years of their life not giving any information, not providing any tools or resources then we can't expect, they can't expect us to go create a great democracy if we've never seen one modeled or if we've never been told how we can make one or been given resources to make one.

The popular narrative that youth need to be educated and prepared for democratic participation provides a way for young people to remind adults of the importance of youth politics and to claim their participatory rights. Here, Diana deploys a developmental discourse, suggesting that adults should support youth activism in order to help teens develop into proper citizens.

However, although Diana and several other teens occasionally draw upon this developmental democratic discourse, using it for their purposes, others point to the limitations of this narrative, actively refusing the suggestion that their politics is only relevant in a deferred future. In this view the discourse of preparation is, in the end, incompatible with their efforts to claim authority because it makes no space for the democratic participation of youth *as youth*.[14] Girl activists do not see themselves as being "in training" for later, more meaningful, involvement as adults. Instead, they emphasize their current participatory and democratic rights as teenagers, not merely as future adults. As one young woman in Venezuela put it, "we don't, because we're minors, we don't have the right to vote, but we do, right now, have the right to defend what we have and to fight for what we want." Ixtab concurs, saying that "I don't believe that we are the future. We are the present, right? Okay, sure we'll be around in the future, but we are also here right now and we can do things starting now so that the future is good for us and good for those who come after us." Josephine and Megan, the two Vancouver teens who were quite vocal about their anger at the idea of their exceptionality, have also thought a lot about the issue of their current rights to participation. They even have a standard statement on this topic that they use to close the presentations they give to groups around the city. Megan shared it with me: "Young people need to stop being addressed by everyone else as the leaders of tomorrow, because that closes us down, because if I'm the leader of tomorrow, and I see that garbage there, I don't have to do anything because it's not my issue right now, tomorrow I'll grow up. . . . So youth are not only the leaders of tomorrow, but also the leaders of today." Josephine looked at her friend, smiled and added, "We're not gonna inherit [the world], we have it now." Girl activists make many direct claims about their rights to political agency in the present, and are thus modifying and expanding the symbolic relationship between young people and democracy.

By emphasizing their own *current* potential, girl activists suggest that youth is not an irrelevant social identity, a mere phase that one passes through on the way to adulthood. Youth are not only adults-in-training; they are also real people who matter in the present. Instead of only caring about youth for what they might become, or how their present experiences will influence their futures, girls' narratives on youth activism demand that adults pay attention to their present-day political lives as important in and of themselves. This approach to understanding the experiences of childhood and youth is also relevant beyond political participation; Alan Prout and Allison James argue that scholars need to attempt to look at childhood as significant in its own right rather than through the lens of adult concerns.[15]

A developmental discourse on youth politics implies that youth activism is *only* valuable for the future and dismisses the possibility that youth activism does actually make a difference or that youth activists can create substantial social change. As Hava Gordon articulates in her analysis of citizenship-in-the-making,[16] the assumption that teenagers can't really make a difference during their youth is rooted in conceptions of the inherent inequality of young people. In contrast, underlying girl activists' discourse on their democratic rights in the present is a firm belief in their own competence and their equality with adults. For example, several girls argued that many adults are more ignorant about politics than they themselves are but that they [adults] still have the right to vote, just because of their age. Rachel, a Vancouver seventeen-year-old, said:

I think the whole age thing is kind of a controversial issue. . . . Some teenagers who are so into the political issues, they actually do research on things, but they're not, they can't vote because they're not old enough. Whereas you have adults, some adults who will not vote and or they just go and pick [their] favorite name or something. . . . And sixteen is kind of like, at the age range where, in high school, you are learning and thinking and studying how government works. Kids are more aware than you think they are.

Rachel, and organizations like the National Youth Rights Association, in discussing lowering the voting age, propose that young people are capable of making political choices and of being informed citizens.[17] Other girl activists emphasized that youth activists are smart, critical thinkers. Lolita, a Buenos Aires sixteen-year-old said: "It seems to me that youth know very clearly what it is that we want. We know what kind of education we want, what kind of country we want, but people still think that we don't have a critical position, that we aren't able to speak or form our own ideas. From my point of view, they are wrong. I believe that we can discuss everything equally." Several other girls indicated that they are just doing what they believe all people (of any age) can and should be doing—getting involved in their communities and taking action on issues that matter to them. According to Yasmine, from the San Francisco Bay Area, "I just think, like I'd be a waste of space and energy if I didn't do all I can to make a change, or you know, and especially I can't afford to be ignorant and I can't afford to not know what is happening in my community and like, I just have to know, otherwise I'll just, I'm a victim. So I just feel it is my duty." In this view, if adults have responsibility to be involved, to make the world a better place, so do youth. Instead of letting their youth be an excuse or reason for inaction, these girls see themselves as equally responsible for making the world a better place. The logic of democracy and the extension of citizenship rights to a previously excluded group rely, in part, upon that group arguing that they are not inherently inferior to those who currently have such rights. Girl activists are certainly not unique in expressing this particular facet of oppositional consciousness; similar citizenship and equality claims have played a role in many movements including, but not limited to, numerous women's movements, post-colonial independence struggles, and the U.S. civil rights movement.[18]

Girl activists believe that youth activism is as legitimate as the activism of adults and that it should be seen as being equally important and meaningful. Lisette, a San Francisco Bay Area teen who organizes around environmental racism issues, said, "I kind of feel like, in a way, wherever we go we usually get tokenized, like, oh, you know, youth are doing such a good job, and you're so smart and it's just like, no. This is really like what we do, and we actually do work that matters. . . . I just wish that they would take us like more seriously, like you know, this is stuff that we actually put a lot of hours into." Youth activism is not just "cute" or about training youth for the future, but it is a politics that matters. Lisette suggests that she and her peers are doing "real work," that their contributions should not be seen as less than those of adults. It is "serious" activism.

In most of my research locations, girl activists criticized adults for not taking their contributions seriously. They acknowledged that they were, for the most part, excluded from meaningful democratic participation and political power in their schools and communities. The one exception to this was in Venezuela where many girls believe that youth capabilities and potential contributions are being recognized for the first time. On one of my last days in Caracas, I attended an event that was the kick-off for the formation of a new national organization of secondary-school students. Student representatives from schools around the country had gathered to discuss the formation of this organization and to meet with President Hugo Chavez to discuss their hopes for changes in the educational system. During President Chavez's on-stage and televised conversation with the national council of these representatives, he listened to them nearly as much as he spoke, and there were several teens who felt sufficiently comfortable and empowered to speak out that they freely interrupted their president when they felt he was dominating the conversation and not hearing their voices. Sitting in the audience, I was amazed to see teenagers who were so sure of their own political authority on student issues and so confident in their rights to be heard that they were willing to actively demand that the president stop talking and listen. President Chavez handled their interruptions with good grace, and as the event progressed, he seemed increasingly intent on keeping his own statements short and providing room for the young people to talk to each other and to him.

One of the teens who participated in this discussion was Catalina, a sixteen-year-old from the outskirts of Caracas. She described the current role of youth in the Bolivarian revolution in the following manner:

Look, the role of youth is important and now, well, we have been given the opportunity to express ourselves. Before, we didn't have even the chance to know the president except through television and only sometimes. This is an opportunity to know really what is happening in our country. This, it is one of the things that they have insisted to us, that we will be taken into consideration because before, in what was called the Fourth Republic, they never took us into consideration, they never asked us, "do you agree with this educational system? What do you think?" No, never. So I think that the most important thing is that we have been given this right to have opinions, because we are people and we are thinking and we are conscious of what is happening. For me, this is the most important.

While Venezuelan youth felt that they were finally being acknowledged as legitimate political actors, this was not the case for girls in the other four countries in this study. Most girl activists continue to be frustrated by their lack of democratic inclusion or equality in the present. The language of democratic inclusion is a useful discursive tool in girl activists' struggles to construct their social movement identities and to claim authority, but, so far, these assertions of standing have not yet yielded the desired results in most locations or circumstances.

Difference and Unique Contributions

Alongside their assertions of political authority based on discourses of equality and democracy, girl activists also make claims to social movement standing that are rooted in ideas about their difference or uniqueness. These difference-based statements do not, of course, preclude or contradict statements of equality but can instead be seen as complementary. As Mary Bernstein has argued, movements and activists shift between making identity claims that highlight their "normality" and claims that celebrate their differences from the norm.[19] Rather than emphasizing similarity to adults, when framing their agency and authority in this second manner girl activists draw attention to how they are different from adults and how this difference means that they have something distinct to offer to social movements and social change. Reminiscent of standpoint theory, the discourse of difference suggests that youth should possess political authority not *despite* their age but rather *because* of it.[20]

Girl activists regularly argue that they are different from adults and that this difference makes their political action necessary and valuable. Nenetzin, a Mexican media activist, asserted, "We think differently. . . . The times have changed and now the youth, we see it from the point of view of our own problems." Youth perspectives, she suggests, are distinct from those of adults, and so youth are likely to focus on issues that matter to them, to address different social problems. Nenetzin continued, "We still have to study . . . we fight for our education, for teachers that teach us. A group of adults won't fight for that anymore." Teenage activists directly assert their authority to organize around "youth issues" like educational policy and school privatization, student bus fares, juvenile justice system reforms, teenagers' reproductive rights and sexual education, child abuse and youth rights, and curfews and police harassment precisely because these are topics that impact their lives but are not, in their view, part of the political concerns of most adults. Their youth perspective, then, gives them insight into a set of social problems and injustices, which would, in their view, otherwise be left under-addressed.

Even when adults are involved in these youth issues, they tend to look at them from a different angle, a different social location. One example of this can be found in approaches to child labor. Laura, a Venezuelan activist with a youth rights organization, says that adult organizations and her own organization see child labor issues very differently. Most adults, in her view, are primarily concerned with "eradicating child labor in all forms." In contrast, her organization, as an organization of child and adolescent workers, focuses on young workers' rights to good working conditions and their rights to have enough time for school, in addition to their jobs. Discussing a project she is working on with youth who work in the fields, she said, "what we want is to improve the work conditions. How? By forming cooperatives." Laura and the youth in her organization are addressing child labor together *as workers*, not as concerned outsiders. Youth labor activists see the issue of child labor as an issue of rights, equal treatment, and justice, rather than as an issue of youth protection. Their perspective is fairly unusual: their work on creating youth-led and youth-organized workers' cooperatives suggests a distinct and innovative approach to improving the lives of child workers, rooted in their standpoint and experiences as young people.

Youth activists are not, however, exclusively involved in specifically youth-oriented issues. Their identities and experiences cannot be reduced to simply "youth," but are also informed by their race, class, and location in the global economy. Girl activists are concerned about many of the same issues as adults from similar social contexts. In fact Nenetzin's newspaper collective and activist organization, Las Voces, doesn't actually spend substantial time and energy on topics that are obviously about youth. Instead, the talk about a distinct "youth perspective" on youth topics provides a discursive entry point for claiming young people's social movement standing and authority. It is easier to claim political voice for youth on those issues that are most obviously addressing the conditions of young people's lives. This claim, then, can be a springboard for other assertions of youth authority. Las Voces, after establishing that youth voice should be heard on youth issues, can then assert, throughout their publications, that they are offering a distinct youth perspective on a wide variety of political topics of relevance to their community.

Nenetzin and Laura both make claims to authority on the basis of the idea that youth have a unique perspective because of their current experiences as teenagers. In contrast, Patricia was one of many girls who argued that youth have something special to offer social movements because they are growing up in a different historical moment, or because of their generational, rather than their age-based, identity. Patricia, a seventeen-year-old from Peru at the World Social Forum, was especially interested in talking with me about how she saw her generation. She argued that youth do their activism differently from adults "because of the era too, right? Because before it was all, I don't know, the Cold War influenced everything, I don't know, the Russian Revolution. Well, at least in Peru, this stays with the adults, right? I didn't live much in this era. The Berlin Wall fell when I was born, so, sure, there's a difference." They might be looking at the same set of issues and concerns as adults, but some girls argue that they will see the world differently based on coming of age and becoming activists in the era of globalization, the "war on terror," and digital culture. This claim not only dovetails with Karl Mannheim's theoretical work on the significance of generations,[21] but is also well supported by the findings of empirical research on political generations, which has concluded that "when society changes rapidly and cohorts come of age under different conditions, the members of each cohort are likely to develop their own perception and style of politics."[22]

Mostly born between 1987 and 1991, these girls are in the middle of the generation that has been called Generation Y, the Internet Generation, and the Millennials.[23] This is a generation that has been variously described as self-oriented and individualistic, civic minded and engaged, curious and innovative, demanding and impatient, or responsible and optimistic despite facing serious hardships, challenges, and scapegoating.[24] The research on this generation's identity is clearly conflicted. And, although each of these conflicting generational characteristics may indeed be part of the lives and social contexts of girl activists, they don't really capture the *political* generational identities of this group, and certainly not the political identities of activists from this generation. In addition to coming of age amid globalizing forces and digital technologies, the girl activists in this book came to their activism between 2001 and 2005, a particular moment in the history and development of social movements and social struggles. On the one hand, this was a period of significant political repression, of empire, war, and state-sponsored violence. On the other hand, it was also a period of significant political experimentation, creativity, and the proliferation of new forms of transnational and local resistance within contemporary movements.[25] (My analysis will take up the question of generational identities and girls' affiliation with a specific set of contemporary movements in order to explore how this generational context matters to girls' political practices in chapters 5 through 7). However, the effects of growing up in this historical time frame are complex, and the girls themselves rarely articulate specific influences. Instead, girls are more likely to reference a vague and generalized conception of generational difference in order to claim authority.

The claim that young people have a different perspective on the world than adults can be rooted either in ideas of age-specific experiences or generational difference, or in some combination of the two. Nenetzin and Laura articulate the first perspective, while Patricia articulates the second. Sorting out the differences between age effects and generational effects in youth politics is not an easy or clear task since age as social location and generational dynamics are both present within youth movements.[26] Girl activists also reference both age and generation when articulating their difference from adults and, therefore, their rights to social movement standing. As they discuss these generational and age-based differences from adults in order to claim political authority, girl activists also make a series of assertions about the meaning and importance of this collective identity, about what it means to be *youth* activists. These specific articulations of their differences from adults are the many threads that make up the broader claim to social movement standing on the basis of their unique contributions and distinctive skills.

Kate, a San Francisco Bay Area teen, is involved in both a school-based women's rights club and an adult-run women's health organization. As someone who works in both youth-oriented and adult-oriented spaces, she has a strong sense of the different approach that young people take to their political work. The most significant difference, in her view, was that young activists were more likely to try out new ideas, new tactics, new ways of doing politics, rather than to always return to trusted and familiar actions and tactical repertoires. She said it was even "kind of cliché or something, but maybe it's just true, that young people are . . . more willing to take risks and do things that might not work to see if they do work." Innovation, Kate recognizes, is risky, but according to many teens it is more likely to be practiced by youth. The idea that youth are more innovative than adults is probably not an accurate perception of social movement innovation. Empirically, research has not necessarily indicated that tactical innovation is the province of the young, but this does not prevent youth from treating it as if it were. What is important about these claims (and the others which I address below) is not that young people *are* more innovative, but rather that they see innovation as one of their strengths and, as we shall see in the following chapters, this construction of their collective identity shapes their political action and practice.

Another important set of strengths and skills that girl activists see as giving them a distinctive place in social movements is their ability to be rebellious and militant without fear. Nenetzin claims that this makes young activists bold: "I feel like it is good that we are youth. We can do things that the older people don't want to do anymore. . . . The adults already have fear of doing some things." This is one space where being below the age of majority can help; as Chantal, also from Mexico, noted, "if you are arrested when you are minor, you get out the next day. If you are older, they keep you there longer." Minors sometimes have a slight legal advantage when it comes to engaging in civil disobedience—their arrest records are usually erased once they turn eighteen. I met several teens in different countries who, when interacting with adults, gladly offer to play key roles in acts of nonviolent civil disobedience because they are confident that it will not cause them as much legal trouble.

This youthful boldness is not limited to street protests, but it can infuse youth politics more broadly. According to Lisette, "A lot of people would like to have us around and invite us to things because we would speak our mind and not be so like what is this person gonna think of me. . . . I found that they enjoyed, adults enjoyed us having around because we would say things like how we saw and not be so afraid of what others think." Lisette's comments here indicate that young people can play a valuable role in radical movements—they can speak directly about what they really think without having to be diplomatic or play by the rules of conventional political discourse. Rebellious, abrupt, or troublesome behaviors and speech are allowed during youth in a way that it is not always permitted in adulthood. In this case, the image of youthful defiance is clearly useful for adolescents. However, in most instances, classifying young people as "dangerous," "rebellious," and "defiant" can also lead to the intense criminalization of teens. How youthful rebellion is treated is deeply racialized and class-specific; white, middle-class rebellion is more frequently allowed as "normal" youthful troublemaking, while the defiance of youth of color and of poor teens is often harshly punished.[27] Taking up the image of youthful rebellion, then, carries greater risks for those teenagers who are more likely to be treated as criminals, or as dangers to the social order, most notably teens from marginalized racial or ethnic groups, indigenous teens, or those from impoverished families. Although it is an identity claim that many girls use to authorize their politics, the potential social impact and risk of its use is greater for some teens than for others.

Innovation and rebellion are characteristics of youth that are, to a degree, rooted in social narratives of youth as a time of becoming, of exploration, rather than following already fixed social rules, including rules for political engagement and action. The idea that young activists are still "in process," is also vital to a third identity claim made by girls: that they are more open to each others' ideas and insights. Diana said that youth organize better educational events than adults because they are "less rigid, more about open discussion and less formal, less of a classroom setting, like I'm talking to you and you're gonna listen and then you're gonna like learn something. It is more about sharing perspectives and I'm not saying that all adults do that, cause I know there are good adults out there . . . but that is a big difference . . . youth kind of give you open space." Creating open space is thus not only seen by girls as a good practice for the building of oppositional consciousness, (see chap. 5), but, the fact that they do this better than adults is another way that they authorize themselves as important contributors to social movements. Further, such openness not only makes them effective educators but also better organizers in general. According to Clare, young people are especially effective activists because they listen to each other and work more cooperatively:

> Youth can be more effective. . . . Our groups work really really really well together and like probably you would assume that because we're sixteen to eighteen that we're like fighting over everything and we can't get anything done. But we absolutely work amazingly together. . . . I think that youth work a lot better than some people think. Yeah, just not even necessarily in like getting their faces out there but just in like teamwork and community building.

Like Clare and Diana, many girl activists argued that openness, listening, and cooperation are more often found in youth organizations than in adult-led social movements.

As these quotes indicate, girl activists define their youthful strengths largely in opposition to adults. They claim a set of strengths and skills as "youthful" and simultaneously argue that these are things that adults are less able to do, or are less interested in working toward. Girl activists not only see themselves as different from adults, for reasons of age and generation, but they also suggest that these differences make them more effective in some aspects of their activism. They may not be as good at some components of political organizing, but they are better at others. Chantal indicated that youth activists are especially effective at reaching other youth: "There are very few youth involved, but it might be because when they see only adult activists they aren't interested, but when they see young activists of their same ages, well, then they are going to ask what is happening and so it is a few more." If there aren't enough youth involved, according to Chantal, and others, then youth just won't feel welcome. By emphasizing the fact that adults don't really know how to involve youth, and that they do this better, girl activists carve out a niche for themselves in social movements.

Brenda, a San Francisco Bay Area peer health educator, spoke extensively about how being a teenager makes her better able to speak to her peers and educate them on social issues.

I keep promoting that I can serve as a resource and that people can have my resource books if they want them. . . . So I've had females come up to me and ask like where can you get the pill. Females that I don't know, but the fact that I'm just like young and I go through it too kinda like boosts up my credibility so much, you know what I mean. And also, being a young woman of color from a low-income household in a low-income community, a poor community lacking a whole bunch of resources, and you hear a female that's been through it and is currently going through it promoting that kind of stuff, it is just so much more powerful.

Brenda contrasts her approach with that of adults where, "it feels like maybe they're preaching to us, you know." Many adult activists talk about the importance of teaching young people but, according to girl activists, they are not always the best ones to do this work. Also a peer educator, but in Colombia, Yelitza also articulated the belief that it more effective to have organizations that are "for children by children. We kids teach other kids." The idea that youth themselves are the best people to educate youth gives young activists an important and distinctive role in struggles for social change.

In the San Francisco Bay Area, many teens also argued that they are simply more efficient and organized when compared to adults—they get tasks accomplished. Lisette described a recent meeting she had been to where they were planning for their campaign against a local toxic waste facility:

There was two groups that were mostly youth and one that was mostly adults and we had like twenty minutes to discuss and come up with next steps and the goal and everything. And so the two youth groups were able to have everything laid out, the adult group—nothing. And I was in that group, and I just found that this guy that was facilitating it was so kind of like in love with himself, like he would use all these big words and like elaborate and everything. And I think he's so used to people wanting to listen to him that he wasn't listening to other people and that therefore he didn't get anything done.

Ella also expressed frustration at adult meetings that just were "logistically ridiculous or even like, only two people are talking. . . . Even though I'm a kid I feel like I've been trained to be able to plan things really well and adults—how come they don't know how to do this?" Interestingly, this claim that adults are less-effective organizers was made primarily in the Bay Area. The girls in this metropolitan area were largely part of formalized youth organizations where they had received some sort of training on facilitation, meeting planning, and organizing. Many of the adults around them, on the other hand, have never been through such trainings. Adult organizations, perhaps, assume that most adults know how to plan a meeting so do not include extensive training in their regular practice. Youth organizations in the Bay Area, on the other hand, have usually had extensive conversations about different ways to approach action planning, building their facilitation skills, and developing their communicative styles. In the Bay Area, then, it may be the case that youth are actually better prepared to run an activist meeting than many of their adult counterparts.

Youth skillfulness at political organizing may surprise many adults, but so too does youth activism more generally. Surprising adults with their actions is, in fact, a way to capitalize on their youth status and use it to achieve their political goals. Haile, from Vancouver, said she's learned that "youth have sometimes more impact than adults. Because if youth do something, people pay attention because that stereotype kind of helps in a way, because when youth do something, people are like, whoa, they're actually doing something, right?" Similarly, Emma, also from Vancouver, noted that "when people see just students on the media, it definitely turns heads" and Yelitza remarked, "It is very striking that a girl is influencing things because in Colombia you only have the perspective that girls are only there to clean up and to sweep." An irony of the prevailing discourse of youth apathy is that when youth break out of this assumed disinterest or silence, their actions can garner more attention and therefore assist in the successful achievement of their goals. Because their involvement is unexpected, and youth activism is, in part, seen as "cute" or "endearing," youth activists are occasionally able to capture the attention of the media, to surprise school boards into hearing their demands and concerns, or to gain access to policy-makers who might otherwise be disinterested in the critiques and analysis of their movements.

Challenging adult expectations, youth activists can surprise adults with their thoughtful political knowledge and analysis along with their commitment to community and social change. Although young people are often marginalized within the political sphere, their youth can also occasionally be an asset. Seeing youth as an asset is indeed a substantial component of girl activists' narratives of authorization and social movement standing. By proposing that youth are different from, and even occasionally more effective than, adults, these girl activists carve out a distinct space for themselves as political agents. They recognize their own unique skills and perspectives as valuable to social movements and social change. As girl activists articulate their differences from adults and claim value in youthful identity, they also define a set of youthful traits that they see as relevant to their activism. Some of these traits belong to young people for structural reasons and are the result of their exclusion from formal politics, while others are better understood as commonly ascribed cultural characteristics of youth that young activists choose to emphasize as they claim their authority to be political actors in the present.

Youth Responsibility and Adult Failure

The students in Mexico City (with whom I opened this chapter) took over their school in part because the adults who were supposedly responsible for their safety had let them down. In Buenos Aires, many teens claim that it was a similar lack of adult concern for the safety of youth that led to the tragic fire in the Cromañón night club that killed 194 young people in December 2004. When adult officials did not respond to the ceiling tiles falling onto the heads of the students of a school in Buenos Aires, the teens also took action, taking over their school and refusing to attend classes until authorities agreed to make renovations. Such adult failures are not, of course, limited to Latin America. In Vancouver, a group of teens managed to draw attention to the potential instability of their school during an earthquake, pushing the city for a seismic refit. Cases like these have led many youth activists to lose faith in the ability of adults to look out for them or to even take their safety and needs into consideration. Given this, youth have a justification for taking action themselves.

Girl activists not only criticize adults for failing to look out for young people's immediate needs, they also often talk about adults as having given up the broader struggle for a just world. Daniela, a Mexico City Communist, talking about her mother said, "She is a little disillusioned. She thinks that she couldn't change the world, that she couldn't change anything." Similarly, Mariana, from the same group, says of her formerly active father, "he dedicated a lot of time to this. But for him it wasn't worth it. He doesn't have this hope anymore." Like many in Argentina, Julia attributed this cynicism to the Dirty War, the disappearances, the dictatorship: "There's a lot of fear and frustration in the adults. There is a lot of feeling that everything was in vain."

The experience of living with parents who have ceased to believe in the possibility of change was notable across the Americas. These girl activists see adults, sometimes including their parents, who used to be active, but who, disheartened by what they could not accomplish, have given up. In this context, they feel that if they want to make a difference, they will have to do it themselves. Even some girls with parents who are still politically involved often think that their parents remain active in part, because they, their daughters, keep pushing them in this direction. This was Emily's view: "I don't think my parents would go to peace rallies if I didn't make them. Even though, like, they really care about it, I sort of feel like they maybe feel like it is pointless. They've been activist forever and it hasn't gotten anywhere."[28] This close-up view of disheartened and inactive parents often frustrates girl activists. Their parents' inactivity, while they may understand it, also makes them angry. This frustration animates their discourse of generational necessity and provides the force behind their claim that youth need to act because their parents can not accomplish what they want in the world.

Many young women suggested that adults think that accomplishing much is impossible, that they have stopped dreaming big. Ramona, from Mexico City, stated that "youth are dreamers, more utopian, and adults aren't. They are more realistic, calmer." Ramona's parents are still activists, but she suggests that they aren't as visionary as the young people she knows. Adults may still be trying to make change, but according to Ramona, they are not likely to create the kind of world that these dream-filled, hopeful teenagers imagine to be possible. Angela, also from Mexico City, said that this is partly because young people are not as set in their ways: "I think that an older person, like a fifty-year-old woman, she's already very stuck in capitalism, in how she lives and is already accustomed to this way of life." Other girls, like Emily, argued that even if adults might still have dreams and hopes, they don't really want to take action: "I think that adults are lazy. They want their Sunday afternoons to do the crossword puzzles, not to go to peace rallies." In this view, youth not only dream big, they take action more willingly than adults. These multiple perspectives on adult inaction all lead girls to a common conclusion: adults are not going to create the kind of world that girls want to live in and therefore it is their own responsibility, as young people, to make the changes they want to see in the world.

In Caracas, however, this youthful dissatisfaction with adults was completely absent. None of the girl activists I met in Venezuela ever expressed the view that adults were not doing their part for social movements. In the context of the many substantial social and political changes taking place as part of the revolutionary Bolivarian process, it would be nearly impossible for teenagers to feel that adults are no longer trying to improve the world.

Instead, Venezuela provides a striking example of how youth can be inspired by the adult activity around them. Youth and adults were more likely to collaborate on projects in Caracas, and they seemed to be heartened by the fact that "nearly everyone," in their words, is concerned about politics, democracy, and social justice.

Unlike Caracas teens who believe that there is, at present, a steady march toward progress in Venezuela, teens in the other four cities articulate a strong sense of urgency. Contributing to their narrative of the necessity of youthful activism is the perception of a world in crisis. Camila argued that if they (youth) don't take action soon to improve social conditions, the state of the world is just going to keep getting worse. "It's very important to me to worry about what is happening now in this country and to try to improve it. Because I think that if this is the country now, what's going to happen when we are forty? It's going to be a disaster, a giant *villa* [slum]." For both environmental and socio-economic reasons, this particular historical moment is seen by girl activists as requiring immediate youth attention and action. If they want to have positive futures, they suggest, they will need to take action in the present. They can not wait until they are adults to begin to care about the world; their political intervention is necessary right now. Again, they are not just future activists, but must be activists today.

For Julia, an eighteen-year-old Argentine, youth have consistently been important to social struggles: "In general, the adults are less than the youth, there are [fewer] of them. This is very common." Unlike those young women who emphasize the current global situation in their understanding of young people's generational and historical responsibility, Julia spoke extensively about the continued importance of youth in creating social change. She said that she was proud that her generation was finally starting to come into its own, to become more involved, and spoke about several major student strikes and movements from the previous year.[29] "I think now we're starting to take a more active role in the political scene, not only in Argentina but also in Chile, in Greece, in France. . . . Especially with the issues of education on one hand and labor flexibility on the other, which affect youth more." Julia's stress on the vital role of young people in creating change is also reflected in a long history of scholarship and popular writing on youth movements. As Braungart and Braungart point out, the developmental characteristics of youth are "likely to make youth critical of their elders, society, and politics, and this has been interpreted by some to indicate that youth have a 'predisposition' to generational conflict, rebellion, and revolution."[30] What is perhaps most noteworthy in these girls' articulation of this position about the centrality of youth in social change efforts is that, for them, the task of creating change belongs not just to college-age youth—the focus of most writing on youth activism and student movements—but to teenagers as well.

In Mexico, Argentina, and Venezuela girl activists regularly referenced long traditions of youth activism in their countries as evidence of the ongoing centrality of youth to social change. In Mexico City and Buenos Aires, there are annual marches commemorating the dates of significant acts of repression against student activists, which serve to highlight the connections between today's youth movements and those of the past. Every October 2, Mexico City student activists commemorate the Tlatelolco Massacre of 1968 with a student-led march and vigil. Each September, Argentinean high school students plan and lead their own vigil to remember the Noche de Los Lápices, a night in 1976 when ten secondary school student activists were disappeared by the provincial police. Those students were fighting for a low-cost student bus pass, something that girls in Buenos Aires today note that they are still fighting for. Today's teens, then, remember the disappeared youth not just as predecessors but also as comrades in the same ongoing struggle. This sense of connection to previous generations of youth activists, this memory of a past full of teenage activists, is another way for these young women to justify and legitimate their political engagement.

Compared to their Latin American peers, the girls I interviewed in the United States and Canada demonstrated very little knowledge of high school students' participation in social movements through history. This lack of knowledge is not the result of teenagers' absence from social movements in North America, but is instead the result of a lack of explicit discussion of their presence as young people in most of the commonly taught histories of these movements. Girl activists in the United States may have heard of SNCC in their U.S. history classes, but they don't usually know that many of the activists were teens. Similarly, they may have learned about labor struggles in the mill towns of the Northeast, but not specifically about the role of teenage girls in these struggles. Because of this, they tend to see their own generation as uniquely active, rather than as part of a historical tradition of youthful activism. Girls' deployment of discourses about youthful rebellion, resistance, and activism is substantially shaped by these distinct national historical traditions. The Latin American girls draw on historical memory and a shared story about teenage activists' past accomplishments, activating a discursive resource that is not available to their North American peers.

Teenage girl activists see the multitude of problems around them—in their schools, their communities, and in the world—and, instead of waiting for adults to solve these problems, or waiting until they grow up, they are taking political action in the present. Partly this is done out of necessity: they feel as if their safety is being threatened. They can not wait until they turn eighteen to deal with the political, social, and economic violence that they are experiencing. But they also act on the belief that they, as young people, have an important role to play in social change. Frustrated by what they see as adult inaction, cynicism, and fears, they suggest that if they want the world to be different, they are going to have to start trying to change it themselves, today. Instead of being only "future citizens," they must be citizens now. According to teen activists, adults have failed to look out for young people's immediate and long-term well-being, and so youth must take action on their own.

Teenage girl activists, in emphasizing their roles as history makers and agents of social change, are reclaiming and reworking the social and political responsibilities of youth. By focusing on how these girls infuse their identities as youth with political authority, this chapter sheds some light on a very significant part of the process of collective identity formation within social movements. The discursive threads of democracy, equality, and difference play an important role in this process, as they have for many other marginalized and oppressed groups. Youth, however, also use a third, distinctive narrative to claim authority: youth responsibility. This narrative takes different forms in different cities, indicating that claims to social movement standing and political legitimacy are deeply shaped by the cultural contexts and histories from which they are made.

Youth, as a discursive formation, has simultaneously been linked with social change, social movements, and rebellion along with political naiveté, future (rather than present) citizenship, and apathy. This duality of meanings deserves a deconstructive eye. Instead of seeing rebellion and inability as polar opposites in the semiotic field of youth, we should also ask how they are related to one another. First, I would argue that the discursive association of youth with both political inability and political rebellion implies that youth activism and youth social movements are an irrational, silly, or ill-conceived approach to politics and social change. Further, through their shared link to the category of youth, rebellion and the lack of political acumen or skill become bound together in a symbolic cluster. This has far-reaching implications for social movements, as their more disruptive activities are often described by commentators and the media as immature, irresponsible, and ineffective.

Girl activists embrace the association of young people with social change and social movements, claiming that their youth is a reason for their political activity. Youth, they remind us, are not always rebels without causes but are also important social innovators and can act as a collective force for progress, growth, and transformation. In order to authorize their youthful political identities, they can not simply proclaim the virtues of youthful rebellion but must reconstruct this trope, showing that they are not just "causing trouble" but are thoughtful, well-informed political actors. My research with girl activists clearly suggests that youth activism can not be dismissed as an irrational developmental stage, but that youth activists often act with careful consideration, well-articulated political theories, and smart strategic planning. In short, youth activism is no more or less rational than that of adults.

In addition to these contributions to our understanding of the discursive relationship between youth and social movements, and to the process of collective identity formation and the production of social movement standing, teenage girls' narratives on their political authority also offer several important lessons for adult activists and social movements, pushing us to pay attention to the dynamics of age-based inclusion and exclusion. In their calls for equality with adults and their emphasis on their democratic rights, there is also an implicit request for greater involvement in organizations and movements that have currently done little to incorporate young people as equal partners. On the other hand, girls' statements about their unique contributions and differences from adults should encourage adults to consider the ways that they can act in solidarity with young people in youth-led organizing. Girls' feelings that adults are no longer with them in the struggle for a better world should also lead us to consider the ways that adult activists have failed to connect with young people and thus encourage us to show them that they are not entirely alone.

Teenage girls' attempts to reclaim youth as a space of political agency are not, in their view, sufficiently supported by the majority of adult activists. They argue that many adults continue to see them as "cute," as incapable, or as needing adult guidance in everything that they do. These perceptions of youth do not build a positive foundation on which to build cross-age relationships. On the other hand, as girl activists discursively construct the category of youth as one of political capability, responsibility, and innovation, they contrast it with adult cynicism and inaction. Teens' negative view on adults and their rejection of what they see as adult complicity, passivity, and ineffectual organizing poses another challenge to productive cross-generational and cross-age collaborations. However, girl activists often told me that they would like to improve adult/youth relationships within social movements. Such relationships would not only be beneficial to them but also for adults. While there is much that adult activists can teach these young women and a lot that adults can do to support their development as political actors and social movement participants, there is also a great deal that these adults can gain from interacting with teenagers. Their unique perspectives on a variety of issues from education to consumerism can shed new light on some of these struggles. And, perhaps more importantly, their enthusiasm, hopefulness, and openness to new ideas could do much to revitalize contemporary social movements.

4

We Are Not Girls

Escaping and Defining Girlhood

I first met Manuela at the mall. She and several other members of the local chapter of the Juventud Comunista de Venezuela had selected this location, and we were to meet for dinner and socializing with the youth delegation I was traveling with after the World Social Forum. A few weeks later, when I went back to their town to spend more time with Manuela and interview a few of the young women involved in the JCV, I was taken to the mall again. At one point partway through an evening of eating hot dogs and salsa dancing (badly, in my case), I asked Manuela if she thought it was at all odd that the Communist youth hang out at the mall so much. She smiled, laughed, and said, "just because we are Communists doesn't mean that we aren't like other youth. And many youth go there to sit, to talk, to hang out. So we do too. We're still young and like things that other youth like." Of course, I thought, just because you are an activist doesn't mean that you can't still be a teenager.

Being a teenager is a very important part of girl activists' collective identity claims. Manuela's youthful activist identity, though, is also gendered. The coexistence of a specifically teenage girl identity with an activist identity was highly visible in Manuela's bedroom: pink gauzy curtains, a dresser covered in glittery belts and fringed scarves, and posters of Lindsay Lohan and Harry Potter alongside a pile of books by Marx and Lenin, bright red JCV T-shirts and a World Social Forum tote bag brought back by a friend. Manuela's room and our conversation about the mall made me think that she was smoothly integrating her teenage girl and activist identities—that these two aspects of Manuela's self were complementary, not conflicting or mutually exclusive. Later, during our interview, I discovered that it was not quite as easy as it looked.

As we were discussing her experiences at school, some of Manuela's frustrations with other girls and young women began to emerge: "At school I have to interact with people that don't, people who don't know anything, or who are so alienated that—how should I say this—they know and think the things that the capitalist system has told them . . . well, we don't have much in common. I think they are people who don't read, who don't know, who are mostly focused on the newest music, the newest bars and clubs." A few minutes later, I asked her, "Do you think you are different from other girls your age?" She vigorously replied "Yes, yes. Because there are girls (*chicas*) my age who don't have consciousness, and I do have consciousness, consciousness in the sense that we are talking about: political, revolutionary. There are people that don't know and that are just completely stopped." She also criticized other girls for "spending all of the weekend at parties . . . and walking around saying stupid things with friends, I don't like that. I'm more, more relaxed, and if I'm going to say something, it is something more productive, not just saying stupid things." Manuela expressed very few positive associations with girls and girlhood, and she was quick to distance herself from what she sees as "typical" girl traits and behaviors. Girls, in her view, make stupid statements, just care about parties, and don't have political consciousness. However, alongside her criticism of girls and her distancing from them in order to distinguish herself as an activist, Manuela also acknowledged that she has some characteristics in common with other girls: "I like to dress fashionably. If I see someone on television and I like how they look, I might try to look like that. And sometimes I like to go out, but not a huge amount." Manuela acknowledges she can be girl-like, but she is quick to remind me that these girl-like elements of her identity don't mean she is really like other girls. Her activism makes her qualitatively different. It is not just an addition that sits alongside her girl identity, but changes it and sometimes negates it as well.

Complex and shifting relationships to the category of girlhood are typical of girl activists. Collectively and individually, girl activists simultaneously remake and reject girlhood. On the one hand, many of them say that they are still sometimes "just a girl" and like to do "girly things," and that there are some aspects of girlhood that enhance their activism and social movement participation. But on the other hand, these same girls suggest that becoming activists means that they are no longer girls and that the traits of girlhood and the traits of activism are diametrically opposed to one another. This tension and ambiguity raises important questions about how girl activists understand and engage with ideas about girlhood as an identity category. What are the meanings they attach to "girl"? When do these young activists identify as girls and when do they not? For what purposes?

In trying to make sense of these seemingly contradictory relationships to girlhood, it is important to remember that, as an identity category, it is in fact quite fluid and flexible. There is no singular moment in which a young woman stops being a girl. Instead, most of the activists in this study suggest that they are sometimes girls and sometimes women. They might be girls when they visit their grandparents, teenagers when they are out at a dance club with friends, or women when volunteering at a local health clinic. They are girls when they make mistakes or say something they think is stupid, but women when they make important decisions about their futures. Their relationships to girlhood are perpetually shifting and unstable, changing with the social context and their own feelings. Only three of the young women I interviewed stated that they never feel like girls anymore, that they are always women or abstract, genderless youth. Mostly, they acknowledge being somewhere between girl and woman, sometimes one and sometimes the other, sometimes both simultaneously, and sometimes a third position that is just "in between." Some girls, like Marguerite, an eighteen-year-old Asian Canadian in Vancouver, love and embrace this shifting status: "I think the good thing, or the thing I love about being a—I'll use teenage woman right now—is that we morph so often. Like one moment you can be childish, you can be innocent, and the next moment you can be this serious lady that is getting things done." Others wish they could be done with all the negative experiences and traits that they associate with girlhood and just be women. Emily acknowledged that "it is sorta hard for me cause I want to be a woman, but I'm not a woman—I'm seventeen."

Talking about the gendered terrain of growing up is, of course, different in different languages. In English, the choices are minimal. There are girls and women, or you can add some qualifiers to either word: teenage girls, teenage women, young girls, young women. This linguistic shortage frustrated Emily: "I am a teenager. I'm not a woman, so calling myself a woman is sort of a leap, a leap of faith, or . . . I mean, I guess that I feel like there should be a different word than teenager. Like I'm not a girl, I'm not a woman, but teenager just seems so reckless and un-responsible, and doesn't care about anything, and like that's not who I am." I responded by telling her, "It's different doing these interviews in English and in Spanish, 'cause in Spanish there's a whole bunch of in-between words." She replied, "Yeah, we should create one." I had a similar conversation with Hayley, a seventeen-year-old from Vancouver. I asked her, "So, do you consider yourself a girl, a young woman, a teen woman?" She laughed and said, "That's so funny! Me and my friend were just having this conversation. We don't know. Especially in high school, you have no idea. You're sort of a girl, a teenager, you don't really, you know you're kind of a young woman but then you're like, I don't know if I'm a woman, I don't know, I don't even have a boyfriend, I'm like so single right now." In English, there are fewer options for discussing the distinctly gendered process of moving from childhood to adulthood. The terms "teenager" and "youth" allow girls to name their age-specific identities and affiliations, yet these same terms do not allow them to articulate how this period in their lives, and thus their experiences and identities in it, are also very much shaped by their gender. Naming one's gendered and aged location as a high school female is not always easy or self-evident in English.

Spanish has a great deal more linguistic richness in this area. My interviewees and I would variously talk about the meanings of *niña* (girl), *chica*, *chava*, *chavita*, *chama*, *muchacha*, *muchachita*, *mina*, and *mujer* (woman). While the English speakers were stuck navigating the girl/woman binary, most of the Spanish-speaking girls identified themselves most often with one of the many, often regionally specific, "in-between terms" associated with female adolescence. This closer association with the various words for female adolescence did not mean that these individuals identified only with the in-between words. Instead, they described shifting between the three (or more) different identities as they moved through different contexts and spaces in their lives. Having more linguistic options gives them more choices for talking about the transition between girlhood and womanhood, but it does not mean that this process is necessarily straightforward or entirely linear. (Because English can not capture these words, as I translate these young activists' statements on the meaning of girlhood, I will continue to use Spanish.)

The activists I write about here are constantly shifting in and out of girl-hood. And, as much as their presence inside and outside of this category fluctuates, so too do the meanings associated with it. Depending on the situation and context, they describe girls as compassionate, hopeful, and socially engaged, or as silly, superficial, and stupid. The meaning of girlhood is not fixed but is constantly being defined and redefined. These changing meanings of girl and girlhood must also be seen in the context of the many important differences in girls' experiences and lives. The intersecting forces of race, class, nation, religion, and sexuality all shape what it means to be a girl in complex and ever-changing ways. There is no universal girlhood, but a multiplicity of girlhoods.[1]

Girl-Dominated Activism

Teenage girls outnumber boys in many youth activist organizations. Girls were a sizable majority in all but one of the North American youth-based activist groups from which my interviewees emerged. Although their presence was not so overwhelming in most of the Latin American organizations, girls still outnumbered boys in exactly half of the youth-based organizations in which these young women participated. Only four of the forty-two youth organizations I encountered in this project had larger number of males than females involved. Significantly, these four male-dominated organizations were groups that were not focused explicitly on high school students. Girls' majority status in activism, then, seems to be especially the case in high school organizations, rather than broader youth groups.[2] Other recent studies, conducted in several different national contexts, have also concluded that girls and young women are more likely to be interested and active in both conventional politics and social movement activity than boys and young men.[3] This preponderance of girls within teenage activism and social movements calls into question the assumptions of much of the "classical," Birmingham Centre for Contemporary Cultural Studies research on youth subcultures, which positioned boys as resistant and girls as conformist. Since the 1970s, feminist cultural studies scholars like Angela McRobbie have questioned this implicit association of girls with conformity and boys with rebellion and have identified some of the many ways that girls too engage in anti-hegemonic cultural practices.[4] Recent findings about girls' dominance within radical youth organizing indicate that girls are not only resistant actors but they appear (in high school settings) to be more likely than boys to channel their anti-hegemonic energies into collective action for social and political change.

Teenage girl activists are highly aware of the gender disparity in participation. As they explain, describe, and think through this difference in participation, girls develop a set of narratives about the meaning of girlhood and its role in their political lives. Occasionally girls deploy a developmental or biological discourse of difference, arguing that girls mature more rapidly, but more often girls argue that this imbalance is based on the social construction of gender roles. In the context of discussions on their numerical dominance within high school politics and organizing, teenage girls spoke extensively about how being girls encouraged their activism. Drawing on highly prevalent discourses about the meaning of femininity, Megan argued that more girls are involved in activism because "guys aren't nurturing. And girls, if they see something, if there are people that are sad, that we see, we go, 'you know,

I want to do something.'" Girls' greater involvement is, according to Hosang, "a projection of their expected roles in society, like the helper, the nurturer." They suggest that because they are encouraged to care about people, girls are more likely to become active in social change movements. Similar to the narratives about gender and activism told by many adult women activists, these girls also argue that their activism is an extension of their concern and responsibility for the well-being of communities.[5]

In their study of conceptions of girlhood within contemporary media, psychological, pedagogical, and academic discourses, the authors of *Young Femininity* find that girls are often depicted as "caring figures concerned for the global community" and that "active citizenship for young women frequently means taking responsibility for themselves economically and at the same time taking care of others."[6] Kimberly Ann Scott suggests that these messages to girls about their responsibility to take care of others are shaped by race and class. Her research found that while white and privileged girls can sometimes expect to be cared for if they are quiet and docile, black girls are consistently "expected to 'reach out' and serve others, especially those of higher status."[7] Responsibility for community and family also takes on very different meanings for girls based on their class-specific local contexts. Carmen, for example, is a Venezuelan teen who migrated to Caracas to find work as a domestic so she could send money home to her family in the economically depressed rural region where she grew up. Her activism with a young workers' organization to improve domestic workers' rights and wages is deeply connected to the work she is doing to care for her family. In Mexico City and the San Francisco Bay Area, many working-class girl activists spoke about how they do significant labor in their homes, taking care of younger siblings, cooking, and cleaning. This familial responsibility keeps them busy, giving them less time for activism than they might want, but it also means that they are quite skilled at time-management and balancing their different obligations. When they say they will do something, they can be counted on to do it. In contrast to working-class and poor teen girls' direct obligations for care-work, middle-class and wealthier girls spoke of a responsibility for taking care of others in far more abstract and generalized terms.

As girls articulate and deploy a discourse about gender and femininity that claims women's responsibility for community well-being, they also suggest several other substantial differences between girls and boys, including the idea that girls are just generally more "serious" or "responsible" than their male peers. Camila and Milagros told me that this difference was a big part of why girls do more activism in high school. And, after my experience at a "work day" with their organization, I was inclined to agree with them. The work day had been planned by the youth group coordinators of a Buenos Aires organization that brings together unemployed activists (*piqueteros*) with more middle-class allies. Youth from all over the city were going to meet up and collectively offer their time and energy to several grassroots projects located in one of the poorest *villas*, or slums, of the city. Camila, Milagros, and I spent the whole day helping to build a community center and conducting community-designed surveys about public health needs. Participating in this action required a major commitment of time and energy, and a willingness to wake up early on a Saturday morning.

When I interviewed the two girls a few days later, I commented that there were many more young women at the work day than young men. They both nodded, and Camila said, "What happened is that a lot of the guys went out the day before and so they were sleeping. It's not that there aren't guys, but it is more that they don't see this as their number one priority. . . . And *chicas* are more—" Milagros chimed in here, and, in unison, they finished the sentence: "more hardworking." There may indeed be as many boys involved in youth organizing as girls within some organizations, but they don't always put as much time and energy into it. The girls, these young women argue, are more consistently active, while the boys drop in and out, as it suits them.

Closely related to girls' articulation of their duty and responsibility as community care-takers is girls' assertion that their gender socialization encourages them to feel deeply, to have strong emotions, and that activism requires such emotion. Diana described how emotional passion is something that is more acceptable for girls than guys:

> I would have to say I see a lot more teenage girls being activists than teenage guys. . . . I think in a way it is easier for us . . . to really like get motivated to do something . . . because I feel like activism is something that you really have to be passionate about, you really have to put your heart and soul into an issue that you care about and I think like because of the way that gender roles are set up, it is not, like teenage boys don't really want to show that they really love something and that they really want to make a change.

Diana suggests here that the ability to express love is one of the reasons that there are more activist girls than guys at the high school level.

According to my interviewees, girls are also more likely to be activists because they are idealistic. Part of what makes them different from boys is that in general they are not cynical. Violet says that there are more girls who organize in her youth group because "in terms of my friends and other peers that I have, I feel like males . . . in my community, tend to be more just frustrated with the system and cynical. Not apathetic, but just cynical in a way that makes them want to disengage. Whereas more of my female peers, like, stemming from the same issues and the same problems will say 'this is really fucked up right now, so what can I do and how can I help.'" And, in the words of Azul, from Buenos Aires, "*niñas* can be more naïve in some things, but at the same time they are dreamers more than other people. Maintaining that *niña* inside is beautiful." Transforming girlhood's association with thoughtless naïveté and innocence to an assertion of girls' inclination toward politicized optimism enables these young activists to place political value on the fairly common image of girls as "dreamy" and hopeful. These claims to emotionality, concern for others, optimism, and hopefulness substantially shape girls' political practice.

As young women draw upon popular, widely circulating, and even fairly stereotypical discourses about femininity to describe the reasons for girls' higher levels of participation in activism, they also place substantial narrative attention on the limitations of boyhood. Camila, when talking about why the guys didn't come to the work days said that they [boys] think that they can do everything: "they want to be the most macho, 'I'm the Macho Perez, I can do everything.'" But, she said, they overestimate themselves and can't do it all. "So the *chicas* are more conscientious, and, well, if I have to get up early tomorrow, that is fine, I just won't go out tonight." Camila placed part of the blame for guys' lack of responsibility on the pressures they face to appear macho or masculine, indicating that girls' presence in activism is not just about the social construction of girlhood, but also about the construction of teenage boyhood. Camila's analysis about the gender differences in youth activism implies that the pressures of masculinity are a sizable part of the reason for boys' irresponsible behaviors.

Clare also noted that there are gendered expectations that lead boys to be fearful of expressing compassion and concern for other people. She said, "In my community, I see young women doing it more. I don't know if there's an expectation of them or maybe in reverse there's an expectation of young men to not act, so in a way it is also to me about gender roles. Like girls are allowed, and boys are not, to . . . really care about stuff." Many girls argue that boyhood is, in fact, a much more restrictive identity category than girlhood. According to Kayla, from Vancouver, "It is harder for guys to—they have a more rigid image than girls do." Erica, also from Vancouver, agreed, saying that "girls don't have as much of a pressure on them by their friends to be a certain way." Girls' assertions that girlhood is a more open and flexible identity category than boyhood is intriguing, and suggests that these girls are critically reflecting on the gendered construction of both femininity *and* masculinity. Furthermore, their belief that there are many ways to "be a girl" reflects their experiences growing up in an era of visible feminism and explicit discussions of gender equality. Although these particular statements might dovetail with the growing social discourse on how "feminism has gone too far" and that boys are now often marginalized within schools, this tendency is mitigated by many girl activists' explicit commentary on the continued structural inequalities and gender-based injustices faced by women and girls around the world.

When discussing and reflecting on their numerical dominance within youth activism, teenage girl activists tend to embrace their girlhood and to suggest that some aspects of their (socially constructed) identities as girls enhance their activist identities and practices. In these moments, they simultaneously replicate and reconfigure powerful, and often quite conventional, narratives about girlhood and girls' cultures. They assert that girls are, indeed, more emotional, more caring, more sensitive. They then take these stereotypical characteristics into new social terrain, carrying them over into the world of activist politics, giving them a slightly different meaning and significance. In short, they make some of the conventional understandings of girlhood rebellious.

We Are Not (Those) Girls

In the context of describing the differences between high school girls and boys, girl activists draw on discourses of girlhood in order to construct their activist selves. In other conversations and contexts, however, the same young women engage in a reverse process: they draw upon their identities as youth activists in order to critique and resist dominant and traditional forms of girlhood. For these young women, being girls might make them better activists, but being activists also makes them different from other girls, and, in many instances, so different that they are no longer girls at all. In their study of alternative girlhoods, Canadian girls' studies scholars Dawn Currie, Deirdre Kelly, and Shauna Pomerantz explore the processes that encourage and enable some girls to resist traditional femininity and the norms of "popular" girlhood. They note some girls in their study "embraced or actively fostered an identity that earned them the label 'weird' or 'different.' Many did so by consciously positioning themselves against the 'girlie girl' symbols of an emphasized femininity that gave popular girls currency in the gendered economy of school culture."[8] Girls who participate in critical youth subcultures often draw upon elements of those subcultures as resources for the construction of a different way of being a girl.[9] Youth activism, as an alternative political community and subculture, can therefore enable teenage girls to find the space to critically reflect on and refuse conventional gender rules and the constraints of "typical" girlhood. Being an activist can help girls as they construct identities that are alternative to the dominant forms of girlhood but that still "fit" somewhere within peer and school cultures.

Mass media presentations of girlhood play an important but complex role in girls' understandings of this identity. Girls' relationship to the mainstream media and to popular culture is simultaneously global and local. As Sunaina Maira and Elisabeth Soep write in the introduction to their edited collection on globalization and youth culture, "the cosmopolitan and transnational imaginaries of youth culture are always in dialectical tension with both national ideologies and local affiliations."[10] Girls in all five of my research locations are watching some of the same television shows and movies, listening to some of the same music, and reading magazines about some of the same celebrities. They read these texts through their different experiences, locations, and perspectives, producing their own local interpretations. There are also some features of girls' media landscapes that are not the same, but are instead rooted in national and local culture industries. Despite these differences in media content and media context, I found that girl activists consistently describe the mainstream media version of girlhood (whatever it may be in their local media culture) as a singular, hegemonic, and destructive force in girls' lives.

In general, girl activists distinguish between media stereotypes of girls, which are, in their words, absolutely awful, and the girls that they actually know. They truly despise the transnational media's version of girlhood, but are more subdued in their criticisms of "real" girls, demonstrating a complex and nuanced understanding of the power of media images and discourses of girlhood in shaping (other) girls' identity practices and lives. A fairly typical response to questions about what they think of the media's portrayal of girls was Patricia's: "Don't even talk about it. They are horrible. They are just horrible. *Chicas* are stupid people who only want to be like models. They want to be Cindy Crawford . . . putting on makeup, listening to music, being with boyfriends, focusing on boys. At the end of the day, that is what they want us to be, right? I mean, you have to be like this to be beautiful, to be loved and wanted. But they are just stereotypes that they show us." Dara, from Vancouver, also had a visible reaction. Shaking her head, she said, "Teenage girls have a very negative image sometimes. You know, teenage girls wanting to experiment with sex, experiment with guys, experiment with stuff like that. And they have the stereotype of being, you know, stupid and self-obsessed." Some girls acknowledged that the portrayal of girls might be shifting, citing the cosmetic company Dove's "real beauty" campaign and various images of women athletes, but they primarily saw the media as a source of stereotypes and negative portrayals of girlhood.

As they criticized the version of girlhood presented by the media for its emphasis on appearance and its depiction of girls as weak, dependent, and foolish, the activist teens regularly stated that they themselves are not actually influenced by these images. In contrast to the vast quantity of scholarship that suggests that media depictions of girls have a powerful sway over their perceptions and are harmful to girls' healthy development,[11] these young women repeatedly stressed that they do not let these images have that kind of control over them. These assertions do not mean that they are completely unaffected by the media versions of girlhood, but they demonstrate, at a minimum, a reflective and critical distance from such images.

In some cases, girl activists' dismissal of the media was rooted in their sense of their own girlhood as being very unlike that portrayed in the media. Rae's description of this separation between her life growing up and the girlhood she saw in the media sheds light on the ways that race and class differences can enable a critical response to dominant images of girls and girlhoods:[12]

> When I see things, they're mostly like . . . really blonde, and you know, how they're all running around, prancing around, doing that kind of thing. I just kind of thought it was, I knew they were silly. I knew they were goony and I knew that the girls in the magazines were almost passing out and things like that. I always knew that because I never thought it was, oh, I want to be that way, I want to dress that way, I want to bleach my hair and things like that. So I guess that's how I'm, I'm not those girls. I've never tried to be them or to—I don't really know how to answer that. . . . I just see that as a different lifestyle and a different culture. It's not mine and I'm never gonna claim it. So, it is just another way of life, but it's not mine.

Rae suggests she never really believed in the media version of girlhood partly because it was so distant from her own lived experiences growing up as a First Nations girl in the Vancouver area.

Some of the girls who perceive more race, class, and cultural similarities between themselves and the stereotypical girls portrayed in the media also maintain that these images do not define their own identities as girls but do so on different grounds. They were more likely to reference their own internal sense of self-worth, parents or teachers who taught them about media literacy, or a group of supportive friends. Emma is just one example of a girl with this type of relationship to the media images of girls.

> Well, you've got the beautiful model girl, really tall, you know, but not even the big boobs anymore, just the skinny tall girl. That's a big thing in the media and magazines. But I have a really strong group of friends that range from every size and shape but they are all totally gorgeous girls who are really empowered. . . . I've realized that when you open a magazine, all the models look the same and I think people know it's not realistic. I think people know it's a stereotype. Yeah, I just don't, like it really doesn't affect us that much. . . . I guess it must affect some girls, but I don't, on a personal level, I don't think it affects me and my friends that much.

Emma acknowledges that some girls might be impacted by the media discourses on girlhood, but like many of the other activist girls in this study, she does not accept these images as significant to her own identity and sense of self. The media may be trying to get her and other girls to "do girlhood" in particular ways, but Emma's responses indicate how some girls critically analyze and resist these influences.[13] Such media literacy is likely, at least in part, a result of the growing number of programs and organizations that focus on girls' relationship to media.[14]

Although these girls' responses to the media stereotypes of girlhood are probably heartening for many readers, their critical commentary on the media does not mean that girl activists are completely unaffected by pop culture ideals. Rather, Manuela's Lindsay Lohan posters are just one example of girl activists' much more complicated relationships to dominant versions of girlhood. Girl activists do continue to participate in the consumption of pop culture versions of girlhood. They worry about dating, boyfriends, and popularity, and they go on shopping trips to the mall with their friends. However, they claim that they do all of this in a conscious manner. They say that they are aware of the stereotypes and can therefore resist them. They act like "typical" girls only when *they* want to and are not just dupes of the media industry. But, even as they say they take up girly and feminine traits consciously and with awareness, these young women do not ascribe the same consciousness to many of their peers. In contrast to their own perceived agency and ability to resist the media, they often imply that the other (non-activist) girls they know are much more passive consumers of girlhood. In their view, "typical" or nonactivist girls aren't critical consumers of the media, but they accept and emulate dominant models of femininity. Of course, this does not mean that activist girls are entirely media-savvy and completely unaffected by popular culture imagery. Rather, it is an example of how they narrate themselves as resistant subjects and, in doing so, distinguish themselves from other girls whom they see as much less self-aware.

Like many other youth who are part of subcultures, teenage girl activists describe "a homogeneous mainstream group against which they position themselves in order to further define their own sense of self."[15] Despite the fact that they refuse to see themselves as exceptional because of their activism, these young activists tend to see themselves as very different from other, more "mainstream," girls. My questions about the other girls in their schools would lead them to wrinkle their noses with disgust, sigh in exasperation, and immediately claim their difference from their peers. In constructing their own identities as different from those of "typical" girls, girl activists outline and reject a series of characteristics that they see as "girly" and instead claim a set of opposing traits, which they associate with having an activist identity. Their activist identities thus offer them a way of being in the world that is different from that suggested by conventional gender roles and the pressures of emphasized femininity.

One of the most pervasive criticisms of girlhood made by the activist girls was that other girls are superficial. Girls were frequently described as interested only in fashion, *telenovelas*, gossip, appearances and beauty, or going to parties. Lucy, a Mexican sixteen-year-old, when comparing herself to other girls her age, said, "*Chicas* are really superficial. They worry about how they look. . . . They are empty-headed, have empty ideas." Similarly, Greta, also from Mexico, said, "The majority of *chavas*, generally all they talk about is music, television stars, all of these kinds of things, which I don't think are interesting." Greta's criticism of girls is not that they talk about music, television, and similar topics sometimes, but rather that this is *all* that they talk about. Most of the girl activists who criticized their peers for supposedly superficial behavior and interests similarly suggested that the problem was that these were the entirety of girls' concerns. It is okay to go out to parties, to have fun, to talk about boys, and gossip about celebrities, but these should not be *all* that girls care about. To put this in terms of Manuela's story, according to most girl activists, going to the mall is fine, but girls who *only* go to the mall and who don't think about the world around them are superficial and deserve criticism. In fact, many girl activists say that playfulness, having fun with friends, and enjoying life were features associated with girlhood that they love and appreciate. The critique of superficiality is not a call to live a politically and morally "pure" or entirely serious life, but is instead a rejection of excess: too much emphasis on having fun and not enough attention to what really matters.

The superficiality of girlhood stands in contrast to an image of activist identity as doing something important, something significant. Chantal described how important this is for young women activists:

> There aren't many *mujeres jovenes* activists so you have to show that *mujeres* think and that you are not only concerned about your hair, or how people see you. . . . As an activist woman you have to demonstrate that you are also interested in other situations, you are concerned about society, politics, what is happening to your neighbor. . . . You have to show that you aren't the typical *chica*, or the stereotype of the stupid, materialistic *chica* who doesn't think about anything.

Because girls are superficial, becoming an activist means that you have to distinguish yourself from this trait and from this identity. Being an activist means caring about things that matter, not things that stereotypical girls care about. And, therefore, in the eyes of many of my interviewees, activists are not really girls. Activism, then, provides girls with a community of young women who are all resisting the narrow confines of a version of girlhood that emphasizes appearance, fashion, and popularity by focusing their energy on politics and social change.

Superficiality and concern with unimportant topics can lead to even worse traits that some girl activists associate with girlhood: pettiness and meanness. Hayley said, "I'm not a girl in the way that I don't fight about petty issues. I don't think it's good to waste your day worrying if so-and-so is mad at you or if so-and-so thinks you're mad at them and you're not mad at them." Girls, according to many girl activists, can be horrible gossips and brutally mean to each other as they attempt to make themselves feel better or gain status. Describing her middle school years and the beginning of high school, Emily shared her perspective on girls' mean and selfish behaviors:

Girls were really mean to me. . . . I fought with my girlfriends all the time, but it . . .well, it was sort of like backstabbing. They would like sit me down and tell me all the reasons why I'm flawed in personality. Two of my best friends checked my email, like found my password, like stuff that you don't think happens, but it did, it happened to me. . . . And I really think that it just comes down to insecurity. I just think girls are really insecure and the easiest way to make yourself feel better is to make someone else feel bad at the most fundamental level.

Emily's view on girls' behavior is expressed very differently from Hayley's; instead of seeing this as just "how girls are" and presenting it as a rationale for avoiding other girls or not identifying as a girl, Emily sees girls' meanness as a response to a bigger problem. Without this more nuanced and compassionate view on mean girls, the association between girlhood and pettiness replicates stereotypical images of women as catty, bitchy, or just plain unable to get along with one another.

There has been a significant amount of public and institutional attention given to the phenomena of "mean girls" and relational aggression in recent years.[16] It is therefore not surprising that girls themselves, particularly in the United States and Canada, where this discourse has been especially visible, would suggest that meanness is a typical attribute of girlhood. In the context of so much discussion of girls' petty, judgmental, and competitive relationships with one another, the notion of girl solidarity and supportive communities of activist girls can appear practically impossible. Even girl activists sometimes imply that girls are too used to mistrust, betrayal, and unhealthy relationships with one another to organize together. Therefore, instead of trying to forge relationships or political communities *as girls* they emphasize that their activist communities are based on shared youth status, thus downplaying the fact that they are numerically dominated by girls (often quite dramatically).

In order to work together and to organize as part of a community, activist teens say that you have to stop being a girl—someone who is petty or mean—and instead grow up, become a woman, and have "real relationships." As Ramona described her youth activist collective, she said that "within activism, the *mujeres* support each other a lot . . . there isn't that rivalry of *chicas*. There is always strong support." In contrast to relational aggression found in "girl" spaces, teenage activists say that in their political communities they become women who support one another. Being an activist thus gives them a social network that is much better, stronger, and healthier than the peer relationships of "typical" girls.

Paralleling and intersecting with the institutional and organizational concern with girls' relational aggression is a broader public interest in girls' self-esteem and psychological well-being.[17] And, much as teenage girl activists affirm the widespread notion that girls are mean to each other, some of them also regularly reproduce the common association of girlhood with insecurity, depression, and unhealthy self-image. Kate talked about girls' "self-monitoring behavior," Haile described girls' "unhealthy body image," and Megan said girls are "really lost and eager to please anybody." In each of these cases, the activist teen then argued that she had overcome her own girl-like feelings of insecurity through the process of becoming an activist. Their more typical peers, they argue, have not yet dealt with or moved beyond these feelings of inadequacy and self-doubt. Therefore, they are still girls. Notably, this narrative of overcoming girlish insecurity was primarily expressed by white, middle-class girls in the United States and Canada, the targets of much of the public discussion of this "crisis."

Whether activism provides opportunities for girls to become more confident or more confident girls are drawn to political activism, it is evident that being an activist bolsters girls' sense of their self-worth. The girls I encountered, even though they were occasionally shy, uncomfortable, awkward, or dismissive of their skills, were much more frequently self-assured, direct, and proud of the young women they were becoming. They speak and carry themselves with confidence and in no way resemble the passive victims or "Ophelias" described in the institutional and discursive domain of pop psychology.

According to many girl activists, girls' insecurities make them vulnerable to becoming overly dependent on other people, particularly boys, and their opinions of them. Describing how she is different from other girls, Daniela said, "I don't want to be completely attached to a boyfriend like they do. I don't want to let men direct everything like they do." Marguerite also felt that girls are too dependent on what others think of them and on how they are seen by guys.

> I find that there's a huge dependence on being able to find somebody of the opposite sex, like I have a girlfriend right now and all she can talk about is "Oh, I don't have a date for whatever," and what I often find myself saying "why worry about this?" She keeps asking, "What is wrong with myself that I can't find somebody, I can't find a guy." Why aren't you asking yourself what is the best for me and to understand that I have my own self, my own image. . . . I don't depend on somebody else's approval of me. I don't depend on somebody loving me.

In a world where women and girls continue to be devalued and have less social power and authority than men and boys, girls experience significant pressure to gain the approval of boys. As the girls' studies scholar Lyn Mikel Brown argues, girls are socialized at an early age to "look to boys and men for approval and acceptance . . . and sacrifice other girls for success, popularity, and boyfriends."[18] Girls are taught that they have value primarily through their relationships with men and boys. According to Brown, the devaluation of other women and girls and the drive for male approval are the sources of relational aggression, betrayal, and competition within girls' relationships and friendships.

Youth activist communities, to the extent that they encourage and enable a critical analysis of gender and power, provide teenage girl activists with a way to make sense of and resist this troubling version of girlhood and gendered relationships. For the young Bay Area activists who are part of Students for Women's Rights (SWR), a feminist discussion group in their high school, the community of resistant girls is a substantial benefit of participation. They see the group as a space in which they, as young women, can analyze these pressures and develop their own critical responses. In SWR, teenage girls come together every week to talk about precisely these dynamics and problems. Such discussions are a major part of SWR's political practices, but they are a much less common occurrence in the other youth activist groups I encountered in this project. Some girls in each location see the quest for male approval as a social and political problem, and then draw upon this critical consciousness as they define themselves outside of such a paradigm. More frequently, it is activist identity itself rather than a critical feminist analysis of gender and the male gaze that gives them a way to see their own worth outside of relationships with boys and men. Many girl activists speak about how they are making contributions to the world and to social change, placing value on themselves as political actors and agents, rather than as girls who just want to be accepted. Activism, as an alternative community with its own set of values, thus gives girls another set of traits upon which to assess their worth.

As activism helps girls to reject and refuse some of the constraints of conventional or dominant girlhood, it also leads to a discursive bifurcation of girl identity and activist identity. Girls, these young women say, need the approval of others, but activists must have enough confidence in themselves and their beliefs to be willing to be seen as "different" or "weird" by many of their peers. Furthermore, many activists actively disassociated such confidence from girlhood. For example, when I asked Madeline, from the San

Francisco Bay Area, when she felt like a girl and when she felt like a woman she said, "Being a young woman, I guess, is taking the lead for what you want to do and deciding what you want to do . . . and what you want to stand up for." Similarly, Zitzitlini, from Mexico City, said, "When I am making decisions and when I am showing myself what I am capable of doing. That is when I feel like a *mujer.*" Confidence, being skillful, being sure of oneself, and being able to act politically were all traits that young women activists saw as not girly and instead as more "woman-like" and adult.

At the conceptual center of this series of oppositions between "girl identity" and "activist identity" (superficial/serious; mean/supportive; insecure/confident) is a pervasive and powerful narrative about the transition from innocent, ignorant, or stupid girl to conscious and empowered activist. Emily says part of why she likes to call herself a woman is "because it's empowering, yet oftentimes I feel like I'm just a stupid teenage girl." And part of why Erica doesn't identify as a girl is because of its link to a lack of knowledge. She said, "I don't like to be called a girl." When I asked her why, she replied, "it sort of assumes a bit more innocence, or maybe ignorance." Lolita also discussed girlhood as representing both innocence and stupidity:

> Being a *niña*, generally there are two things. One is "oh, how cute, she's so little, let me give her a candy, let me help her." Or, when someone takes a different perspective, maybe one that isn't quite as innocent, it is, 'Okay, but she's little, she doesn't understand anything, she is saying that because she doesn't understand." I think these are the two positions. It is like, she's a *niña* means she is dumb or it means she is really innocent, very good, still unaffected by the bad things in society.

Specifically referring to the girls she goes to school with, Lucy said, "I know lots, well, lots of *niñas*, yes, they are *niñas* because they are really closed in their thinking and they don't know much." The figure of the girl is thus frequently linked by girls themselves to stupidity, ignorance, and innocence.

In my Latin American research locations, not knowing anything about the world around you was primarily associated with being a *niña*, or a little girl. As such, it was a more excusable and acceptable personality trait than the ignorance or stupidity that North American girls associated with teenage girlhood. Many of the Latin American activists described the transition from *niña* to *chica* as involving a shift from living in a dream world, unaware of what is happening around you, to becoming conscious of political, social, and economic conditions. As Celia described it, "When you are a *niña*, you don't yet realize things about the world that is around you, you live with dreams, with your imagination and that is all. When a *niña* grows up and becomes a *chica*, she begins to realize more about the world where she lives. I don't really know how to explain this, but I think that it is like, you grow up inside, but you also grow in your relationship with the world." Lucia, from Mexico City, talked about a very similar transition: "You are a *niña* when you see everything as rosy and your world is all right there, and everything is beautiful because you have everything. When you are an adolescent, that is when you don't see everything as so beautiful anymore because you begin to grow and you begin to realize what the problems are and you begin to explore the world." This distinction between the innocence of being a *niña* and the growing knowledge and consciousness of being a *chica* is one of the places where the value of the multiple terms for "girl" in Spanish becomes visible. The Spanish-speaking girls can still be some kind of girl (a *chica*) and also have some knowledge about the world. English speakers, on the other hand, continue to link girlhood, including the teenage version, to ignorance, stupidity, and innocence.

The claim that girlhood is a time of blissful ignorance where you have no problems ignores the diversity of childhood experiences and assumes a comfortable, middle-class, and privileged life. This persistent social image of childhood innocence has been deconstructed by numerous scholars who argue that innocence and complete isolation from the problems of the world are not the experience of most children, even those from more privileged backgrounds.[19] Surprisingly, girl activists from a wide range of class backgrounds and national contexts participated in this narrative of innocent childhood. The only girl who explicitly commented on how such an image is actually not universally accurate was Aura, a sixteen-year-old in Mexico City, who described her class background as "proletarian." She said that "a *niña* can't really talk about [what is happening in the world] because really, she doesn't feel it quite so much. Obviously not all of them, we could talk about *niñas* who at twelve years old live on the streets and maybe already have kids while they are constructing super-luxury freeways in the country." Aura reminds us that many girls are not untouched by the problems of the world and therefore can and do have a complex understanding of such problems.

Even if ignorance about the world and the happy innocence of child-hood are more fiction than reality for most girls, these traits are still seen as "girl-like" and incompatible with an activist identity and social movement participation. Therefore, it is not surprising that these would be traits that young activists separate themselves from. The depiction of the development of political consciousness as part of the process of leaving girlhood is a key part of the definitional separation between girls and activists. In Dara's view, doing activism and having knowledge matures you: "I think girls the same age can be called different things, like one can be called a woman and one can be called a girl because of where they are mentally. But I think that . . . now that I'm aware of the world a bit more . . . I think I can call myself a young woman." According to these young activists, as you develop your sense of the world and its problems, as you come to be engaged and take action, you leave girlhood behind you. In this formulation, girls (or *niñas*) are those who don't know enough to be activists. Developing critical knowledge about the world is a crucial feature of an activist identity, and to the extent that it is dissociated from girlhood and their experiences as girls, activism also becomes de-linked from girlhood.

One of the most striking features of girl activists' relationship to girlhood is their claim that being an activist means you are no longer a girl. Their narratives of becoming an activist are frequently tied to narratives of leaving girlhood. This is not surprising given that the traits that they most often associate with girls are opposites of the characteristics they associate with activists. Activists are, in their view, concerned about important issues, care about other people, are confident, independent, and have knowledge about the world around them. Becoming an activist means that you are not a superficial, selfish, insecure, and ignorant girl. In this sense, the meanings of girl and activist are constructed through a series of definitional oppositions where the negative traits are always associated with girlhood and other girls. Throughout the Americas, the young women I interviewed often said that they were *not girls* in the context of their activism and political organizing. As with participation in many other youth subcultures, being part of activist communities gives teenage girls opportunities and spaces from which to challenge the constraints of conventional girlhood. Being an activist can enable and empower girls to work against and outside of expectations of how girls "should be." Girl activists, as I've indicated here, use their activist identities, knowledge, and experiences to resist the pressures to conform to a narrow version of girlhood. In this process, they also produce and reproduce a series of binary oppositions, with political and activist traits on one side of the divide, and passive and apolitical girl traits on the other. Despite saying that their girlhood makes them more likely to be activists than their male peers, these young women articulate "girl" and "activist" as mutually conflicting identities.

Gender, Politics, and Alternative Girlhood

Despite the numerical dominance of girls within high school activism, teenage girl activists' conceptions of girlhood replicate the ongoing de-coupling of women and girls from politics and social struggle. According to feminist political theorists, women's marginalization from political space is partially accomplished by this type of discursive de-linking.[20] The binary hierarchies of public/private, active/passive, and masculine/feminine combine with a set of institutional practices to obscure and exclude the political agendas and practice of women and girls.[21] The implicit masculinity of politics is also reflected in research on youth subcultures, which has emphasized young men's rebellion and young women's consumerism and conformity.[22] Although girl activists' actual practices challenge those who would see girls and young women only as passive, private, conformist, or nonpolitical subjects, by articulating girl and activist as mutually conflicting identities, they unwittingly reinforce their own gendered marginalization and collective invisibility from the terrain of social movements and social struggle.

However, girl activists do not just define *girl* and *activist* through these oppositions; they also talk about how being a girl encourages their activism. When we look at these two tendencies simultaneously, we can see how these young women are reconstructing and redefining what it means to be a girl, enacting an alternative version of girlhood. In my interviews, after asking girls about their thoughts on girlhood, other girls, and their own relationships to the process of growing up female, I would raise the idea of an "alternative girlhood." This concept itself was certainly not part of young women's own way of talking about themselves or other girls involved in social struggles, but it did seem to resonate for them. My conversation with Haile provides a view of this. I asked "do you think of yourself as a girl, as a teen woman, as a woman, both, depends on the situation—how would you identify yourself?" She replied, "I associate girlhood with my insecurity in girlhood, so I remember once . . . my mom was asking me to do something that was kind of time-consuming, and I was like, I am a working woman, I screamed that out, then I was like, wait a minute, I'm not a working woman. And that really showed me that deep down I want to be a woman." I asked her, "Are there times when you feel more grown up, more like a woman and times when you feel more like a girl?" She replied, "Yes, yeah. . . . In my public life, I feel more like a woman and, well, even with my family, I feel like they treat me as a girl. So . . . it makes me feel like a girl when I feel not like a girl, and I have my prejudices toward the word 'girl,' which is biased, right?" Finally, after more discussion of the characteristics and experiences she associates with girlhood and with womanhood, I brought up this idea of an alternative girlhood, commenting that "one of the things that I think is interesting about girls that are involved in things like you, girl activists, girls who are doing social change work is that they offer the world sort of an alternative image of girlhood than the ones that we see most of the time. . . . So it's an alternative vision of girlhood, a different way of being girls. What do you think is alternative about how you are girl?" She replied: "I feel sorta guilty for being so sick of high school life and rejecting that label, even though I am a girl, obviously. And what you just said kind of makes me want to own up, like, okay, I'm seventeen, I admit it. And you just kind of reminded me how me being proud of being a girl would help change that image so that I'm not as annoyed. Yeah. Thank you." Haile herself would not necessarily have considered herself as enacting an alternative girlhood without my raising this question.

Throughout my interviews and participant observation with girl activists, I saw evidence of an ongoing tension between girl activists' desires to escape the limits of girlhood and their narratives about how being a girl can support and enhance their activist identities. Unlike a full refusal of girlhood or the construction of a girl/activist binary, the idea of alternative girlhoods creates space for an acknowledgment that girls, as a socially constructed group, also have some valuable collective knowledge, skills, traits, and strengths to contribute to social movements. Despite young women's sometimes positive feelings about the idealism, responsibility, compassion, and creativity of girls, more often than not their primary orientation toward this category was one of rejection. While they have some interest in reconstructing girlhood in an alternative fashion that associates it with these traits, they are generally more concerned with moving beyond such categorization all together.

As I've traveled around the Americas, talking with adult activists about my project, I have come to appreciate one of the many reasons why my interviewees de-emphasize their girl identities in activist spaces: the narrow perception of "girl politics." Frequently, when I would mention to various politically engaged adults that I was looking for girl activists, I would be told about organizations that work with girls, programs that develop girls' leadership capacity, or youth groups who work on issues that are seen as specifically "girls' issues" such as minors' reproductive rights and health education. Basically, people heard my request for help finding girl activists as a request for help finding girls. To them, the group I was seeking was primarily defined by their girlhood. They generally assumed that girl activists work on "girls' issues" and are part of girls' groups. I would then explain that I was not only interested in girls who are part of girl-oriented spaces or projects, but those who are engaged in a wide range of political and social struggles.

The adult assumptions that girl activists are primarily engaged in what we might call "girl politics" mirror a variety of similar ideas about the activism of marginalized peoples: women activists are often assumed to be involved in a narrowly defined conception of "women's issues," disabled people are seen as only organizing around disability, and so forth. Underlying these ideas is the deeper philosophical assumption that the only universal is the white, Western, heterosexual male. All else is reduced to its own particularity. Not wanting to be limited or forced into this narrow understanding of "girls' politics," these young activists' disassociation from girlhood helps them lay claim to a broader, more expansive political authority and engagement. Their politics, they imply, are not merely "girl." This is not to deny the specificity of girlhood, but rather to suggest that girls' politics, like the politics of any other activist group, are relevant beyond simply the issues most closely associated with a singular or monolithic understanding of their identities. Girls are affected by neoliberal globalization, political repression, poverty, racism, environmental crises, war, and militarism in diverse and uneven ways. They are not just impacted by an assumed, restricted set of "girls' issues," which includes only social problems that have a direct impact on girls more than anyone else (media portrayal of girls, gender equity in schools, or minors' reproductive rights are just a few examples).

The limiting of girls to a narrow political terrain that holds only a small portion of the many social problems that impact girls and their communities, and the presumption that they are not engaged in broader political activity, is directly contradicted by the fact that girl activists are involved in a wide range of social movements. Many adults assume that "girls' issues" are the focus of girl activists' political activity, but this is actually far from the truth. The girl activists I encountered actually spend very little time focused on such themes. Although this is partly an indication of their more expansive political engagement and the fact that there are a wide variety of political issues that shape their lives and communities, it is also possible that the disregard for these (stereo)typically girls' issues is tied to the low-status and disregard given to girlhood, in general. Clare, taking a position quite different than many of the other girls, argued this point:

No one wants to take on girls' problems because they think they're so self-absorbed and so complex that who would want to deal with that. . . . There's almost like a disrespect for the issues I guess. . . . if you went and said, well my community service is that I go and volunteer with autistic children . . . because of the innocence of children there's a thing where . . . okay, I'll respect that work. But if you were saying I'm working with . . . whatever particular thing for teenage girls, it's almost like people would think, 'Well, why are you doing that?' I don't know. Just like no one respects that, no one sees that as valuable work. Almost like no one sees working with gender at all as valuable.

Clare points to one of the dangers of girl activists' tendency to see their girlhood and their activism in opposition to each other, but she does not necessarily imply that girl activists should focus on only those social problems that are most often associated with girlhood.

In conceiving and planning this project, I had not assumed that girl activists would be engaged only in a narrow version of "girl politics." Rather, I was looking for activists who were girls working in numerous social movement spaces and contexts. Although I did not think that their girl identities would necessarily limit their political engagement to "girls' issues," I was especially interested in the role of their collective identity *as girls* in shaping their political practices and social movement experiences. But, in frequently de-linking their girlhood from their activist identities, and telling me they weren't girls when they were activists, these young women seriously challenged many of my initial questions and ideas. I went into the field looking for girl activists, only to find that they did not really exist. I found many teenage women (and even many girls) who are involved in activism, but the more thoroughly interwoven "girl activist" identity was one based more on my own understandings of who they are than on their own. As I continue to refer to them as "girl activists" in the chapters that follow, I hope readers will remember that this is a shorthand in place of the longer, more complicated (and therefore more accurate) designation of "high-school-aged people who sometimes identify as women, sometimes identify as girls, and sometimes as youth, and who are also actively involved in social movements."

Navigating the sometimes conflicting and sometimes mutually supporting identities of "girl" and "activist" is clearly not a simple process for the teenage women I interviewed. Girls draw on a variety of stereotypical and traditional discourses about girlhood in order to argue that "girl" is an identity category that can support and enhance their activism. They also suggest that this is an identity that must be overcome in the process of becoming an activist. Unlike their relationship to the category of youth, which is substantially more positive, girls do not tend to authorize their movement standing on the basis of their girlhood. However, as we'll see in the following chapters, this does not prevent them from occasionally referencing their "girlish" identities and skills when articulating their reasons for emphasizing particular political strategies in their movements and organizations.

"Being a girl" is clearly very complex. Previous scholarship on the discursive construction of the category of girlhood has illuminated this complexity through an analysis of media, culture, and text. This study adds depth to our understanding of this identity category by focusing on girls' own narratives about the *meaning* of being a girl. It suggests that girlhood is not just a flexible, shifting category within cultural discourses but is also unstable for girls and young women themselves. These young activists indicate that girlhood is not a fixed state or a stable identity—a girl does not become a woman in a singular moment. Rather, my research suggests that people shift in and out of girlhood, sometimes claiming and reworking this identity, and other times refusing and rejecting it in favor of other forms of identification.

This raises important questions for the developing field of girls' studies. It highlights the inherent difficulty of defining our object of study, of determining who is and is not a girl. Does a girl cease to be one when she decides she is not one anymore? Or are there objective markers scholars can rely upon that make an individual subject no-longer-girl? Work? The age of legal majority? Reproduction? Sexuality? Financial independence? We need to think carefully about these questions, but not necessarily answer them with any one, unified definition. The answers, of course, are context-specific, complex, overlapping, but this remains a theoretical and empirical issue that scholars of girlhood need to grapple with. When we ask the important question of 'what makes someone a girl' it forces us to really consider the constructed, messy, shifting, complicated category that we study. It turns our focus from just "girls" as individuals to "girlhoods" as projects of subjectification. It also reminds us that the meaning of girlhood is not fixed but is constantly being defined and redefined in historically specific and located ways.

Narratives about being (and not being) girls, youth, and activists play an important role in girl activists' self-presentation and their conceptions of who they are both individually and collectively. Through narration, they produce themselves as particular kinds of subjects, drawing on and rejecting various widespread discourses of youth and of girlhood, reinforcing some common perceptions of their social groups, but challenging and redefining others.

Girl activists' identity talk is clearly a method of telling others how they wish to be seen, but it is also a method of telling themselves who they are. It is a form of self-creation. Girls' identity talk is important partly because it tells us who they think that they are and who they are trying to become. It gives us insight into the discursive regimes that shape their lives and into their ongoing projects of making themselves in relation to such regimes.

It is my view that girls' stories of the self matter not just to girls' individual lives, to the process of political authorization, or to the ever-changing and always negotiated discourses of gender, age, and citizenship, but also to the collective social movement strategies that girl activists emphasize in their political communities and organizations. Girl activists' identity narratives mirror and foreshadow the shared tendencies found in girls' activist practices. Girl activists also regularly draw upon these identity claims as they discuss their political practices. The following three chapters look at girls' political strategies, and their narratives about those strategies, analyzing not just the convergences and divergences in their modes of doing activism, but also how their identity narratives weave in and around their articulations of the rationale behind these political actions.

Part 2 —

Making Change Happen

5

The Street Is Our Classroom

A Politics of Learning

The courtyard in front of the Oakland City Hall was full of teenagers, all chanting for their rights to quality education. It was Take Back Our Schools Day, a San Francisco Bay Area activist event organized by a coalition of youth organizations fighting for educational justice. Approximately four hundred teenagers were gathered, holding signs and banners with messages like: Education Is a Human Right, Not a Privilege; Student Power; Unity and Justice; Hella [Bay Area slang for "lots" or "really," depending on the context] Children Left Behind; and Education Is a Civil Right. The group had four key demands: noncompliance with President Bush's educational policy No Child Left Behind (particularly the punishment of "failing" schools); the return of Oakland schools to local control; an end to the high school exit exams; and the full funding of Proposition 98, which guaranteed a minimum level of funding for public education in California. Standing at the microphone in front of the crowd, a young black woman shouted out: "People have asked me why I'm not in class today, and I say the street is our classroom! We can teach each other here!" Education, she told her listeners, happens in social movements and social struggle, not just in the school building.

Throughout the rally, student speakers expressed frustration with adults who might think they don't know enough about the issues to take action, and they also encouraged their peers in the audience to make sure to educate themselves and take advantage of the day's opportunities to learn more. A thirteen-year-old Chicana let everyone know her anger at the *Oakland Tribune* for saying that the youth activists were parroting somebody else's view. She replied, "But we came up with our own point of view. We know about things—this is our reality! We have messed up bathrooms, and bathrooms that are locked half the time. We have teachers who don't care about us and our learning, and we know that it isn't totally their fault—the ones who do care, the state isn't giving them enough money to teach us or to provide the things we need to learn. We know this. We know what the problems are. No Child Left Behind left all y'all behind!" When she finished, a young black man came up to the stage and reminded everyone that there would be workshops all day "to learn about the issues, to educate ourselves. We are here educating each other today. We are all peers and we can learn from each other, so I encourage y'all to really participate, to ask questions, to make comments." A school board member also took the stage, building on the message of education outside the classroom. "Be sure to ask questions and learn while you are here. Some people say that adults are using you as puppets, as their political toys. This is not true! We know you'll speak for yourselves, we know you'll think for yourselves. You are like the children of Selma, the children of Soweto, the children of Sharpeville, of the civil rights movement who started the sit-ins. People probably said they were manipulated by adults too. They were not, you were not. To those who say you are, prove them wrong." Following these and other speeches, several of the event organizers (all teenagers) stood up and told the crowd where to find a series of workshops, including sessions on the politics of the exit exam, on how to take back control of the schools, on No Child Left Behind, on "five hundred years of miseducation," on organizing and youth action, and on shutting down the California Youth Authority (juvenile prisons). This education, they suggested, is just as good as, or better than, what they'd be learning in school that day.

A few weeks later, I interviewed Chela, the eighteen-year-old education coordinator for one of the organizations that spearheaded Take Back Our Schools Day. Like most of the other girls I interviewed, she continually emphasized the importance of education to social change and social struggle. "We don't get real education in our schools, I feel like. A lot of times I sit in a classroom and I feel like what I'm learning is completely irrelevant to my life. And, what we get taught in my organization, or what we put out through the organization is . . . I don't know, I would say it is life changing because so many things that are meant not to be known by people who are willing to make a change. And it is knowing that information that motivates you to make that change. So, I've been more attracted to that part of organizing." Education is at the heart of Chela's political practices.

According to the girl activists I interviewed, the vast majority of their political events and activities are designed to educate. These activists spend a significant amount of their activist energy organizing and planning events aimed at developing political knowledge. They write and perform plays and puppet shows, and organize rock, punk, and hip-hop concerts with political content. They make and distribute videos, run youth radio stations, and write and publish their own newspapers, zines, and blogs. They paint murals, organize photo exhibitions, and post fliers. And they organize and host countless workshops, film screenings, assemblies, debates, study circles, and open discussions. Political education is a central feature in nearly all of their campaigns and projects.

This chapter looks at three different approaches to "knowledge-creation" used by girl activists, and discusses some of the major differences in their educational strategies, showing how each is rooted in its own localized political culture. Alongside these major differences, however, I also find that girl activists' political education practices across locations consistently emphasize learning new feelings, emotions, and desires in addition to facts, analysis, and knowledge. Finally, I show how their practices are generally non-dogmatic and process-based, focusing on ongoing learning and questioning rather than fixed answers. Girl activists' politics of learning encourages critical thinking and critical feeling, and it is deeply open-minded and open-hearted. Analyzing girls' talk about these strategies, as well as some of the practices themselves, I find that their emphasis on the ongoing process of political education is supported and shaped by their local political cultures and contexts, by girls' identity narratives, and by a transnational social movement culture—in this case, the many iterations of Zapatismo, the political philosophy of the Zapatista autonomous indigenous movement in Mexico.

Political Education as Knowledge Construction

Beth believes in the power of facts. A Vancouver activist involved primarily in organizing around humanitarian issues outside of Canada, she took the position that making people aware of the world's problems is all that is required for change to occur. I asked her, "If you could have a conversation or say anything to the CEO of some big corporation, like the Gap or Nike, what would you say?" She responded, "I'd ask them how do they justify using child labor and see how they'd respond to that because I don't think they could. I don't know how they sleep at night. I don't get it. I don't know. I think it must be that they are just so unconnected and they just don't understand. It would be interesting to take them there and see." Beth implies here that the CEOs of corporations that use sweatshop and child labor must not realize the consequences of their actions. In her view, giving them facts about this would perhaps lead them to change. Earlier in our conversation, Beth had also said that the goal of her global issues club is "mainly to promote awareness in our school because a lot of the root of the problem is that people just don't know or understand what is going on. And I think that if we educate our peers— I mean it is easy for us to educate our peers—and once people know, they start caring and start doing something." This firm belief that people (including corporate CEOs) will do "what is right" once they have the information implies that social awareness is all that is needed for social change. Unfortunately, the history of social movements and struggles indicates that this is not often the case.

Compared to Beth, many girl activists were less sure that *all* that people need to create change is knowledge. For most of the girls I interviewed, knowledge is central, and it will hopefully inspire action and change, but it is not necessarily going to move everyone. Dara, for example, made a statement similar but not identical to Beth's when she said "the main thing for me is to raise awareness, 'cause . . . with the knowledge comes the passion to do something. And a lot of people, most people, I won't say most, but like a lot of people, they can't have the knowledge that something like this is going on in the world without doing something to erase it. So that is what we strive to do in the club." Dara isn't sure that everyone will act upon the knowledge offered by her organization, but she hopes at least some people are inspired to do something with what they learn.

Beth, Dara, and many other Vancouver girls were the most confident about the power of information to change people's actions and therefore change the world. Their political education practices reflected this faith in facts. Many of the Vancouver girls' political actions promoted critical knowledge primarily in the form of "becoming aware" of what is happening in the world around us. They were more likely to provide information about specific problems, rather than discuss more comprehensive understandings of the social structures beneath these problems. Their organizations sponsor workshops, films, and assemblies that tend to focus on single issues or particular campaigns. These girls held events to inform their peers about refugee issues, child soldiers, land mines, the small arms trade, global poverty and hunger, fair trade, and green consumerism. Their educational tactics were often creative, such as a bake sale where people would, in addition to their cupcakes, get a picture of a paper soccer ball to paste over a picture of a paper gun, and information about "the right to play." Such creativity was part of an approach to political education that was much more circumscribed in terms of scope and depth of analysis than were the approaches I encountered in other locations. In Vancouver, political education was largely understood to be the provision of new information about specific issues and topics.

This approach to knowledge and political learning does not develop in isolation. It is typical of the kinds of mainstream organizations in which the Vancouver girls participate, and it is distinctly Canadian. First of all, many of the Vancouver teens were part of large, formalized nongovernmental organizations with a political perspective far less radical than that of most of the student-led organizations in the other four cities in this sample. Given that they have been, in part, trained by these large organizations, it is not surprising that the Vancouver girls would have a more issue-specific and less comprehensive and ideological approach to doing political education than their peers in other types of organizations. Second, the Vancouver girls' faith in change through information is also partly rooted in the deep historic denial of Canadian racism and colonialism. In this national context, the problems that need to be addressed are framed as specific social issues to be tackled, rather than as manifestations of larger and more thoroughly structured injustices. Within a national discourse about Canada as a "just" and "fair" multicultural nation, each problem is an error that needs to be corrected, rather than an example of a system of inequalities that benefit some but not others. It is also within this cultural context that we can understand why these girls might believe that most Canadians would want to fix these problems, if only they knew about them. The Canadian national self-image is, in general, one of well-intentioned and generous leaders who will look out for those less fortunate, both at home and abroad. Part of these girls' cultural toolkit, then, is this long-standing idea that Canadians will consistently "do what is right."[1]

In contrast to the Vancouver girls' collective emphasis on disseminating facts and information, girls in other locations frequently highlighted the importance of developing beliefs in the possibility of a better world; they aimed to create political education practices that would teach others to enact potential solutions to the problems they see. Marisa, a Mexican teen working with a maquiladora workers' support organization, emphasized that people need to know how to defend their rights, not just to know that they have rights. "The reality is that people know that they have problems, and they have courage, but they feel like they can't improve things because they don't know how to defend themselves. A lot of times they don't defend themselves because they aren't aware of how they can. So we want to help people to realize this and to defend themselves." Marisa points out that information about the problems is not always enough (and that many people already know that such problems exist). She argues that political education should also help others see that change is possible and that they, collectively, can contribute to making those changes. It is this perspective that leads to workshops and educational events that not only provide information about a problem but also spend significant time and energy strategizing about how to address that problem.

This dual emphasis on identifying problems and solutions was by far the most common political education style used by the San Francisco Bay Area girls. With historical ties to youth development organizations and foundations, their organizations frequently draw upon the tools of community needs assessments and participatory action research.[2] Bay Area groups often teach teens how to research problems in their schools and communities, and to study what the larger community sees as useful ways to address these problems. Political education is often achieved through the research process and then again through the presentation of research findings, both of which center on an analysis of specific problems and a discussion of proposed community solutions.

In addition to engaging in community and school needs assessments as political education processes, some of the Bay Area youth organizations also have an extensive, planned political education curriculum for new members. This is especially the case for the more structured, foundation-funded, community-based youth organizations. In Jewish Youth for Social Justice, for example, each year the "new group" goes through several months of weekly meetings primarily focused on political education including such topics as facilitation training, connections between Judaism and social justice, and youth leadership and youth empowerment. More senior members of the organization help facilitate this process as peer leaders. Then, when the new group joins up with the older members, the teens collectively choose a series of issues and topics that they want to learn more about that year. They split into groups, do research, and present workshops on each of these topics to one another and, eventually, to other members of their school communities.

These Bay Area youth activist groups are all building collective youth knowledge about the institutions that shape and constrain youth choices and futures. Their workshops (for youth and led by youth) build consciousness of these problems and encourage youth to collectively develop strategies for how to change and challenge these institutions and power dynamics. According to Mattie Weiss, "a key emphasis in many [U.S. youth activist] groups' political education is developing analytical connections between individual and community issues, between problems at the local and federal level, between national and international phenomena."[3] These organizations sometimes highlight the ways local school and community problems are embedded in some bigger "isms," such as racism, classism, or sexism, and in broader social processes and patterns. However, my own conversations with Bay Area girl activists suggest the political education practices in these groups do not often provide sufficient time and space for youth to develop their political vocabularies or to learn more theoretical tools for analyzing the many injustices they see around them. The problem/solution approach to political education includes some important attention to addressing (or at least naming) the root causes of a set of problems, but it doesn't always give teens the space to develop and strengthen their own understandings of these root causes. For example, teens organizing around educational justice and privatization of the public schools say that this issue is related to No Child Left Behind, racism, and classism, but they don't have the language to do much more than name these possible connections. They would say that something is the result of these "root causes," but not often articulate *how* this process functions.

Diana, a seventeen-year-old San Francisco Bay Area Latina who attended the World Social Forum in Caracas, noticed this difference between her U.S. classmates and the youth she met in Venezuela. She and I were discussing globalization during our interview:

> When I think of the word globalization, first of all I feel very stupid because I don't think we get a lot of education on it and maybe it is because of our government's point of view that it is not something they want incorporated into the curriculum, so maybe that is why we don't get to talk about it a lot in class and in school. But, I know, especially after the World Social Forum, that it is something of great importance and that even if I haven't heard of it, it is affecting me. And I really wish that I could, that there were places that you could learn about it and have it be normal to learn about that, because here, if you ask a random teenager what globalization is, I don't think we would know, and in a lot of other places they know and, yeah, that is frustrating.

This lack of familiarity with the terminology of globalization doesn't mean that Diana is ignorant about global inequalities, corporate power, or transnational relationships. Instead, Diana and many of her U.S. peers have a strong generalized awareness of power, authority, and inequality. They truly understand a great deal, but lacking a politicized vocabulary to name these problems, they frequently struggle to express what they think and feel about the world. As Clare explained, "I'm trying to grab all these thoughts and . . . process them in a cohesive way and not rambling forever. . . . I think that there's that epiphany that you have a lot more frequently when you are younger of maybe I can't talk about it, but I really do understand it. I feel it."

Trying to communicate what they know but can't always explain has led some Bay Area girl activists into some frustrating interactions with adults. Yasmine, a sixteen-year-old black girl from the Bay Area, is involved in a local educational justice organization. In our interview, she expressed a great deal of critical knowledge about the prison-industrial complex, racial inequality in schools, economic injustice, and sexism, to name just a few of the topics we discussed. But she has been frustrated by her inability to communicate what she knows, particularly to adults who, "all they respect is facts." This was her experience with her history teacher:

> I was just sitting in class and I knew that there was something wrong with the curriculum because it was just . . . really culturally biased and that's just 'cause otherwise I wouldn't have felt the way I felt. And like in my heart, or I guess you could say even in my soul, it didn't feel right. . . . And I was trying to express myself to him, but . . . obviously he went to college and he has more factual knowledge and so whenever I would try to say, well, I feel this is culturally biased, he'd say . . . yeah, but, we are gonna learn about the African American movement, and he would always try to water down what I was saying and . . . dis-validate or un-validate or whatever what I was saying.

Yasmine was getting more and more frustrated about having to defend her point of view as the year went on and told me that sometimes, "I just like tear up, because I can't put it into words." She found some support from another teacher who told her that he understood how she felt, but that "all these people understand is like rational thinking, like all they understand is . . . facts and knowledge, book knowledge." Yasmine is very clear that she already knows a lot about what is wrong: she understands the problems in her school and in her community, but she says she needs to learn the facts in order to communicate them to skeptical adults. What she is doing now, as an activist, is "really trying to acquire as much knowledge as I can so that I'll be real grounded in what I know and what I'm sure of." Yasmine knows a lot about how oppression works, but she can't always explain it. She needs to learn a language for talking about these issues, but she has had a hard time finding places to develop that language and the skills involved in expressing oppositional consciousness and her own critical knowledge. She can name the problems but hasn't had space to develop her own, more extensive political discourse on these topics.[4]

North American youth organizations have emerged, in part, out of the tradition of community organizing.[5] As such, they carry some of the challenges and pitfalls of this tradition's approach to political education. Community organizing, particularly the model developed by Saul Alinsky in his *Rules for Radicals* has been criticized for its intensive focus on specific, localized problems and their potential solutions at the expense of more open discussions of larger political structures and systems, notably racism and sexism.[6] According to Alinsky and many who followed his method, this focus on the specific, particular campaign was necessary to help organizers avoid the pitfalls of ideology. However, as Rinku Sen writes, "activists are beginning to recognize that the nonideological organization doesn't exist. All individuals and organizations operate from an ideology; an ideology is simply a worldview, and everybody has one, whether stated or implicit."[7] She argues that contemporary community organizations need to begin to take on more complex and difficult issues as part of their political education practices because "it is virtually impossible for an organization to achieve long-term change without a coherent picture of the world and a theory of how change is effected."[8] While youth organizations in North America occasionally try to connect young people's problems to these broader conversations, their political education practices still tend to be dominated by the older community-organizing focus on issues, rather than more open-ended critical analysis and dialogue. Thus, girls like Yasmine, Diana, and Clare can name racism, classism, sexism, homophobia, and capitalism because they have learned that such things are the "root causes" of local injustices, but they have not had much experience in actually discussing how they think these causes operate in the world.

In contrast to North American girls' frequent frustrations about the difficulty of expressing what they know about the social world, I found that Mexican, Venezuelan, and Argentinean girl activists from a variety of class backgrounds drew upon and deployed extensive political vocabularies. They were very comfortable discussing and proposing theories about how to understand the social and political world. This is possibly the result of their political education practices. Unlike the generally issue-specific political education found in North America, their youth organizations tend toward the development of more systematic critical analyses and knowledges and, in some cases, ideologically informed oppositional consciousness. While Latin American teens, like their North American peers, organize workshops, speakers, and films about a wide array of specific issues, they also intentionally conduct workshops that create space for more holistic political conversations and debates.

For example, Rosa, a Mexican seventeen-year-old, told me that her organization had organized workshops and conferences "about neoliberalism, capitalism, the consequences of these, the histories of guerillas, of revolutions, *magonismo* [the ideas of Mexican anarchist Ricardo Flores Magon], and other informative forums, like those to inform people about what is happening with the *porros*, with educational reforms, and all the other things that are harming us." Clearly, the topics of some of these educational events are of a different type than those addressed in the events of the Vancouver teens. Part of political cultures that are openly intellectual, Latin American youth activists approach political education from a more comprehensive perspective. Furthermore, these girls also live in countries with a much more diverse political terrain than that found in North America. Communism, socialism, Marxism, and anarchism are all traditions of political thought with visible presence in the democratic debate and political discourse in Mexico, Argentina, and Venezuela.[9] The historical tradition and contemporary persistence of a radical, Left-wing political culture in Latin America informs and inspires girls' political education practices, providing them with a set of intellectual resources upon which to build their own politics of learning.

Study circles and reading groups are an especially vibrant part of these young women's political education practices and a key space in which they develop their political vocabularies and critical knowledges. When I asked Alicia to describe what meetings are like in her Venezuelan Communist youth group, she said, "We talk. We always bring documents, like from Lenin, Che. We read them and then analyze them, we give our opinions, say what we think about this, and what we should take from these examples for ourselves." Similarly, Liliana said that her *cubiculo* "is more like a study group. We study Zapatista texts, but not just Zapatista things. Also things on human rights, on homosexuality, literary texts, things from wherever, things that we want to address. But mostly Zapatista readings because we want to understand and learn from this point of view. So we are trying to educate ourselves and teach ourselves and from there, in some form, teach others. And this is how we move forward, developing our voices." Both with their peers and individually, the Latin American teens read extensively. They use books, articles, and literature to help them make sense of and talk about the world and thus develop their own political analyses and voices. Azul talked about reading social theory, history, and Marxist analysis; Julia mentioned reading Marx, Lenin, and Trotsky; Alicia was just finishing Eduardo Galeano's *Open Veins of Latin America*; and Zitzitlini told me she began her studies of political theory with the works of the Russian anarchist Peter Kropotkin.[10]

Reading history and political philosophy gives these girls a set of intellectual and analytic tools for making sense of the world around them, informing their political practices, enhancing their critical knowledges, and helping them develop their own political voices.

But reading and discussing history and philosophy are not the only ways that girl activists in Latin America develop their critical knowledges and political vocabularies. This more formalized and fixed resource is complemented by the creation of extensive informal spaces for casual political discussion and collective dialogue. They talk about politics regularly with their friends, families, and classmates. For example, in many of the Mexico City high schools I visited, student activists gather together in their *cubiculos* to hang out with friends and chat between classes, after school, and during other free time. The casual conversations that happen in these social spaces include not only gossip about who is dating who and plans for the upcoming weekend, but also personal support and advice for each other and a great deal of discussion of current issues and political theory. Gathering in the *cubiculos* gives these youth time and space to develop their political insights and ideas. Compared to their North American peers, Latin American girls have more places where they can practice expressing their critical knowledges, expand on their skills of political analysis, and learn more extensive political vocabularies.

These ongoing political conversations and the formal and informal spaces for sharing and developing critical knowledges provide girl activists in Latin America with opportunities to sharpen their skills of politicized talk. Their political education practices emphasize not just learning facts about social problems or thinking through ways to address these problems, but they try to make sense of the ways that these problems relate to one another, examining the social structures, systems, processes, and institutions that underlie a given situation. In some groups, this involves reading political philosophy, and in others it is more likely to occur in the form of sustained conversations about how people in the group make sense of what is happening in their lives and in the lives of people around them. No matter what the specific form, however, it is clear that these young activists are engaged in an ongoing process of developing theoretical and systematic critical knowledge.

As I spoke with girl activists in Mexico, Venezuela, and Argentina, I was frequently impressed by their critical knowledge and political insights. These young women had well-developed ideas about the world around them and were using these ideas to shape and construct their political strategies and actions. A few of the Communist youth in Mexico spoke stiffly about capitalism, the bourgeoisie, and the power of the proletariat, talking with me as if they were reciting memorized lines, but most of the girls had much more personal and comfortable relationships with social and political theory, putting their ideas about politics into their own words and expressing their own, distinctive political voices. They were sharp, analytic, thoughtful, and seemed to be generally well-served by their political educations. Unlike their North American peers who often struggled to name and describe the problems that they experience, see, and feel, and were frustrated by their inability to communicate what they know, the Latin American girls were obviously at ease talking politics.

Learning is important to girls in all five of my research sites, but they don't have the same ideas about what they and their peers need to know in order to effect social change. These differences matter, and not all forms of political knowledge-building serve girls equally well. Specifically, the U.S. and Canadian teens' tendency to focus on specific issues and their potential solutions without sufficient space for theorizing the relation between these issues leaves them struggling to formulate their political beliefs. On the other hand, the Latin American girls draw upon a much wider range of intellectual resources and ideas, and create many more opportunities for the development of their own oppositional vocabularies.

My comments here are not meant to be a celebration of book knowledge at the expense of embedded knowledge or the theories and philosophies of regular people and communities. Nor is this a prescription for all activist groups to start study circles on Marx, Lenin, or Kropotkin. Rather, I mean to highlight the value of political education practices that enhance and develop· people's vocabularies and provide the intellectual tools for political analysis and self-expression. These can be developed in a multitude of ways, not all of which require a return to metanarratives or singular and monolithic understandings of "the system." Activists of any age don't need "the right analysis," but they do need some analyses as starting points for ongoing conversations. Activist groups don't need fixed lines on every topic, but they do need to be able to think and talk about the world with other members of their political communities. This is the real value of the Latin American girl activists' approach to political education: they create spaces for talking about politics and power in a deeper and more sustained fashion than North American teens. In doing so, they develop and strengthen their abilities to contribute to the ongoing conversations about both the current state of the world and desirable alternative futures.

Political Education as Feeling Production

In the previous section I have highlighted some of the different ways that girls' political education practices construct oppositional and critical knowledges. But knowledge creation is not the only goal of girls' political education strategies. Political education, according to teenage girls, is not limited to teaching and learning new ideas, but includes teaching and learning new ways to feel. Indeed, many girls suggested that the reason they are engaged in political education work is because, in Josephine's words, "we want people to care, to feel something." Political education should draw out people's concern for others, opening up their hearts. To do this, girl activists make extensive use of films, theater, photography and other artistic mediums. In Mexico City, several groups set up regular photo exhibits in their schools. Others present pieces of political theater that they have developed, hoping to spark a sense of anger and energize their peers to chant and march alongside with them at the conclusion of the play. Angela told me about a play that she and her peers were developing that was about a student strike that had happened at the school a few years previously. The play, she hoped, would help the audience not only learn about that event and about current problems of repression at the school but also inspire "political feelings." In Vancouver, many of the global issues clubs show films that highlight social injustices in other parts of the world so that other teens can learn about these problems from the mouths of those who experience them. Watching films, they say, is more emotional than simply reading about an issue. Ideally, people come to the films and actually feel something for the people they see on the screen. This is a form of political education that is not limited to providing information or analysis, but instead intentionally aims to produce certain kinds of oppositional feelings: compassion, anger, outrage, shock, and the like. In using these methods of political education, girl activists are intentionally cultivating emotional, and not just rational, responses to social problems.

In addition to using art to heighten feelings of empathy, compassion, and outrage, some girl activists spoke about the utility of simulations and role plays. Several Vancouver girls described their own strong emotional reactions to a simulation about refugee issues that they experienced at a youth activist conference and symposium. They were awakened early one morning, told their "village" was under attack, rushed from their rooms, and were taken to a "border" and then to a "refugee camp." They were given names of "family members" whom they were meant to find, but most could not. Describing the experience, Beth said "it sorta made me understand, but not completely understand, but begin to understand what it would be like, and that was really powerful for me." She continued by saying that the simulation "only lasted six hours, and these people didn't even hurt us and yet we're all like so affected by it, and I can't even imagine what it would be like if it were real." The emotional charge of this kind of educational event, these girls suggest, makes them much more effective as pedagogical tools for social movements.

Estrella, a girl from a small town outside of Mexico City, is deeply concerned about the ongoing destruction of the ecosystem in the area. But she notes that far too many of the youth don't feel a need to do anything about it because they don't really engage with the environment that much. She and the group she is part of regularly take people out on hikes in the surrounding forest so that they can see what is happening to the ecosystem, but also so that they begin to appreciate the nature that is around them and feel a stronger desire to be in this environment and thus a stronger desire to protect it. A healthy forest is something Estrella feels she needs, and she hopes that by taking other youth hiking there, they will also come to need the forest as well. Estrella's educational approach combines the creation of new knowledge about what is happening to the forest with the encouragement of new desires and needs.

In *An Essay on Liberation*, Herbert Marcuse argues that oppositionality is a position of the body, the sensibility of people, and is not just located in the mind. He writes, "liberation presupposes . . . different instinctual needs, different reactions of the body as well as the mind."[11] The subject who seeks liberation is a subject with different needs, not just different thoughts. This moves opposition from a purely intellectual realm into the realm of emotion, physicality, desire, and need. For Marcuse, the free subject is an "organism which is no longer capable of adapting to the competitive performances required for well-being under domination, no longer capable of tolerating the aggressiveness, brutality, and ugliness of the established way of life."[12]

Marcuse's writings also remind us that such feelings and instincts are socially produced. He writes, "The needs and faculties of freedom . . . can emerge only in the collective practice of creating an environment."[13] He goes on to state, "Revolutionary forces emerge in the process of change itself; the translation of the potential into the actual is the work of political practice."[14] Oppositional subjects are, for Marcuse, universally possible but developed only in social space, in interaction with a social, cultural, and historical framework. Marcuse's instinct for freedom is partly within individual bodies, but it is expressed and made actual only through a collective process of social struggle. Part of this process is political education.

Films, cultural events, and emotionally charged simulations are all methods of political education, but their goal, according to girl activists, is not to provide a lot of information or facts. Instead, the goal of these methods is to encourage participants to understand something of the emotional significance of social problems. These methods of political education are designed by girl activists to encourage participants to *feel* something, whether it be empathy, compassion, shock, outrage, or anger. Recent sociological research on social movements has addressed some of the emotional work done by activists in building and sustaining their political communities.[15] Much less, however, has been written about activists' intentional use of emotion within their pedagogical practices. Girl activists' political education practices suggest that critical social movement pedagogy can do more than simply develop analytic understandings of the world, and that these educational practices are an important force in the production of what scholars variously call the "emotional infrastructure," or "emotion culture" within a given movement.[16]

Hayley, a Vancouver activist, indicates that anger is an important part of the emotion culture that she and her peers are trying to create through their educational strategies. She said, "Look at the faces of children ravaged by war, and if it doesn't make you angry, you gotta consider, should you be doing this? Do you really care? It should make you think about how you see the world if that doesn't make you angry and upset." And Camila noted "When you go there [to work in the *villas*] and see—it really made me angry, not because of what I have, but because of the inequality that there is in the country." Hayley and Camila suggest that people should *feel* something when they look around them, that opening one's eyes to the inequalities and injustices of the world should lead to an emotional response.[17]

The anger that Camila and Hayley describe emerges from empathy and seeing the problems around them, but girls' anger is also sometimes rooted in their personal and immediate experiences of oppression and systemic violence. Lisette told me about how her experiences in a political education program led to a greater understanding of structural racism, which drew out and focused some of her anger. "Seeing like, I'm missing out just because of where I come from and what I look like, that's not fair. So I got really mad . . . and a lot of that anger drove me." For Lisette, increased consciousness and deeper analysis of racism led not just to more knowledge, but to anger. This anger, she says, is what kept her going.

Many scholars have noted that anger has a very important role to play in political mobilization, so it is not surprising that it would be a desired emotional outcome in teenage girls' political education strategies.[18] But it is also a more complicated and problematic emotion for women activists to embrace and navigate than men.[19] Furthermore, Lyn Mikel Brown, in her research on girls' anger, argues that as they grow up, girls "learn that their expressions of anger are inappropriate and unacceptable within the narrow framework of the dominant culture."[20] She states that staying in touch with their emotions, particularly the emotion of anger, is difficult for girls during adolescence. One way girl activists try to negotiate this difficulty is through attempting to balance their talk about cultivating and producing anger with an equivalent emphasis on love and compassion, far more "acceptable" feminine emotions.[21] Azul indicates how these two emotional positions can in fact be treated as two sides of the same coin. She said, "It is because I love humanity, because I want a better world that I hate that people are dying of hunger." Girls' anger at injustice, their hatred for the problems, stems from their love for those around them and for the greater community. Anger is useful for social movement actors, so girls do not want to abandon it as a desired outcome of their political education practices. Therefore, they manage this unfeminine emotion by linking it back to and rooting it in the more gender-appropriate feelings of love, care, and concern for others.

Treating political education as an emotional task, and not merely a cognitive one, is a strategic choice. Not all approaches to political education have this kind of emphasis on feeling. But such an emphasis seems to be an obvious choice for girl activists when we place this strategy in the context of their identity claims. Girls often suggested that the reason that there are more girl activists in high school than boys is precisely because of their emotional socialization. Lolita, referring to the differences between teenage girl and teenage guy activists, said, "We [women] are a little more emotional in our perspectives, and maybe it bothers us more to see people with economic problems, social problems, and so for that reason we are more mobilized." Girls' focus on emotional political education makes complete sense for a group that claims their emotions are an important part of what make them "better" activists.

An emotion-based approach to political education is not just supported by girls' gender-based claims, but also by their age-based identity claims. In Emily's view, "I think there can be more of an emotional drive from teenagers because I think teenagers are really reactive, like hormones, whatever it is. We react. And I think reactions and like anger can really drive a lot of teenagers, and I think that is really important, whereas with adults, it can be more of an intellectual sort of push." In the same vein Azul said, "I'm not sure if it's good or bad, I don't know, but youth sometimes do everything very passionately. I think it is beautiful, but sometimes it's bad because you need to rationalize or be rational a little more. . . . But I think it is beautiful to feel strongly and to feel good with what you are doing. I think that sometimes when someone already has twenty years of experience with activism they do things more mechanically." Emotion, both Azul and Emily argue, is an important part of youth activism, something that can and should be facilitated and channeled into action. But as Azul indicates, this does not mean operating only on the basis of feelings: emotion needs to be accompanied by reason and knowledge. Emotion can not be the entire foundation for political mobilization and action, but by talking about the importance of emotion, girl activists bring a different tone and quality to discussions of political education and oppositional consciousness. They highlight a mode of understanding that is at least partly outside of rationality, scientific diagnoses, or what the Marxist theorist Georg Lukács describes as a theoretically informed "knowledge of the totality."[22]

Girl activists' focus on the emotional, intuitive, and feeling-based elements of oppositional consciousness suggest that there is more to building consciousness than simply supplying people with information and knowledge. Their political education strategy involves not only creating spaces for sharing facts, discussing solutions to problems, and developing philosophies, theories, and vocabularies but also developing dissident feelings, intuitions, and desires. These practices open people's minds to new ideas *and* open people's hearts to new feelings. They do this through the intentional use of art, culture, and other pedagogical activities designed to help participants "put themselves in someone else's shoes" and, as the example of Estrella's actions indicates, by prefiguring other ways of living and being, thus creating new needs and desires. In doing so, they suggests a distinctive, and often underacknowledged, pedagogical strategy for social movements.

Political Education as an Ongoing Process

Given their location as students, it is not surprising that teenagers would place a particular emphasis on education and learning within social movements. To a certain extent, this identity position partially explains why they prioritize this social change strategy. According to Manuela, "in youth, you study." As teenagers and high school students, girl activists are highly aware of what they don't know. As new activists, they continually express that there is a great deal more that they want to learn about politics, social change, and the social world. In our interview, Zitzitlini casually mentioned reading works by Flores Magon, Kropotkin, Proudhon, and Bakunin. She has probably read far more anarchist theory than many sociologists. But, Zitzitlini also said that there is a lot that she does not yet know about the world. She is glad to have the chance to spend more time with slightly older students in her activist *cubiculo* because "they are teaching me. As I told you, I'm just starting to get involved." Drawing on their claims about their own not-yet-fully-activist identities and on developmental discourses about adolescence as a time of growth, Zitzitlini and other girl activists define and describe themselves as activists who are "still learning." They argue that they themselves are still "in process" and have much more to learn about politics, movements, and social change. Thus, their student and youth identity narratives support their strategic emphasis on political learning. Furthermore, these developmental narratives play a significant role in shaping their political education practices. Girl activists' workshops, educational actions, and reading circles are not designed only to educate other youth but also to develop their own knowledge, feelings, and perspectives. As Dara succinctly put it, "the point of the club is not just to educate others, but to educate ourselves." Girls' narration of their youthful and student identities encourages them to see themselves as still learning about the world, which then supports their strategic tendency to take a nondogmatic and process-based approach to political education.

But girl activists' open-ended pedagogy is not unique to girls or to youth: it is also closely tied to the contemporary social movement cultures that surround them. More specifically, this is a movement pedagogy that draws heavily on the transnational diffusion of Zapatista ideas, practices, and theories.[23] Like Zapatismo, which "relies on a community of people to mentor one another in order to appreciate how to move forward together, thereby challenging the role of the elite intellectual and producing 'incarnated intellectuals' in the process,"[24] girl activists don't see political organizers as teachers with all the answers but instead position themselves as part of a larger community of learners.

Emily was part of a student-led walk-out against the Iraq War that captures this idea of learning together through social action, rather than being taught by experts. Describing this event, she said, "It was maybe like sixty students, sitting on the steps, and there was a megaphone being passed around and people were just like talking about why they were there and it was really empowering." She says this was her "favorite rally that I've ever been to," because instead of being a rally where "every speaker says the same thing," this one involved "just listening to each other in a really honest way . . . and it was like one of the first ones I had ever been to and I didn't even know exactly why I was there . . . but I could say something and I could hear other people." This kind of listening, Emily suggests, was a more empowering learning experience than when she stands in a crowd and listens to someone on a stage. Protest is often seen by activists as an opportunity for political education, but such education tends to rely on a few well-known speakers addressing the rest of the crowd. Youth-led protests that have a strong political education component, however, sometimes take a different tack, creating space where the participants talk to each other in a learning-community.

Listening is a central component in many of the political education tactics used by girl activists. Frida, a Mexican seventeen-year-old, said that she loves to give workshops because "it is the most gratifying . . . you teach what you know and other people teach you. You always learn something new from each person. Always." As I sat in on some of the planning meetings for workshops in each city, I noticed that girl activists were consistently attentive to making sure that there was scheduled time in the agenda for discussion, for people to listen to each other. In Vancouver, for example, as the teens in one global issues club planned an educational event on the genocide in Darfur, Dara kept reminding her peers that they needed to have time for people to "talk about it, and about how they are feeling about what they learn, and what it means." In each of their groups, as they plan their political events and educational strategies, girl activists emphasize the importance of conversation and dialogue.

When I asked Ramona, a Mexican student who is part of a collective explicitly inspired by the theory and practice of Zapatismo, to tell me about her activism, she said, "First, listen. The most important thing in being an activist is first to listen to people and to not isolate ourselves. One thing that we always do in my collective is to listen to other people to know what they are thinking and to base our work on this. I know collectives that are only ten people and that isolate themselves and only talk to each other and do their work. Our tactic is to listen to people and to do work for the people and not to only stay among ourselves, to invite others."

Writing about Zapatista *encuentros*, or encounters, as an innovative mechanism for doing politics, Manuel Callahan describes a pedagogy that resonates strongly with that practiced by many of the girl activists in this study, not just the members of Ramona's *cubiculo*. He writes, "An *encuentro* is not a space to impose an already established political program in order to 'conscientize' a community to a specific issue. It is not a chic approach to capture activist market share. Rather, *encuentros* are spaces for a collective analysis and vision to emerge."[25] The learning outlined by Callahan and practiced by girl activists is not one of teaching people "correct" interpretations and analysis, but rather of producing spaces for communities to engage in collective learning, dialogue, and discussion.

In addition to being supported by the transnational diffusion of Zapatista ideas throughout their political contexts, the emphasis on listening and on learning as an ongoing process dovetails with girls' narratives about both their youthfulness and their gender identities. Describing what she sees as a difference between youth and adult organizations, Camila said, "youth groups are more flexible. We don't know a lot, we have a ton of things to learn." Hayley also argued that adults "have . . . firm beliefs and traditions that you hold and they're not as free to just talk about the issue as a whole, but they have more firm opinions about it. And they're not as open minded. [Youth] are still trying to find out who they are and they don't have . . . a firm opinion about everything so they're more . . . more open minded to kind of taking other people's ideas." By embracing and discursively emphasizing their own continued learning processes, these girls suggest that they remain open to the ongoing development of their critical consciousness and knowledge. They suggest that their identities as youth, and as students, help them to stay curious and to continue to listen to the voices and opinions of people around them.

Listening and the associated open-ended approach to pedagogy and consciousness-raising is also distinctly gendered. As Chantal put it, "Well, we're girls and I really like to talk and talk and talk with people. I really like to know their problems." Girls' analysis on the gendered dimension of this kind of political education, of course, resonates with the extensive research and writing on the importance of consciousness-raising, discussion, and conversation to numerous women's movements and organizations around the world.[26] Describing the difference between the Alinsky model of community organizing and what they call a "women-centered model," Susan Stall and Randy Stoecker argue that the latter has often tried to "create an atmosphere that affirms each participant's contribution, provides the time for individuals to share, and helps participants listen carefully to each other."[27] In focusing on learning and listening, girl activists are contributing to and drawing upon a political strategy found in many women's movements. Feminist pedagogy and dialogic learning play a central role in girls' activism, but this does not mean that there is any essential or natural link between women, girls, and a politics of listening. Rather, as I've suggested throughout, this link is much more the result of girls' identity narratives than the result of their identities per se. They talk about themselves as being good listeners; therefore, when developing their political education practices, they draw upon something that they see as one of their unique strengths.

Girl activists' identity narratives about their capacity to listen, and about their own ignorance and the need to keep learning can be an important resource for shaping their approach to political education. More specifically, it is my contention that these identity narratives help them to avoid some of the most troubling aspects of dogmatism and sectarian politics. Even in more sectarian groups known for their ideological rigidity, girls are for the most part wary of becoming too fixed in a given ideology. Azul, for example, is a member of the youth wing of a Trotskyist political party in Argentina. But she expressed concern about those members of her party who want everyone to take up their particular political positions.

> You don't need to say to other students, "Oh, you're not a Communist." No, that doesn't help. This is why I think we need a coordinating group of secondary students. Now, there's so much prejudice and the people don't participate and it is a complicated vicious circle and it stresses me out. . . . I don't like that the party prioritizes the party over the secondary student movement. I think that you don't need to say to fifteen-year-olds, you should be Trotskyists. You should say to them, find your place and help out with the rest of your secondary student *compañeros*. . . . I don't sell the newspaper at my school. I may sell it to someone I see as a contact, someone who might become involved in the party, but I don't try to sell it to the whole school.

Azul is clear that she doesn't want to push her ideology, her "line," on other students. Instead, she, like many other girls, proposes that youth movements need space for multiple perspectives. Rosa, from Mexico, made a similar point when I asked her, "What things should change or be improved within your movements?" She replied, "The main thing is to get rid of the personal and ideological questions. Of course we have a diversity of ideologies and it is very respectable for one person to be an anarchist and another to be a Communist, but the point is to share ideas. This is what we need to focus ourselves on, not on the differences that we have between ideologies." Spending time with the Venezuelan Communist Youth, I was struck by their willingness to work across ideological lines. Jesus, a university student and

Communist, told me that his group has worked together with an anarchist collective to run candidates in university elections. When I seemed surprised by this, mentioning that such coalition work is not as frequent as we would like it to be in the United States, that sectarianism and dogmatism unfortunately divide us too often, he responded: "But we are all trying to destroy capitalism. And we are the minority, there are so few of us. We should work together to get rid of this system."

Such openness to diverse ideological perspectives was not, of course, universally present. Acknowledging my own semi-anarchist leanings to one group of Mexican Communist youth led to a long-winded attempt (on the part of one of the older, male activists) to convince me of the error of my ways. The girls in this group, while somewhat less interested in changing my mind than the young men, also would periodically tell me why I too should become a Communist. And, not all girl activists maintained the kind of open, in-process perspective on their own positions and ideologies that I've been describing. For example, Gloria, from Venezuela, proclaimed that her "ideals are very clear and well formed, and I'll maintain them until I die." But speaking of one's beliefs in this firm and fixed manner was not very common among these girls. Most of the young women instead emphasized their own ongoing learning, listening, and developing ideas.

Developmental narratives about youth, a clear connection to schooling and student life, and girl activists' gendered notions of themselves as good listeners all play important roles in supporting their politics of learning. A strategic emphasis on education coincides with girl activists' numerous identity claims, and they regularly draw on these identity claims when articulating the reasons for their political education practices. Because they are paying attention to their own learning and not just that of the people around them, girl activists infuse their workshops, reading groups, and educational events with a sense of curiosity and collective purpose. They do political education not only to teach others but to continually teach themselves as well. They listen, question each other, and continue to rethink what they already (don't) know. However, girls' educational strategies are not unique to them; they also resonate strongly with the contemporary transnational practices of Zapatismo. Marina Sitrin also notes the spread of these ideas across the Americas: "Similar to the Zapatistas and other movements, many in Argentina speak in terms of process and walking. The Zapatistas often refer to the importance of the walk, and not of the goal or destination per se."[28] In discussing consciousness as a process and approaching political education with the belief that their own ideas are continually shifting and open to change, girl activists embody and participate in shaping this distinctly postmodern approach to consciousness raising. John Holloway suggests that the Zapatista saying *caminamos preguntando* ("we walk asking") "acquires a particular resonance because we are conscious that we do not know the way forward. . . . The politics of rebellion is a politics of searching—not for the correct line, but for some sort of way forward. . . . There is no party to tell us which way to go, so we must find it for ourselves."[29] For girl activists, as for many other contemporary social movement participants inspired by Zapatismo, political education is the perpetual process of collectively seeking a way. As Holloway indicates, this walking and questioning is very different from the modes of political education found in traditional Left political parties, many of which have long sought to teach new members the value and correctness of their ideologies, analysis, and already-known strategies.

Although girl activists in all five cities emphasize the importance of the process of political learning, the content and shape of their educational conversations vary greatly. If political education is an ongoing dialogue about power, social problems, alternative solutions, and dissident feelings, it is also strikingly uneven. Some girls did not have the words to say what they wanted about what they felt and knew. Others stiffly repeated lines from party documents. These two examples, when placed side by side, remind us of the importance of language, vocabulary, and spaces for the development of systematic ideas about how the world works, but they also warn us against seeing the world as easily and completely encapsulated by metanarratives or singular truths about history and social change. Instead, the pedagogical approach of some of the girls I encountered, particularly the approach taken by many girl activists in Latin America, suggests the deep value of creating spaces where people can talk and share ideas about political problems and solutions without being sure of all the answers.

Girl activists regularly suggest that building consciousness is both an important goal and strategy in their political practice. Whether they are gaining new information, constructing new theories, or creating new desires, they continue to grow and learn in the streets and through activism more generally. Their Zapatista-inspired version of political education and the knowledges it aims to produce can not be reduced to a Marxist notion of the promotion of class consciousness, nor to the development of the somewhat more expansive "oppositional consciousness" described by Morris and Mansbridge in their edited collection on that subject.[30] By looking at their practices of political education, activists' embedded theories of oppositional consciousness are made visible. Oppositional consciousness exists not in isolation but in social movement action and conversation. Scholars interested in these topics can benefit from a careful analysis of different social movements' approaches to education (and the extent to which they center educational work in their political organizing), looking at their pedagogies in order to understand how movements and activists see the relationship between oppositional consciousness and resistance. Attention to activists' pedagogical strategies brings to light movement-based theories about consciousness, knowledge, and social change, some of which are explicit and some of which are not. In the case of girl activists, their political education practices suggest that mobilizing young people for social change requires the production of a form of oppositional consciousness that is not merely based in knowledge and facts, but in feelings and desires. Further, they also promote a version of political consciousness that is nondogmatic, process-based, and both open-hearted and open-minded, articulating and enacting a political strategy that is supported by their identity claims and by the transnational diffusion of Zapatismo as a political and cultural practice.

6

Join the Party

A Politics of Participation

Having a democratic and participatory student center is slower, Marina tells me over a cup of coffee and *medialunas*. But, she adds, she is glad that her school has transitioned away from the vertical, top-down structure that many student centers still use and put in place a new, "horizontal" model. It increases student participation, and that is a very good thing in Marina's eyes. A seventeen-year-old delegate in one of Buenos Aires' most active and most innovative student centers, Marina is a vocal supporter of horizontalism, a continually developing mode of political practice that emphasizes the ongoing processes of building democratic, participatory, and nonhierarchical relationships and communities.[1] In contrast to the other student centers in Buenos Aires, which, she says, "all have presidents and vice-presidents and are vertical, instead we have delegates for each class. And the delegates are in charge of having votes and discussions in their classes, then bringing the results from the classes to the delegates meetings, which is where we share all of the proposals and votes from the classes. We vote, we look at what is happening in the classes, then we go back to our classes with information on the votes of the others."

Using this method for identifying problems and planning actions, the students decide what outside events to participate in, such as the annual marches to commemorate the "Noche de los Lápices" (the Night of the Pencils), a night when several secondary school student activists were disappeared during the Dirty War. They also decide what actions to take within the school, as in 2005 when they took over and shut down the school to demand repairs be made to the building. All of this, according to Marina, "takes more time to prepare, because every student has to vote and then get together again when the votes have been put together and again to discuss and share all the information. . . . But it is a little more participatory, in general. And it works well because we can achieve more things than if everything was being generated by one person."

Transitioning to this model is not always easy—people aren't used to participation, and there are a lot of challenges involved in trying to actually create a participatory student organization.

In theory there is more participation. But in practice, what happens is there are a lot of people who feel like the student center monopolizes things and so we have a moment where some people don't participate as individuals. They feel like, for example, the delegates are the only people who can get involved in things and others can't. So, even though the statute says that there isn't, that the delegates don't have power, or as we say, don't have political power over the others, what happens is that they do end up having a certain amount of power because the delegates are in charge of transmitting voices and so they can manipulate a lot of information. In reality, we try to make it so that this doesn't happen, but it could.

Marina's comments here touch upon just a few of the challenges to creating nonhierarchical participatory spaces. Power, particularly *power-over*, is not so easy to erase or remove and replace with shared *power-to*—many students have a hard time seeing their own participation as vital, or as potentially equal to that of the delegates.[2] In the habit of representative democracy, students sometimes fall back on the notion that delegates are the ones who really do the work and that they, as nondelegates, have little political responsibility or opportunity. Despite this, though, Marina is still hopeful about the potential of the horizontal model. She says her objective is "the participation of everyone. And for the center to be a place where people can express themselves freely, give their opinions, whether they are political, or social, or whatever. . . . I want us to know ourselves, and do something for youth and for the society, and to be a type of community."

Marina recognizes that there is a divide at her school between those, like her, who approach political participation from a horizontalist and autonomous perspective, and those who are part of leftist parties.[3] After our interview Marina introduced me to another girl from the student center, Azul, saying that I should hear her perspective too, since it is very different. And she was right: Azul doesn't really like the horizontalism of the student center, arguing that it depoliticizes the students. She acknowledges that the horizontal structure "would be really great if it worked well, but what it has done, in my opinion, is depoliticize. I prefer verticalism where I vote, and where there is a concrete platform, to a horizontalism where, in order to not be above anyone, nothing happens. Since the center doesn't have platforms, it doesn't have, or follow, a political position." In "vertical" centers the *agrupaciones*—student political groupings with clear standpoints and platforms—have majorities and, therefore, political authority to move the center in particular directions. In contrast, the horizontal model, in Azul's view, ends up being "incoherent." She says that the supporters of horizontalism have created prejudices against those, like her, who want a more vertical structure. "They say that those of us who want verticalism or centralism . . . only want this because we are part of a political apparatus." According to Azul, the horizontalists tell others that "we follow particular parties so whatever we say is bad." In her view, horizontalism has made the politics of the center too personal, too much about individuals and which groups they are part of rather than about the ideas. While Marina supports the horizontal structure, Azul says that the student center needs to be able to take more concrete, specific positions.

Building on the work of Massimo De Angelis, I emphasize horizontality and verticality as "modes of doing and relating" rather than as "states of being" or fixed identities.[4] Referring to the conflict over the European Social Forum in 2004, De Angelis makes the following distinction between the two modes of doing politics:

> The two camps held quite different meanings of democracy; they *valued* different aspects of it. On one hand, a hierarchal concept of democracy, rooted in apparatus, in which the powers of the social body (in this case the people involved in the production of the Forum) are articulated through a vertical scale of representations and mediations that constructs and rigidify roles, bureaucratically define the boundaries of the subjects' inputs, of *what* they can or cannot contribute to, of *how* they can and cannot contribute, and confine the free expression of their *powers* within a wall well guarded by bureaucratic socialist principles. . . . On the other hand, a horizontal plateau of encounters, relations, and doing through which the exercise of the subjects' powers, and their reciprocal feedbacks, construct norm, rules, spaces and temporarily defined roles.[5]

Verticalism, as a mode of doing, is rooted in hierarchical and bureaucratic approaches to organization and politics, while horizontalism, in De Angelis's view, leads activists, strategically, to "an emphasis on *relational and communicational processes*" (italics in original).[6] As a political mode of doing and relating, horizontalism emphasizes the ongoing process of creating participatory communities, rather than the mechanisms or fixed structures of participation. Marina Sitrin's conception of horizontalism dovetails well with De Angelis's. Sitrin describes it as "a new way of relating, based in affective politics,"[7] that "implies democratic communication on a level plane and involves—or at least intentionally strives towards—non-hierarchical and anti-authoritarian creation rather than reaction."[8] Horizontalism, as it appears in these texts and in girl activists' words and practices, is not a fixed ideology nor a set procedure. Instead, as a mode of doing politics, it focuses on building supportive, democratic, and egalitarian political communities and relationships.

When we see horizontalism as an emergent mode of doing politics with these general characteristics, rather than as an ideology or an identity, it becomes apparent that even the vocally antihorizontal Azul has many affinities with horizontalism. For example, in the same breath that she speaks of her acceptance of democratic centralism and following the direction of those who were elected in her political party, she also says that democracy is "about consensus" and "everyone constructing something together." She, like most other girl activists, emphasizes the importance of good relationships and listening to other people (De Angelis's "relational and communicational processes"). Azul also thinks that people don't need to become Trotskyists, and that the party is less important than the larger secondary student movement. Instead of wanting to build participation in her own party, it is more important to Azul that people find their own political voice and begin to participate in whatever form works for them. By pointing out Azul's horizontal inclinations here I do not mean to deny or erase the significant differences between Azul's politics and Marina's, but instead to begin to suggest that some elements of the horizontalist mode of doing politics are pervasive features of teenage girls' activism, even among girls in more obviously "vertical" organizations.

Emphasizing participation and the creation of pleasurable, democratic, and egalitarian political communities is a key feature of girl activists' political discourse and political action across all five of my research locations. While this may seem like an obvious movement tendency, it is important to note that not all activists nor all social movement organizations have such a powerful focus on political community-building. The approach taken by girl activists, although not unique, is also not universal. Some movements and groups of activists have much higher degrees of hierarchy and bureaucratization, or may focus on gaining power through work with elites rather than building mass participation, for example. These choices are, as James Jasper notes, substantial strategic dilemmas, and each approach comes with its own strengths, weaknesses, and trade-offs.[9] In this chapter, I look at three strategic emphases within girls' participatory politics: (1) their commitment to building pleasurable political communities, (2) their organizational models for sharing decision-making authority and leadership among participants, and (3) the ways they confront and address issues of inequality and difference within their political groups as they work to create increasingly egalitarian political communities. As I discuss each strategic practice, I highlight the role girls' identity narratives play in their articulation of the reasons for these choices. I also indicate how their strategic practices are linked to and draw upon contemporary social movement culture and widespread discussions of horizontalism, and I conclude with a brief reflection on the gendered dimensions of horizontalism and the relation between that and feminism.

Pleasurable Political Communities

Haile is concerned with the amount of depression she sees among the teens in her school. She said, "a lot of people are really depressed . . . but if being more outside yourself . . . would happen, and if we had a better sense of community, that would help the whole depression thing." Similarly, Megan stated that after doing volunteer work in India and returning home to Vancouver she noticed that "there's this loneliness [here], this deep disconnect, people that don't connect." Megan and Haile point out that many people in their Vancouver communities feel isolated, that they don't have close connections to other people. They see evidence of a society where, in Robert Putnam's famous words, people don't have sufficient social capital and are therefore "bowling alone."[10] Teenagers in particular are often portrayed in the media as being self-centered or self-absorbed,[11] and many experience significant isolation or loneliness.[12] Instead of seeing such isolation as a natural or inevitable part of the teenage condition, girl activists view this as a social problem, rooted in a loss of community and the destruction of public cultures. And instead of only responding to these images and realities with parties, drug and alcohol use, and virtual experiences, they strive to build meaningful political communities and create spaces for participation in social change. These girls are working to reconstruct the fabric of a politicized and activated civil society. To encourage participation, however, one has to work at it, making it a key goal for political actions. Girls' tactical choices and general organizational culture are, by and large, strategically constructed to maximize participation. And most significantly, many girl activists argue that in order to encourage youthful participation, politics must be pleasurable.

When Emma and some of her Vancouver peers wanted to organize an event that would show student support for teachers, they decided that in order to get more students to participate, they would have to make it fun. She says this is why "we made it sort of a party on the street as well as a political event." Similarly, when Manuela and Alicia's Venezuelan Communist youth group wanted to build and deepen their connections with one of the neighborhoods where they were organizing study circles, they put together a barbeque and concert in the neighborhood. Having political events that draw on aspects of local youth cultures, especially music, makes these events more enjoyable, thus bringing in a larger crowd. As Diana put it, creative and cultural activities "call attention in a different way and it . . . will maybe engage people that wouldn't normally be engaged in a discussion or a speech or something." And, just as significantly, the incorporation of music, dancing, spoken word, or other youth-produced arts also ties political events more thoroughly to youth cultural practices, making it clear to young people that these are not just events for adults but are actually by and for youth. By advertising and using particular kinds of popular music in their political actions, girl activists not only bring in new participants who want to go to a fun event with their friends, they are also performing their own youthful identities, showing their peers—and adults—who they are and what it means to them to be a young activist.

These cultural events certainly facilitate participation by making political actions something that young people want to attend. However, they can also sometimes act as a barrier to participation. Rooted in politicized youth subcultures, such as underground hip-hop or punk, these events have their own distinctive music, vocabulary, and rituals. Many teens may, in fact, be turned off by the subcultural styles of their activist peers. Research on youth subcultures as resistant spaces highlights how they make oppositionality and rebellion pleasurable.[13] If these subcultures are felt to be overly "strange" or "weird" by other teens, activists' cultural events can also be alienating and difficult to connect with. Concerts, festivals, and street parties may inspire the participation of other teens by showing them how enjoyable activism is, but this is not always as successful as young activists might hope, particularly if they are enacting a subcultural style that is quite different from the rest of their peers.

In addition to developing public events that incorporate music, dancing, hip-hop, and other aspects of youth culture, girl activists also aim to have fun at their meetings and in other parts of their shared political lives. The young activists in Las Voces structure most of their meetings as a combination of political discussion, planning, writing, and a laid-back potluck dinner. Jewish Youth for Social Justice always includes time for games and group-building activities. And the Mexico City *cubiculos* don't just use their space for political work but also gather in these rooms to simply hang out and chat between classes. According to Diana, a pleasurable approach to politics is crucial to engaging more people *and* necessary for maintaining the interest of those already involved: "I think that if you are gonna have people working for years and years and years on something, you have to keep it fun, you can't just have it be serious every single time." As many other scholars have also found, making the entire process of political participation enjoyable makes it both more accessible to new members and more sustainable for "old" ones.[14]

As these examples indicate, having fun together isn't just an automatic by-product of girls' activism. It is an intentional practice, something that these teens are trying to cultivate through the ways that they organize and plan their activities. Girls in all five locations, while certainly taking politics seriously and seeing it as important work, endeavor to create political spaces where participation is not a burden but a pleasure. In doing so, they again draw upon popular narratives about youth to explain this strategic choice. Many girls told me that they "like to have fun" and still "act like teenagers." Just because they are activists doesn't mean they can't go out to parties, gossip about celebrities, shop for new clothes, or stay out late dancing. Youth activists do not expect each other, or themselves, to sit quietly in dark rooms reading Marx and Lenin through their teenage years. They do not feel any need to give up all of the pleasures of youth culture, nor to live completely "pure" or entirely serious lives. Part of what it means to be a teenager, according to many young activists, is socializing, hanging out with friends, having fun. Given this emphasis on their fun-loving traits and identities, it is not surprising that they would endeavor to create political spaces that build on these identity claims and that let them bring together their political beliefs with their youthful and playful selves.

Pleasurable politics are not linked only to age-based identity claims. Rather, this approach can also be understood to be generational, as it draws extensively on contemporary social movement culture and the diffusion of what Ben Shepard calls "joyfulness as a community organizing strategy."[15] Or, we can also trace this light-hearted, playful politics to the communiqués of the Zapatistas, like Subcomandante Marcos's mock telegram to civil society stating, "The grays hope to win. Stop. Rainbow needed urgently. Stop. If there is dance I want one."[16] But the politics of pleasure, while perhaps more pervasive in this era of cultural reinvention and postmodern movements, are not new. Shepard traces the history of joyful politics back through the dramaturgical and sexual flair of ACT UP (AIDS Coalition to Unleash Power), queer activism, and the anti-car carnivals of Reclaim the Streets to the oft-quoted Emma Goldman statement, "If I can't dance, it's not my revolution." We might also look to Paris in 1968, where one rallying cry of the student radicals, "under the pavement, the beach," envisioned a new, brighter, and more enjoyable world just beneath the surface of the old. Pleasurable protest is thus not only supported by girls' narratives about their teenage identities but also by the legacy of joyful student rebellions, and by the cultural toolkit of the contemporary alter-globalization movements that embrace a light-hearted, playful approach to politics.

In addition to the pleasures of the joyful protest, part of the pleasure of doing politics is the pleasure of friendship, of having meaningful relationships with other teens. Teenage girl activists' political communities are not just spaces for political action and organizing; they are also important social networks for the girls who participate in them. Speaking with girl activists about their organizations and watching them with their friends and peers in these spaces, I was struck by the intensity of their emotional and affective ties to one another. Engaging in activism with other people is often a highly emotional experience, leading to especially powerful and strong relationships and bonds.[17] Combine this social movement research with findings about the centrality of peer relationships and peer culture to teenagers,[18] and the particular importance of close friendships to girls,[19] and it is not surprising that girl activists have such deep and meaningful relationships with the other members of their political groups. Furthermore, in girls' commitment to positive, loving, and enjoyable relationships and communities, we can find an important point of convergence between their activism and the developing theory and practices of horizontalism. As Marina Sitrin writes, "one way people in the [horizontalist] movements describe the territory they are creating is through the idea of *política afectiva*, or affective politics. They are affective in the sense of creating affection, creating a base that is loving and supportive, the only base from which one can create politics. It is a politics of social relationships and love."[20] Girls' focus on relationship, then, intersects with and draws upon the horizontalist politics being articulated and developed in the broader social movement terrain by contemporary theorists and activists.

Julia expressed how valuable these relationships are to her when she said, "Working together in a group, with the people . . . you do activism with every day, and whom you study with at school, and whom you share so many things with . . . creates a closeness that is very important. And all of this working in a group is the thing that I like the most and is the thing I have learned the most from." The companionship, solidarity, and closeness that girls experience within their political communities are central personal benefits that they receive from their activism. Having close social relationships and a community that understands you and how you see the world is a substantial incentive to become involved and stay involved in activism. Activist friends become even more important to girls when their "old friends" don't understand their newfound activism. Valentina, the president of the student center in a large Buenos Aires high school, said she lost many of her previous friends by becoming more involved in activism, but her activist friends have really helped her to handle the challenges and pains of leadership:

> I began to have a lot more friends from the center because I spend so much more time with them and because we have so many more things in common. . . . And a lot of my friends that I had before, I've lost them a little because of this because I can't give them more attention, or more time with them, or fulfill their expectations of me, because, unfortunately, I've been going in a different direction. . . . They don't understand me, or they don't understand what I'm doing and why I don't have more time.

Activist community often replaces other friendships for girls who regret the loss of these previous friendships but who also see this change as an inevitable part of "growing up" and figuring out who you are. Their childhood friends, they say, don't quite understand them anymore, but they have built new (stronger) relationships with other teens with whom they have more in common. They also contrast these new relationships with the increasingly competitive and passive-aggressive tendencies that they see in other friendship circles and social networks of girls.[21] Their activist friends, they say, are much more supportive than other girls. Given their narratives about their own differences from "typical" girls, it is not surprising that they would be especially appreciative of this community of other young women who are also "not girls."

As girl activists state that their activist friendships are much "better" than their relationships with other, non-activist teenage girls, they also simultaneously suggest that their own "girl-ness" is in fact part of the reason that their political communities are so supportive and friendly. They argued that their friendships and their ability to work well with others make them particularly good activists and community organizers. Kayla claimed:

I think it is more difficult for guys to sorta talk to their friends about that kind of thing. Girls can generally, we'll be accepted if we're interested in something and guys, it is more socially acceptable for them not to care very much and just to, you know, not to care. And also, it is harder for them to get their friends to attend because even if a guy is really interested and his friends don't mind, they don't usually want to follow the same path, so it is more, it is considered different. Girls do things as friends more often, and guys more individually.

Violet, however, notes that these relationship-oriented political communities might also be something of a barrier to the participation of young men. Talking about her organization, she said, "there is a big emphasis on community building, just more touchy-feely stuff and that, I think . . . can fit for a lot of young women more than it fits for young men." Girls' gender narratives support the development of "touchy-feely" political organizations, but as Violet acknowledges, a strong reliance on this gendered mode of politics, and the narrative that girls are "better" at such politics than boys, might in fact inhibit the participation of young men.

Girl activists' identity narratives clearly provide discursive support for their organizational approach to creating fun and supportive political communities. This, however, is only one side of the story; their identity narratives are not entirely open and inclusive. In addition to the challenge of involving young men, noted by Violet, some of their stories about who they are create other significant obstacles to the project of participatory community building. More specifically, girl activists' intentions of inclusivity often come up against their own tendencies to see other teens (particularly other girls) as frivolous, stupid, and unlike them. Because of their own sense of themselves as not really "fitting in" to the dominant versions of girlhood, many girl activists choose to emphasize their differences from other girls. Estrella's statement that she has "nothing in common with most of the girls in my school," is quite typical. This sense of separation means that despite their participatory visions, many girls think that most other teens aren't very likely to get involved in activism. Acknowledging that many of their friends and peers just "don't care" and "think activism is nerdy or boring," girls fluctuate back and forth between hoping that they can engage other youth and dismissing the possibilities of getting other students involved in social movements. Although girls draw on their identity narratives to support their participatory and horizontalist mode of doing politics, their identity claims simultaneously create some substantial challenges for encouraging participation and building egalitarian organizations. Girl activists' identity narratives can thus function as both a resource for, and an obstacle to, the creation of participatory political communities.

In addition to the obstacles created by this pessimistic view of other girls, girl activists experience several other challenges when trying to build pleasurable and participatory political communities. Some of these are, while not directly tied to their identity narratives, very much informed by girls' experiences as adolescents. If they want more teens to participate, youth activist organizations need to create welcoming and open spaces. Girl activists frequently acknowledged the particular challenges of high school cliquishness and social divisions as barriers to this goal.[22] Like many other teens concerned with fitting in, popularity, and identity formation, girl activists are trying to construct cohesive, comfortable, and safe communities and social networks in which to explore and construct their own developing identities, and to involve more people in their organizations and collectives.[23] These two desires work against one another. When youth activists appear to be their own tight-knit social group, those who are outside of that group may not feel as if they can easily enter it, despite youth activists' explicit statements to the contrary.

Diana, a San Francisco Bay Area teen, spoke extensively about the possibilities and challenges of bringing together different groups of youth. Unlike some youth peer groups that tend toward homogeneity, Diana said that one of the positive features of teenage activist communities is that they often include youth from different racial, ethnic, and class backgrounds. She said, "activism is really something that can like squash all those stereotypes and boundaries of racial, socio-economic status, sexuality, gender roles. . . . It is something that brings a lot of people from different backgrounds together." Although these diverse youth groups are the ideal that many girls imagine, they aren't always easy to create. Lisette, talking about her own Bay Area organization, noted the current trend toward more and more Latinos, and more and more girls, which can make it less comfortable for boys and other races. She, and other girls, commented that when their organizations are dominated by a particular social group, whether it is rooted in shared class, race, gender, or subcultural identities, they feel less welcoming to those who are outside of that group.

Being part of a close group of youth activists is one way that teenage girls who feel different from their peers can find support for their differences. Finding activist friends has made a major difference in the lives of many of these girls. However, as a response to their own sense of difference and, in some cases, isolation, from other teens, some youth activists become judgmental of "mainstream" youth and youth culture. After traveling to the World Social Forum in Caracas, Diana was struck by how much more open and inclusive the Venezuelan youth were, compared to U.S. teen activists. Despite her comments about how activism "squashes stereotypes" and is open to all kinds of youth, she says that U.S. teen activists can be really judgmental of each other. When I asked her what lessons she wanted to share from her trip with her peers in North America, she said: "I guess inclusion, that there everybody really . . . turns to each other with this, 'I want you to participate' attitude. Here . . . we look them up and down and check them out before we see if we want to invite them to be part of whatever we are. And that . . . inclusion, I think if we look at everybody with a more open attitude, it would be able to make us stronger." Diana's comments here suggest that U.S. youth activist groups, like other youth peer groups, can become cliquish, assessing their peers to determine if they are "cool enough" or "radical enough" to participate.

Girl activists explicitly state that they want other teens to participate in their organizations and that they are trying to build political communities that are open, supportive, and fun. To a certain degree, they are quite successful at this. As an ethnographer getting a glimpse of girls' political communities, I was frequently moved and inspired by the pleasure that these teens took in being together at political gatherings and just "hanging out" and socializing. I have been lucky enough to participate in some truly warm and friendly political groups, but I have also been part of many dysfunctional, divided, and fractious organizations. In contrast to too many adult organizations, these young women's collectives seem strikingly supportive, encouraging, and even joyful.[24] Their honest appreciation of the group and their visible affection for one another was often quite palpable at their meetings and social gatherings. From the group sitting in the courtyard outside a Mexican *cubiculo* listening to Lucia talk about problems with her boyfriend, to the Venezuelan communists singing along to the radio and teasing each other about who is the best dancer, to the Bay Area girls telling me about how wonderful the other girls in their group are and how I *have to* meet them all, it was abundantly clear to me that these young activists truly enjoy being together. These relationships go a long way in encouraging and sustaining political participation, and are evidence of a widespread horizontalist commitment to political communities based on trust, friendship, and affection. Although this participatory approach is well-supported by girls' narratives of themselves as fun-loving and "good at building relationships," girl activists are actually far more conflicted about mobilizing other teens than it might first appear.

Participatory Democratic Organizations

Francesca Polletta argues persuasively that relationships are vital to participatory democratic organizations, informing the democratic models used by different movements and foreshadowing the eventual weaknesses and failures of these models.[25] Friendship relationships, a core part of girls' emphasis on pleasurable politics, are also central to girls' democratic organizational strategies. Girls' friendships with the other members of their organizations provide a foundation and model for their organizations' communicational and relational practices. Polletta's research on participatory democracy has indicated that while friendship has its advantages and uses for social movement organizations, it also comes with its own set of problems, most notably exclusivity, a resistance to formalization, and conflict avoidance.[26] In the case of my own research, the problem of exclusivity was most salient, as I discussed above. Familiar forms of relationship, including friendship, in Polletta's view, generate trust, respect, and norms of behavior that are vital to organizational deliberation and democratic practice. These relationships, however, "may also come with norms that undercut a democratic project." In recent history, participatory democrats have, in Polletta's analysis, come to see the importance of formal rules, structures, and procedures for decision making. As with adults,[27] girl activists have to make many choices about how to construct their participatory democratic relationships and communities. Some groups aim for consensus, others make decisions on a majoritarian system; some have very formalized procedures, others use far more informal methods of decision making; some organizations have elected or chosen leaders, while others are officially "leaderless." Despite these many differences, I find that girl activists consistently articulate and demonstrate De Angelis's horizontalist emphasis on communicational and relational practices.

Mobilizing other youth by making politics pleasurable is only one small part of girls' participatory politics. Once these youth are mobilized, what are they participating in? And what does participation look like within girls' organizations? First, and most significantly, girl activists see political participation as deeply and intensely *collective*. Participation, in their view, is not about individual acts of voting, writing letters to the editor, or even attending protests. Instead, participation means becoming a part of political communities that make decisions, develop strategies, and engage in social struggle *together*. They talk about their activism as "shared work." They emphasize that they want other youth to become part of ongoing groups with them, to participate in shaping and constructing their collective politics. This can be seen in Milagros's comment that "Really, what I want is things to improve for secondary school students, because a lot of the time we aren't given space to participate in things, they don't consult us . . . I want to achieve these objectives that we have in common and that are necessary to us . . . and I can't achieve much by myself, but if I work together with all the people who have the same ideas as me, the same desire to help out the other schools with what they need too, then it seems we absolutely can do it." Milagros makes clear that for her participation, and that of her peers, to be successful they need to work together, in groups, on a collective or shared agenda. Girl activists place a high value on ongoing participation in these communities of struggle and on being part of groups that work together for social change, rather than a politics of free-floating individuals who shift in and out of different political spaces and social movement opportunities.

Like countless other participatory democrats before them, today's girl activists do not generally view potential participants as "followers" of their already existing agenda, but aim to organize other youth to take part in the ongoing, iterative processes of collective political discussion and engagement. This notion of participation is in contrast to both the liberal model that emphasizes the individual voting actor, and the more traditional Left model of mobilization which, in De Angelis's biting formulation, has "forgotten that a process of radical social transformation takes much more than an increasing number of people laid down as 'building bricks.'"[28] Instead of seeing themselves as having found the solutions to the problems of the world and merely needing more members, girl activists work to create spaces where people can come together to discuss and develop their own responses to these problems.

Describing why her group seeks consensus, rather than utilizing majoritarian voting methods, Ramona explained the importance of listening to democratic communities:

In my collective, because it is a Zapatista collective, we say that the first thing to do is to listen. If there are five people and one person doesn't agree, even though the majority do that does not mean that this proposal will win. We go back to discussing until everyone is in agreement with an action. . . . We don't support republican democracy. Forty percent of the population voted for Fox. What is that? It isn't even the majority. If it was 10 percent or 40 percent that were not for Fox, it doesn't matter. You have to listen to the people who are not in agreement.

In some organizations, the consensus process is very loose, without a lot of structure or rules, and based on a generalized commitment to working together to come to agreement. This is the case for Niamh's tiny San Diego collective: "We just sorta work on consensus. Like, if someone has an issue with what we want to do, then we're going to listen to that. We are too small to be like, we block you. And we definitely don't vote." In other cases, groups use particular strategies to mark how people feel about each proposal. Lisette said her group first tries to create unanimity, "But if not then . . . we will start a decision making process. We do a fist of five [individuals show a number of fingers in order to quickly assess how people feel about a decision]. A fist is like no, I'm not at all agreeing with this, and then a three and above is . . . okay, I'm willing to go with this. And so if you have less than three then you put your concerns out there and we try to address them and we talk it out and continue on this really long process." When I asked her, "Do you feel like this works well?" Lisette replied, "It does. I think that it would be much faster to say, oh, yeah, we won, so let's move on, but I think we're trying to make it as democratic as possible so we're trying to hear people out and listen to every little concern that people have." The consensus approach, according to both girls and many others who have written on the topic,[29] is valuable for precisely this reason: it actively requires groups to respond to and take into account the ideas, needs, and concerns of those in the minority on any given issue.

Not all youth activist groups aim for consensus. Most of the Argentine student centers (including Marina's horizontal center), some of the Venezuelan youth rights organizations, and a handful of the Mexican groups make use of a majoritarian decision-making process. When I asked Nenetzin how they decide things in Las Voces, she said: "by majority and minority. If the majority agree, then we do it. Of course, everyone has a point of view, and if a lot of us don't want to go, we aren't obligated to. We talk about it." Decisions are made by majorities, but no one is compelled to participate in something that they think is a bad idea, or that doesn't work for them. Chantal added, "if the majority agree, it is done, but for me it isn't very easy to say, 'okay, fine.' I'm a little disappointed, but yes, I tolerate it and still express my different ideas because it is for the benefit of all of us." Chantal's comments here suggest that voting can, and often does, feel sufficiently democratic and inclusive of different views. Unlike some North American activists who imply that the only way to engage in participatory democratic practices is through a consensus-based model, these young women suggest that majoritarian, voting-based forms can also be sufficiently deliberative and inclusive to "count" as participatory democracy.

Whatever actual structure and procedure is used, whether it is consensus-based or majority-driven, the key point, according to most girls, is a group's commitment to discussion and listening to the whole range of perspectives in order to make the best possible decisions. This agenda coincides with Francesca Polletta's finding that deliberative talk was central to the practice of participatory democracy in U.S. social movements. She writes, "They strove to recognize the merits of each other's reasons for favoring a particular option, even though they did not necessarily rank those reasons in the same order. The point was to make each person's reasoning understandable: the goal was not unanimity so much as discourse. But it was a particular kind of discourse, governed by norms of openness and respect."[30] For girl activists and other participatory democrats, this spirit of openness and willingness to possibly change one's perspective is the defining feature of democratic decision-making processes, rather than the mechanisms themselves. Girl activists' commitment to listening, discussion and process all suggest that democratic participation is defined by communication and relationship rather than formal structures and managerial decision-making mechanisms. Thus, one can have a participatory democratic organization that is either consensus-driven, majority-based, or some combination of the two.

Linking democratic organizational forms to identity, Ella argued that being young helps girl activists to use these democratic forms more effectively.

> I think that youth are really more open to doing things different ways, whereas older people are kind of set in certain ways and it is harder to get them to do things. Kids are more willing to let a conversation go in a certain way that they don't want it to go in and be more flexible about doing this instead of that, on like a personal level and on a group level. So, I think it might take, like with consensus decision making, I'd say it takes kids a shorter amount of time to make a decision than adults because they are just more open to going a different route, like having it get done, but going a different route.

Ella suggests that the deliberative democratic model described above, is in fact, "easier" for teens to put into practice because they are more open-minded and willing to listen to each other. Girl activists' approach to democratic organizational structures is thus not only the result of political choices, but it is also an enactment of their understanding of their collective and individual identities.

Girls' narratives about the meaning of activist identity also provide support for certain kinds of organizational structures. In particular, their discursive rejection of exceptionalism and their emphasis on activism as a collective, rather than individual project (see chap. 2), dovetail with a belief in shared leadership responsibilities. Daniela was just one of many girls who expressed the sentiment that "we're all leaders here. We don't all always get to do what we want, but we all give our opinions and we don't just do what one person says." Instead of emphasizing their own personal "leadership abilities," many girl activists describe themselves as no more important or powerful than anyone else in their organizations. However, despite this common narrative on leadership, their actual organizational practices were much more varied.

A little more than half of the girl activists I interviewed said that they were part of egalitarian activist groups where there are no leaders, or where everyone is a leader. Describing Las Voces, Ixtab said, "we have a horizontal structure. We can all do the same activities, we all have the same role in our work, we do the same things. Each of us writes articles, and among all of us we decide on the corrections, the contributions, et cetera." No one has a particular position within the group; each individual sometimes organizes meetings, puts up posters, writes, edits, or speaks in public on behalf of the group. Groups like these reject formal offices and fixed responsibilities, and instead attempt to encourage the leadership of all participants. According to Violet, one of the things that she appreciates about her youth activist group in the Bay Area is the fact that it "really does try to develop the leadership skills in everybody so that everyone is taking leadership." They do this by rotating facilitators for each meeting, changing spokespeople and media liaisons for each event, and encouraging each other to develop a full range of activist skills. Constructing an organization without hierarchies, however, is quite difficult and is often more of a goal than a reality for girl activists. Marina's "horizontal" student center, for example, still has people with formal leadership (delegates). Most other students think of these delegates as "in charge" of the center, despite their attempts to avoid such assumptions. Even in organizations without formal roles of any kind, like Las Voces, some members have more authority and power than others. As Jo Freeman argued in a classic piece on organizational models, structurelessness is not necessarily egalitarian.[31] Instead, when informal leadership predominates, it has a tendency to replicate already existing inequalities.

Another large percentage of the girls I interviewed were involved in organizations whose leadership models can not be classified as entirely vertical nor as explicitly pursuing horizontalism and completely shared leadership. These in-between groups embrace participatory democracy and try to develop the leadership of all the involved teens, but they continue to place formal "leaders" in charge of some aspects of their group. In these organizations, "leaders" tended to be in charge of tasks like setting meeting agendas and facilitating group discussions, rather than actually making decisions for the group. The groups are not collectively aiming for fully egalitarian organizations, but they do have relatively flat organizational structures with minimal distance between those in charge and the rest of the participants. But what is most interesting is that many of the girls who are active in this type of organization expressed their own personal desires for a *more* inclusive and *more* horizontal leadership structure. Yasmine, for example, is part of a Bay Area student organization with official leaders for each school, and she is critical of the way that such leadership functions. Yasmine notes that the leaders do a lot of work; it is good to know that you can count on them to know what is happening with the organization and to get things done, but, "if you are not a Lead School Organizer [LSO] then you are not—it is just . . . you show up for meetings . . . whereas for LSOs it is such a big part of their life, everyday they are going to meetings and they are planning. . . . So I just felt like if you are not an LSO then . . . what can you do?" Yasmine's criticisms about formalized divisions between "leaders" and "everyone else" come from her perspective as a "regular member" who has lots of friends who are leaders. Seeing what her friends were doing, she felt like she was "in the loop" but couldn't quite offer the same contributions that they were making. Formal leadership structures strengthened the participation of her friends, but it made Yasmine's participation more marginal and more difficult.

Research has consistently found that leadership practices are gendered, with women and girls engaging in more consensus-oriented, participatory, and inclusive styles of leadership.[32] Recent research on U.S. girls' leadership suggests that girls see "boy" leadership as involving "authority, control, and ego," while "girl" leadership "is about being a good listener, building consensus, and ensuring happiness for others."[33] Furthermore, the Ms. Foundation, in their research with U.S. organizations for girls, described a typology of girls' leadership that included a strong emphasis on collective leadership, "built on the concept of the development of the power of the group."[34] Those activists I interviewed sometimes articulated links between their learned gender practices and their approaches to political organization. They noted that girls are taught to "work together" and "be cooperative" and not put one person above anyone else. Given the pressures and expectations of appropriate feminine leadership,[35] it is not surprising that girl activists would, despite their varied political ideologies, tend to focus on building participatory, democratic organizations.

Organizational forms have significant implications for movement cultures and movement outcomes. They also play an important role in shaping the experience an individual has within a social movement. Girl activists do not all share the same organizational forms, decision-making structures, or leadership patterns. But, like Yasmine, most girl activists are vocal advocates of nonhierarchical organizational relationships and practices.[36] Their narratives about participation highlight the central importance of involving people in an ongoing, iterative process of collective political discussion and engagement, rather than merely recruiting them to a social movement with an already set agenda and direction. Communication, listening, sharing power, and building meaningful relationships are all central to the ways they talk about organizations, democracy, and participation. Thus, their narratives, if not always their practices, reflect De Angelis's notion of horizontalism.

Participation and Inequality

Democratic decision-making structures, ideals of shared leadership, and intentionally pleasurable activities and meetings all support the development of highly participatory political organizations. These practices and commitments do not erase or negate the differences between participants in terms of experience or social hierarchies of race, class, gender, sexuality, ability, or age. Participatory democratic structures and supportive relationships make significant strides in the direction of egalitarian and horizontal political communities, but power dynamics and inequalities remain deeply embedded within activist and social movement spaces.[37] Horizontalism, then, is something that is always being aimed for, but is never entirely achieved. It is always in process, existing as a utopian principle that is held out as something to move toward. Girl activists, like many activists, struggle with these internal power dynamics and fault lines on a regular basis, but how these issues are handled varies dramatically by location. The differing racial contexts of each city and their divergent social movement histories combine to produce different locally situated processes and discourses around addressing and challenging inequality within social movements.

The girls in Jewish Youth for Social Justice all spoke about how the few guys in the group tended to dominate discussions, even though there were more girls in the organization. Violet described the situation in the group in the following way: "[The group] is predominately young women, often, and we've had a lot of trainings and stuff, because it has become an issue that the young men in the group are very disproportionally represented. So even though you have a group that is three-quarters young women you'll be hearing from young men just as much if not more, in terms of taking up space. There has definitely been issues within the group in terms of young women feeling silenced a lot in that way." But, instead of allowing this problem to continue, the group has tried to address and change this situation. Violet noted that this willingness to talk about their problems is something that she appreciates about the group.

> Another thing about JYSJ that is really valuable is, I think in many, many activist organizations there'll be internal gender issues or other conflict within the organization that is often overlooked to stay on focus . . . working to save the redwoods or stuff like that. And JYSJ is much more willing to take the consequences of slowing down, so we'll stop and say this is a problem and we're going to look at our internal stuff first and where we're coming from, because what we do in the greater community stems from how we are as our own community.

JYSJ has been committed to addressing internal power dynamics for quite some time. It is an important part of their organizational process, but as Violet notes, this organizational self-reflection isn't a universal practice for social movements.

In the San Francisco Bay Area, there is a substantial collective memory of the ways that race, gender, sexuality, and other social hierarchies led to the implosion and collapse of many of the social movement organizations and communities of previous generations.[38] As Mattie Weiss argues regarding youth organizing in the United States more generally, "This generation is coming of age on the heels of identity politics movements and the lessons learned from those efforts. Many youth organizations heavily emphasize identity and culture and the different oppressions communities face; they generally recognize that all of these variations of oppression developed from similar roots, and that it does not serve to argue about who is most oppressed."[39]

In addition to having heard the stories of movement collapse over internal inequalities from parents, teachers, and other adults, Bay Area youth have also grown up in a fairly distinctive urban area known for its generally liberal political culture, meaning that issues of racism, sexism, and economic inequality are (more) frequently part of the public discourse. In this context, these girls have learned that taking time to address internal power dynamics and problems within their organizations is vital to their survival. Thus, their groups are often highly attuned to such issues. They practice a great deal of collective self-reflection about power and inequality within their movements.

Karen, another member of JYSJ, claimed that willingness to talk about how things are going seems to be more common in youth groups: "I feel like a lot of times adults don't take time to do a vibe-check or talk about how you are feeling about things and really break that down a lot. We take a break and talk about how we are feeling about things." Similarly, Tamara and Niamh also claimed that talking about inequality, in this case race and racism, happens more in youth groups than in adult ones.[40] Tamara, a black seventeen-year-old, argued that "the Left movement is still really racist and has a lot of problems but people aren't looking at it from that direction because they are like, well, look at everything we've achieved. But, you know, still, we have to get ourselves straightened out." Niamh, a white teen and close friend of Tamara, added that she felt as if younger groups were at least trying to address these issues, but the adult organizations around them were not. "We put on a Challenging White Supremacy workshop a couple of months back and [the adults from another organization] were just like, 'oh yeah, well that is great for people to go to, but we don't need to go to that, we are not racist.' . . . But you are going to be racist to some extent and you have to deal with that and learn as much as you can and realize, I may not realize that this is racist, but it is, and you need to change the way you act." Niamh and Tamara distinguish their organization from adult ones, referencing their youthful identities as they articulate their commitment to egalitarian organizations. As with many of their other political strategies, girl activists partly define their approach in opposition to adults and adult organizations. Although this sets up adults and adult groups as a "straw man" of sorts, it also enables them to solidify their commitments to these kinds of organizational practices.

In striking contrast to the depth of the California girls' commentary and practices around internal issues of difference and inequality was the near silence on this topic in Vancouver. Again, the particular sample of girls I interviewed was more predominately middle and upper-middle class, and tended to involve themselves in more politically mainstream organizations than did the girls in the other four locations. Both of these things are likely to impact the quality and extent of their narratives on these topics. Furthermore, there is an additional element here that relates specifically to the national context: a powerful myth of Canada as a multicultural and egalitarian nation. According to the critical poet and essayist Dionne Brand, Canada finds numerous "other ways of saying race . . . without saying that we live in a deeply racialized and racist culture which represses the life possibilities of people of color."[41] Writing about the myth and the silences that accompany it, Brand continues, "I still get asked 'is there racism in this country.' Unlike the United States, where there is at least an admission of the fact that racism exists and has a history, in this country one is faced with a stupefying innocence."[42] It is in this setting we find girls like Dara, a Canadian of Indian (South Asian) descent saying, "In Canada we're really sheltered because we have this wonderful society and high quality of life," and "Canada is very accepting and we're very multicultural." When I directly asked her if she'd felt or experienced any sexism or racism in her own life, she said, "No, it doesn't really happen in Canada." Dara was not the only Canadian (*and* not the only nonwhite Canadian) to make such statements. This refusal to talk about the possibilities of social problems in their own local contexts limits the issues that many of these girls organized around. It also circumscribes conversations about inequality within their political communities. If there are no problems with inequality in Canada, there can be no problems with inequality within their groups.

For indigenous teens like Rae, the idea that everything is fine in Canada is "obviously a lie" and is something that gets in the way of the possibilities for multiracial organizing. She described her negative experiences with the "global perspectives" class and the teens who wanted to make a difference in the world at her high school:

My . . . biggest question for these people, is . . . they're willing to support people in Tibet who have lost their land and their culture and things like that but, we're sitting right here, people who need more help, well not more help, but we've gone through all those oppressions and people who should have their own culture, their land, are sitting right here, but you look at Tibet and, I don't know, maybe the beauty and the color, I don't know what it is, but the foreign part of it appeals, I don't know. Maybe they're afraid that their rights will be taken away, because they're on land that's not theirs. And maybe some of that will be taken away and they're fearful and don't want to help us, I don't know.

Until these "global issues" youth activists start looking at themselves, their own privilege and settler status, and pay attention to the very important issues of indigenous land rights, Rae says, it is hard for her to imagine organizing with them. Teresa, a young white woman who has been an activist since she was thirteen has recently started to create an organization of non-native young people who are trying to stand in solidarity with indigenous movements in the area. Reflecting on Teresa and her group, Rae says, "when I was growing up, I never met anybody that thought the way that they think. I'm still just kinda taking it all in . . . they want to help local people, but they understand. . . . I really appreciate the way that they think . . . but it just kinda took me aback when I met all these people and they were recognizing the indigenous people of this land, because that doesn't happen very often." For Rae and Teresa, working together across these differences is not easy, but they welcome the challenge.

Given patterns of racial and ethnic segregation in Mexico, Argentina, and Venezuela, the girls I interviewed in these locations were generally not working across racial and ethnic differences.[43] Due to the marginalization of indigenous and African-descent communities, and the challenges of accessing youth activists from these communities, nearly all of the Latin American girls I interviewed identified with and were part of the dominant European-descent and/or mestizo populations.[44] Some of these young women expressed critical perspectives on racism and racial inequality in general, or were part of solidarity organizations that support indigenous struggles (particularly the Zapatistas in Mexico), but they had virtually nothing to say about issues of race within their own collectives, seeing themselves as without race (just national identity), or as part of a homogenous mestizo population.[45] As Jean Muteba Rahier argues about Latin American race relations, these "ideologies of national identities have usually downplayed the importance of contemporary racism by proclaiming a myth of racial democracy."[46] The emphasis on their own groups as somehow "raceless" thus plays a significant role in maintaining racial privilege and white supremacy in the region.

In Argentina, discussions of internal power dynamics frequently focused on class identities. During the 2001 economic crisis, social movements in Argentina experienced new cross-class interactions. The suddenly threatened and therefore activated Argentine middle class and the unemployed *piquetero* movements were in the streets together, demanding an end to neoliberal reforms and *que se vayan todos* (the politicians all must go).[47] Coming to political consciousness and action during and in the aftermath of this historical convergence, the teenage girls I interviewed in Buenos Aires were generally highly aware of differences in how people from different class backgrounds approach politics and participation. They often reflected on how class mattered in their own groups.

Many of the Argentinean student centers address issues of scholarships, financial aid, and the rising costs of education, transportation, and photo-copying, thus building a student movement that engages with the needs and concerns of students from working-class backgrounds within their middle-class schools. Girls from both working-class and middle-class backgrounds also noted how the student centers become valuable spaces for cross-class interaction, which rarely happens otherwise in the schools. According to Milagros, when their organizations go to do work in the *villas*, it is "not to do charity" but instead to "have an exchange and learn from each other." Instead of avoiding talk about class, poverty, and the real economic barriers to par-ticipation that some students face (the need to work, etc.), the Argentine girls spoke openly about these issues in their political groups.

Most of the girls in Buenos Aires felt that their organizations were fairly equitable in terms of gender; the only group they criticized strongly for gen-der inequalities was the youth wing of the Trotskyist party. Girls who were part of this group suggested that the group places men at the front of the organization, in visible, speaking roles while the women are more likely to be doing behind-the-scenes organizing work. According to Lolita, men are seen as "being able to express themselves more strongly in front of everyone. Women are seen more as someone timid, someone who is afraid to express her feelings. I think because of this the men are put more at the front of the politics and are seen as being responsible for political questions and organi-zational questions then fall to the women." Lolita, whose words were echoed by other girls from this group, also told me that she challenges these inequali-ties within the organization as often as she can by pointing them out to other girls and to the men involved. Again, the girl activists who are part of these most "vertical" organizations are a critical presence, often trying explicitly to build more egalitarian forms of relating within these spaces.

In contrast to Lolita and the other girls involved in this Argentine political party who were openly critical of the gender hierarchies within the organiza-tion, the girls in the Venezuelan Communist Youth appeared to be more will-ing to accept the ways that organizational hierarchies and leadership struc-tures interact with gender. At a meeting between a group of young people from the United States in Venezuela for the World Social Forum and several activists with the JCV (Juventud Comunista de Venezuela), a young Filipina from the United States, Meliana, asked a question about women's leadership within the organization. She directed her question to the two women from the JCV, Alicia and Pamela, neither of whom had spoken much during the rest of the exchange. Alicia gave a short response about how women in the group can teach people and create consciousness in others, showing that it is not only men who do this. Meliana then said that she'd really like to hear more about what it is like to be a woman in the organization. Immediately, one of the men began to answer her question. She cut him off, and asking if maybe the other woman in the room has something to say. Pamela, a young woman in her early twenties, replied that there is a women's wing in the movement, and that they see women's problems not only as gender problems, but as class problems. As she paused, another one of the men cut into the conversation. He pointed out that a Communist Party woman is currently the president of the National Institute for Women and that one of the most important icons for Communist youth is a young woman "martyr" from the early 1960s. Several more men then began to weigh in on the topic, which then segued to others, and Alicia and Pamela both said almost nothing else for the rest of the evening.

A few weeks later, when I interviewed Alicia, I asked her about her own understanding of that situation:

> JKT: I noticed in the meeting with the group that the guys were talking and talking and talking and the two women—
> ALICIA: Silent.
> JKT: Totally. Why?

Alicia paused then said, "In reality, I think that the ones who were talking the most were the coordinators, and they know, they have more experience than I do, they have more time in the movement. I give opinions and I responded when someone asked me directly. . . . But I think it is because there were more men, and there were so few women and the men that were there had more experience." The issues of hierarchical leadership (they were the coordinators) and of experience (they knew more) thus complicate the situation in Alicia's view. She said that these issues couldn't just be about gender. When I asked her if there were things she might want to change about the relationship between the women and the men in the group, she replied, "Yes, of course." But then she quickly moved to reassure me that "it is not that they discriminate against us. Everything is fine among us. But there are things that have to change, but more on a national level than at the level of our group." Although I am cognizant of the many reasons to be wary of North American feminists' assertions about the silencing of women in the third world,[48] I do think there may, in fact, be something gendered going on here, despite Alicia's claims to the contrary.

The denial of inequality between the men and women within one's organization was a common feature in many other Latin American girls' comments about their own political communities. While I hope that these young women are correct that sexism within social movements is indeed "a thing of the past," I also wonder if they may have been telling me this in order to put forth more positive images of their organizations. Given the historical and contemporary dynamics of North American assumptions about machismo in Latin America and its diaspora,[49] it is entirely possible that teenage girls in these countries avoided sharing their complaints with me. This example of image management raises important questions about the ability of this research to see and address some of the internal problems within girls' organizations. While I did conduct ethnographic observation in some of their groups, it was generally fairly brief. Therefore, the discussion here should not be seen as a comprehensive picture of these organizations' dynamics, but instead primarily as an analysis of the dynamics that girls wanted publicly discussed.

With this important caveat in mind, I want to make a few general conclusions about the challenges girl activists face in creating egalitarian relationships within their organizations and some of the ways that they are navigating these challenges. As with other aspects of girls' political identities and practices, their politics of participation are influenced by context and draw upon some of the histories and traditions of social movements. While power, inequality, and difference within their political communities are significant issues for many girls, how these forces play out are shaped by their particular local and national histories and conditions. Many girl activists acknowledge that creating radically democratic social movements requires directly challenging internal issues of power, difference, and inequality. Girl activists see themselves as having learned from the experiences of previous generations, again drawing upon identities as youth to distinguish their mode of activism from that of adults.

Horizontalism and Feminist Process

Horizontalism is part of the implicit political culture of girl activists across the Americas. Pleasurable politics, participatory democracy, and an attention to internal dynamics are all hallmarks of the horizontalist tendency within contemporary social movements, a tendency that is especially vibrant within alter-globalization struggles. It is certainly not surprising to see this mode of political action playing a significant role in the activism of today's youth.

Emerging from this transnational movement culture and reinforced by girls' identity narratives about the meaning of their gender and age, horizontalism is pervasive. However, I want to emphasize here that this mode of activism is also not entirely new or unique to the contemporary movement context.

For the past thirty years, transnational and U.S. Third World feminists have been articulating many of the ideas now ascribed to horizontalists and alter-globalization theorists. Feminist scholars and activists have frequently discussed the importance of loving and pleasurable political relationships, of egalitarian and nonhierarchical organizations, and of challenging inequality within social movements. Pleasurable politics and the notion of *politica afectiva* is certainly reminiscent of the idea of a "politics of love," theorized extensively by writers like Audre Lorde, Chela Sandoval, and Maria Lugones.[50] Participatory democracy has also been a hallmark of numerous women's movements and feminist organizations. This approach has been so closely tied to women's groups that many activists once called it "feminist process."[51] Barbara Epstein's study of the role of feminist process in the U.S. direct-action movement provides a useful accounting of one of the many threads of connection between feminist decision-making structures and today's horizontalism.[52] Finally, calling attention to internal movement dynamics and to race, class, and gender hierarchies within organizations has been characteristic of the scholarship and activism of feminists of color for many years. Transnational feminists and feminists of color have written extensively on unequal relationships within and between women's movements; they have also argued that addressing internal issues can not wait but must be challenged directly and immediately. Looking at girl activists' politics of participation, I find many striking affinities between their activism and both horizontalism and transnational feminisms. These affinities highlight not just girls' location within a set of ongoing political traditions but also horizontalism's intellectual debt to transnational feminist theory and practice: horizontalism owes much to the work of transnational feminists. However, both scholars and activists who express a horizontalist perspective (including the girls in this study) rarely acknowledge this lineage or history.

Horizontalism is not a gender-neutral theory, even though it is often articulated as such. Rather, it engages with both gendered discourses and symbols, and with transnational feminist histories and practices. As girl activists describe and practice their horizontalist approach to participatory politics, they often emphasize that this approach meshes with their gendered identities and their gender training: horizontalism is about listening, building relationships, sharing power, caring about other people. Furthermore, there is also a hidden feminist history to today's horizontalism, one that deserves to be recuperated and made visible. Although detailing this history is far beyond the scope of this research and the subject of this book, I find that girls' discussion of the relationship between their identities as girls and their organizational practices indicates some of the powerfully gendered and feminist dimensions of horizontalist claims and practices.

To be absolutely clear, I do not argue that horizontalism or feminist process come "naturally" to girls. Rather, it is my contention that today's girl activists draw upon and rework some conventional and widespread discourses about the meaning of their gender and age identities as they develop their activist practices. Girls are not inherently more democratic, more relational, more participatory. They are not automatically better listeners than their male peers, and they are not intrinsically more flexible and open-minded than adults. In fact, as much as girls argue that their identities shape their organizational practices, they also emphasize that horizontalist practices are not inevitable. For example, supportive and loving political relationships do not magically emerge in communities of girls. They are instead intentionally cultivated in political events and meetings that are designed, purposely and strategically, to be pleasurable, supportive, friendly, and fun. Horizontalism, although it is pervasive, is also actively debated, defended, constructed, and redefined in girls' organizations. As the discussion of inequality indicates, girls' experiences with horizontalist, egalitarian, and participatory organizations are not universal but vary by location; their experiences are significantly shaped by the local social movement histories and the local discourse about difference and equality within movements.

7

We've Got Spirit

A Politics of Hope

Rae, an eighteen-year-old Wsanec woman in what is now called British Columbia, is both troubled and hopeful. As a leader in one of many indigenous struggles to stop the encroachment of development and to reclaim some of the sacred spaces that have been lost, Rae's politics of hope is mixed with deep sadness and pain. Her own political education, she acknowledges, came from growing up, "sitting and listening to my uncles and my aunts and my grandparents talk about the indigenous people's struggles here, our land, and around, you know, there was always talk of what had been taken away and different struggles they had gone through." Now, she says, she needs to go beyond talking about the problems and about the violence done to her people; she needs to fight, to move forward, and to try to both recover and create the world she wants for her community. "You get pushed over so many times, and over so many different things . . . so you just start caving into what's going on, and that's what we've been doing and I don't want that to happen at all, you know. I'm just saying . . . we've had so many years of struggle and there's gonna be many more." Rae says that she understands that people are tired, but she thinks that her generation, the youth need to "wake up and stop being lazy" and use their energy to rebuild their culture and community.

Although the past may be bleak, she is clear that the future could be much better, that an alternative to the violence, loss, and displacement is possible, if only they will fight for it. Speaking to her in the home of her mentor, an activist who is something like an older sister to Rae, I would catch occasional glimpses of this vibrant hopefulness. When talking about her motivation for action, Rae voiced some of her hopes and dreams. She said, "I'm very proud of my culture and I want my kids to be able to do the same ceremonies that I know, to know the same things that I know. . . . And I want to know more than I know, to keep the culture. That's my drive, I guess, I want the next generation to have a Wsanec culture." Later, she expanded on this hope for herself and her community to a vision of freedom for indigenous peoples around the world.

> I relate to a lot of people, you know, like the aboriginal Maori, the people of the Marshall Islands, they are my brothers and sisters because we share the same struggle . . . and I refer to them as my brothers and sisters. . . . Personally, in the struggle I fight for, it is for my culture and my land and my freedom to, not just freedom of speech and things like that and all that crap that they say, but for my actual freedom to be a Wsanec woman and carry myself with pride, you know, that is my struggle and that is similar to a lot of the struggles that the people around world carry. I'm Wsanec and I'm gonna fight for that because it is me.

Rae is intensely conscious of the violence and injustice of contemporary society. But, as she talks about these problems, she also voices her hopes and dreams for her community and for a better world.

Rae not only illustrates a politics of hope in her expressiveness about how she wants the world to be, but also in the strategic choices she makes as an activist. Girl activists' politics of hope can be found in their overt willingness to imagine and voice a utopian future, *and* in their practices for creating and building alternatives in the present. Rae's political vision is not aimed at participating in the dominant institutions of government and state power. Rather, she imagines creating spaces for the practice of freedom, spaces where she can truly be a proud and respected Wsanec woman. For her, this means she does not ask the government to solve social problems. Instead, she spends her time and energy reclaiming an important part of her community—a sacred mountain. This mountain, she told me, "is like anybody else's church or temple, or like, I don't know, like my Mecca. We went and prayed there. And that's where our history lies. And anyway, it's being built upon now and I'm trying to save it." To save it, she has gone up to the mountain with other young people, reoccupying the space, thereby challenging the developers who want the land.

> We went there, 'cause, traditionally people would spend four days there and they would pray and they would meditate, four days or longer, and they would seek . . . an inner, an answer that was inside you and you just needed to be alone and be in the forest and be with yourself and seek out an answer. And we tried to do that, we spent three days up there, and then

we were kicked off, so we were not able to do that anymore, and that's one of the things that I want to get back. I'm trying to get the land back, but also trying to just get the rights to stay up there and pray as long as we want because, you know, that's home for us.

Rae went to the mountain in order to make what she wants, a space for her to practice her traditional culture, *and* to demand her community's ongoing rights to this land. She does not ask for space and wait for it to happen but makes that space herself, with her friends and peers. In short, Rae is putting her hopes for the world into practice by making her visions and dreams real in the present.

In his influential book on revolutionary thought and practice, John Holloway begins with a discussion of a two-dimensional scream: "the scream of rage that arises from present experience carries within itself a hope, a projection of possible otherness."[1] Holloway presents the scream as a refusal, an emotional and passionate expression of our outrage at the world. But, much as it begins with negativity, it also carries with it the positive belief that there could be something else, something better. Holloway warns against separating the two sides of the scream since "one-dimensional horror leads only to political depression and theoretical closure" and "if hope is not grounded firmly in that same bitterness of history, it becomes just a one-dimensional and silly expression of optimism."[2] Rae's hope is an example of this two-dimensionality: it is deeply linked to her frustration and anger. She knows the bitterness of history but continues to act on hope, taking the leap into the possible.

In addition to their strategic emphasis on creating spaces for young people's political learning and participation, girl activists want to create "another world." Girl activists willingly and boldly express their hopes and dreams, and they strive to make those hopes real through the creation of prefigurative alternatives. Rebecca Solnit notes briefly that "to be hopeful is to take on a different persona, one that might be considered feminine, childish, or sweet."[3] Girls, then, are already associated with hopefulness, and the girls in this study embrace this association. They regularly argue that their hopefulness sets them apart from adults in some instances, and from boys in others. As Celia stated, "Youth have more dreams. At times they believe in something that the adults already think is impossible. And this is better because, of course, you have to have dreams, utopias, to be able to achieve something." Hope, girl activists suggest, is one of the assets of their political identities. Rather than dismissing girls' hopefulness as "merely utopian," or just "a fantasy of youth,"[4] this chapter asks what girl activists are hoping for and explores how their hopefulness shapes and informs their political practices.

Hope and the utopian imagination have been given a great deal of recent attention from scholars. Some of this attention focuses on a supposed "crisis of hope," and the increasing difficulty of expressing utopian visions. As Sarah Amsler notes, many critical theorists now contend that "utopia—as a genre, a project, and a form of anticipatory knowledge—is either vanishing from public culture or (less often) already extinct."[5] On the other hand, there are also numerous scholars and activists articulating new versions of the utopian, versions that are "a response to its many critics on the Left, to the inevitablism of the right, and to the absurdity of fantasies of perfection." This is utopia not as "a place we might reach but an ongoing process of becoming."[6] Or, as Avery Gordon states, "the utopian is not the future as some absolute break from the past and present, out there. It is in us, a way we conceive and live in the here and now."[7] It is this kind of utopianism, a utopianism that guides the journey rather than fixates on the destination, that I find weaving through girl activists' discussions of their political practices and strategies. To be a utopian, in this context, is to be hopeful about the radical possibilities, the otherness which is part of Holloway's scream, and to actively engage in creating those possibilities, bit by bit.

Hope is the emotional and cognitive foundation of two distinct but related tendencies within girls' political practices: their utopian emphases on imaging how the world could be *and* their collective inclination toward creating practical alternatives, new communities, and innovative democratic institutions, rather than participating in the projects of governance or the search for state power. In providing an ethnographic accounting of girls' strategic use of hopeful discourse and hopeful actions, I illuminate their strong affinity for the utopian and alternative-oriented (rather than purely critical) modes of radicalism. And, in doing so, my analysis also engages with the many scholarly and activist debates about the power of rhetorics of dreams and possibilities versus problems and critiques, and the utility of building autonomous alternatives versus agitating and protesting for state-based political change. Hopefulness as a political strategy and set of practices fuses strongly with girls' identity claims, particularly their narratives about their youthful and girlish idealism. Thus, most girls are thoroughly committed to a utopian approach. This deep commitment makes girls' hopefulness a particularly interesting example of the model of utopian, prefigurative politics found in many contemporary social movements. Their politics of hope is not unique, but instead vividly illuminates some of the larger challenges, complexities, and strengths of this mode of political discourse and practice.

Imagining the Possibilities

Rebecca Solnit argues that many North American activists have a psychology of grimness and "conceive of the truth as pure bad news." They describe and denounce the vast problems of the world without then asking "what prescription, what cure, what chance of recovery, what alternative?"[8] Robin Kelley concurs, stating that "what we are against tends to take precedence over what we are for, which is always a more complicated and ambiguous matter."[9] Furthermore, Avery Gordon writes of radical intellectuals that "we seem to have such an underdeveloped and unmoving vocabulary for these [utopian] longings and these lives, for how people comprehend in a practical way the elsewhere and the otherwise."[10] Gordon suggests that we are quite good at critique but less able to express alternative visions and desires in complicated and rich ways. Unlike those critical activists and intellectuals whose failure to speak about the world they want frustrates Gordon, Kelley, and Solnit, many girl activists throughout the Americas articulate a wide variety of hopes for the world. Collectively, when talking about their political views, they tend to emphasize positive possibilities, alternatives, and imagining a better world, rather than detailed expositions of social problems. Because they willingly embrace and accept the labels of "idealistic" and "dreamer," they do not shy away from expressing their utopian visions of what might be. They express these visions without shame or apology. In short, girl activists often speak in the language of the possible, or, to echo Gordon's words, they are developing a vocabulary for imagining the "elsewhere and otherwise."

Girl activists' visions of another world are frequently quite rich, descriptive, and often very personal. Many girl activists were actively engaging with the ideals of socialism, equality, justice, diversity, freedom, and solidarity, reinterpreting and making these concepts their own as they articulated an array of dreams and desires. Although equality, freedom, justice, and democracy can be referenced for many different agendas and purposes (recall Operation Iraqi Freedom versus the 1961 freedom rides), they continue to play a central role in girls' articulations of their hopes for a better world. Their flexibility, then, does not make them obsolete or irrelevant for analysis. Rather, it is perhaps because of their flexibility that they are useful not just to politicians aiming to convince the populace of the rightness of a certain action, but to activists as they work to name their hopes and dreams. While these terms sometimes, as Gordon notes, function as shorthands without much life or vibrancy, they are also concepts that activists can draw upon and interact with as they struggle to express complex and multidimensional hopes that are often extremely difficult to articulate. The flexibility of these shorthands makes them available for development. Girl activists' dreams and desires for a better world are not only their personal re-articulations and interactions with often vague concepts but are also, of course, shaped by their particular experiences and social contexts, and by the different local and global traditions of the imagination that they have available to them for inspiration and ideas. Their visions are simultaneously their own *and* part of the traditions and innovations of political thought that circulate around them.

In Venezuela, teenage girl activists, like others all around the country, are taking up the challenge of imagining "socialism for the twenty-first century," the goal of President Hugo Chavez's Bolivarian revolution. The meaning of this phrase, however, is not yet fixed or entirely clear,[11] and it remains open to interpretation. Girl activists interact with its many shifting meanings as they construct and articulate their own visions of possible and utopian futures. For Catalina, "Socialism is equality. Equality in education and equality in all of the possible places and ways we could have equality." She went on to say that she doesn't want "a capitalist system where one person gets rich and the majority get poor [but] equality in all of our rights. And that they take us into account equally, all of us. This is socialism to me: equality, peace, justice." Later in our conversation she added that this vision of socialism is what she is struggling for: "For a more just world, a world full of peace, a world full of love, like how they describe heaven: I want the world to be a heaven." Catalina's socialism is not scientific, it doesn't reference the mode of production, and it isn't particularly specific about what egalitarianism would look like, but it *is* a vision of a beautiful and peaceful world, a "heaven on earth" where people are treated equally (and are equally heard) in all parts of their lives. Although Catalina's socialism for the twenty-first century is lacking in some details and is somewhat fuzzy around the edges, it is a vision that inspires her. When I asked her to tell me about what she wants for the world, her eyes lit up and she spoke with true feeling and passion, getting increasingly more excited and engaged in our conversation.

Given her location in Venezuela in this particular historical moment, socialism is the name Catalina gives her vision. She uses the term to summarize her hopes, but she doesn't really draw upon the historical and formalized meanings of the term. In contrast to girls like Catalina who are creating their own interpretations of "socialism" without reference to any particular tradition of radical imagining, the Venezuelan Communist teens see themselves, and their visions for the world, as part of an identifiable line of thought. This is not to say that their visions are not their own, but rather that their articulations of their dreams and desires are informed by a specific theoretical tradition. However, even Manuela, one of the members of the Venezuelan Communist youth organization, did not express a "classic" Marxist conception of what a socialist world would look like:

> It is something equitable. It is when, for example, you give each person what they deserve, when no single person can have a large business, a big industry and manage everything. Poor people are part of the system and they can defend, or they can have things like . . . they can live well. And the workers and the farmers, they don't lack work but have good jobs, well-paid, and they are not exploited like they are now. . . . [Socialism is] something equitable, something equal, where the rights of everyone are valued and the capitalist mode of production has fallen.

Like Catalina, Manuela has a socialist vision that emphasizes equality and decent living and working conditions for everyone. It is only at the end that she tacks on a point about this not being a capitalist vision and that maybe there would be some other mode of production. Instead of emphasizing the "scientific" elements or the nitty-gritty details of socialism, Manuela has a values-based vision of what socialism could and should be. Her language is not one of economic structures or planning, but instead of moral and social values: equity, fairness, inclusion, and a life free from exploitation. This is the vocabulary not of a technocrat but of a dreamer. Modes of production, surplus-value, state ownership, and economic planning committees don't appear to be the words that inspire these girls or motivate their actions. Instead of discussing and imagining "socialism for the twenty-first century" in terms of its economic systems, these young women describe its ethics and principles.

Although Alicia is part of the same organization as Manuela, her discussion of Venezuelan socialism for the new century was very different: "With socialism, we seek the dictatorship of the proletariat, which is the appropriation, or, the worker appropriates the material forces of production and socializes them, and then, working together, they work for a common end that meets the needs of every individual." More traditionally Marxist in her imaginings, Alicia also stated that it is really Communism she wants, which, to her, means "the elimination of the state and a world where human beings work together for everyone." In her view, many of the other Venezuelan youth who say they want socialism don't think the same way: "For them, socialism is Christianity, or socialism is peace, happiness. No, for us, no—socialism is scientific, socialism is studied." Alicia, like many Communists before her, turns to the language of "scientific socialism" in order to distinguish her views from those that she sees as uninformed.[12] But, much as the "verticalist" Azul also expressed many horizontalist ideas, Alicia's "scientific" vision (like that of Engels) is still utopian in the sense that it is an articulation of her desires for the world and the hope that guides her political practice.

Of course, the ideas of socialism are not exclusively limited to the utopian visions of Venezuelan girls. Mexican, Argentine, and even some U.S. and Canadian youth draw upon socialist (and Communist) thought as they formulate their ideals for their communities and the rest of the world. From Aura's "society without classes" to Kayla's "thinking about the general good of society rather than just making money," many girl activists use the word "socialism" to describe a world where profit is not the bottom line, where all people have their economic needs met, and where there is substantial economic equality. In this way, their dreams are very similar to those expressed by countless socialists around the world. But these girls also have their own personal relationships to the ideal of socialism, and they make the concept their own by focusing on particular possibilities that are important to them as individuals. For example, in her vision of a socialist world, Aura, a Mexican teen who is currently organizing against the rising cost of so-called public education in Mexico, emphasized that all levels of education would be free and available to everyone. And Brenda, a working-class girl in San Francisco whose family is struggling financially, said she imagines a socialist world where "a whole bunch of shit would be free. Everything would be hella [really] free. Like resources and everything, and just like all types of aid." These girls are actively interacting with the idea of socialism. Instead of using socialism as a formless shorthand for "a better world," they explore its various meanings, push its edges, and draw upon its diverse facets and faces as they articulate their own dreams and hopes. Girls' visions of a socialist world, then, are not uniform but are personalized. Socialism, for them, has many meanings and refers not just to a Marxist shift in the mode of production but to a wide variety of visions of a noncapitalist world characterized by economic justice, comfortable lives for everyone, economic equality, cooperation, solidarity, and fairness.

As girls' descriptions of socialism and economic justice indicate, their ideal worlds are not merely worlds with different and more equal economic structures and improved material conditions. They are also often cooperative, ecological, and inclusive. In addition to articulating economic visions, girl activists invoke other political, social, and cultural concepts and values as they construct their utopian dreams. Variously informed by anti-racism, feminism, and (occasionally) Zapatismo, and by their own experiences with racism, sexism, and homophobia, many girl activists' visions include talk about creating a world without prejudices, without hierarchies, and with respect and appreciation for difference. Part of a generation that has grown up in the era of multiculturalism, it is not surprising that girl activists' alternative political imaginings included an emphasis on diversity. As Haile put it, "having unity isn't being the same." She went on to say she would like to see a world full of "cooperating and acknowledging differences and more finding the similarities and not having strict borders and thinking just about 'us'—as in us country, or us ethnic or cultural group." But, unlike liberal multiculturalisms that promote diversity without equality,[13] girl activists' utopian visions combine the celebration of difference with a commitment to egalitarian social relationships. For example, referring to the Zapatistas and how they've inspired her, Rosa said, "I think, more than anything, they talk about equality . . . to say that we want a world in which many worlds fit is to say that we want a world that is diverse but equal." Diversity without equality or racial, national, economic, and gender justice is not, for these girls, an ideal world. Rather, their visions of diversity are informed by the anti-oppression analyses of feminism, anti-racism, and other radical ideologies of difference and power.

A world in which everyone is respected, where diversity and multiplicity flourish, where there is solidarity and love across difference, and where all people are treated as full and equal human beings, is not easy to describe in concrete, specific terms. In order to express their hopes and visions for such a world, some girls turned to more metaphoric language. This was the case for Liliana, who said that she wants "to end all the lines of power so that we can all be together equally. . . . I never want us to have to look up [to those above us], but want us all to be able to look forward." Instead of a world in which people are organized into a pyramid and do not have equal power to determine the shape of the future, Liliana imagines a world where people instead stand side by side and can all look outward toward what might be. Liliana's utopia implies not just a vision of equality but also one of freedom, particularly freedom as a radical opening of possibilities for everyone. Several girls were very clear that their visions of freedom do not absolve people of responsibilities or the need to look out for other people, and that freedom means being able to collectively decide the future, together. Carmen stated that "we want freedom not just for ourselves [here in Venezuela] but also for other countries, for other people to have freedom like us, that we are free to do what we want, what we all want. We can decide what we are going to do."

Freedom, for these girls, is not merely about individual rights; it also includes mutual aid and shared responsibility for making the world. In a historical context where freedom is, as Robin Kelley writes, "practically a synonym for free enterprise,"[14] girl activists' reinterpretation of freedom primarily as collective possibility is certainly a radically utopian vision.

Girls' utopian visions are indeed quite varied. They emphasize different concepts and ideals and draw on different philosophical traditions. These visions, like those of many activists before them, are difficult to express and often vague. Girls do not shy away from articulating their ideas for how the world could be better, though. They are, in this way, avid utopians, willing to speak about what that "other place" could be like. They are unabashedly hopeful. They also generally approach their visions for the world not as fixed destinations but as ideals that keep them inspired and inform their political choices. As Diana stated:

> I think the world we live in is always changing so . . . if we're gonna think long term then we have to take into account all the changes that are gonna be happening as we continue to work. So, even like, long term plans are gonna change, and . . . as youth and as people who like want to create change, we have to like keep on changing our plans and keep on changing our vision, and I don't think it is about settling about less or for more, it is just about taking different factors and using it to help mold your plan.

Diana notes that, because the world changes, activist visions of a better world can and will continue to change. Utopianism, for many girls, isn't usually about instituting a particular, already set outcome; it is about having hopes that guide their political journeys. This is the point of Eduardo Galeano's often-quoted poetic notion that "utopia is on the horizon: when I walk two steps, it takes two steps back. I walk ten steps and it is ten steps further away. What is utopia for? It is for this, for walking."[15] Given girl activists' narratives about their own ongoing learning and their attention to process, it is not surprising that their utopian visions also emphasize the open-ended journey rather than the destination.

Many girls' utopian visions center entirely on the ideal of democratic process and participation. Referencing a change in people's subjectivity and a new way of addressing problems, Erica said that she wants "a change in like attitudes . . . they actually want things to happen, they're not jut apathetic about it all . . . and there's this . . . whole community that is like that. It's like the ideal community because everybody works together to solve environmental problems, and they'll all get together and address things, and it seems like the attitude is so different, so that is sort of what I see as an ideal society . . . working together." Erica's utopian vision is of a process, not a product, of people working together to address problems. Here again, a journey rather than a destination. For Diana, one of the reasons that activists can't have a totally fixed ideal in place is because the world changes. For Erica, it is more because they should be emphasizing the process of working together, rather than the outcome. Ana articulated a third reason for focusing on the utopian journey: the impossibility of being able to really know what will come, or what people, collectively, might imagine and accomplish. She said, "the alternative [that I want] is for people to be organized . . . even though it is something that we can create, the alternative is unimaginable. From here, I can't even really name it." For all three of these young women, the alternative, the better world, is a world in which people, collectively, are able to make it work for them. The details of what exactly that looks like must be left at least somewhat open to change. Activist and journalist Naomi Klein makes a similar point when she writes that when people want to know all the details of an alternative, "We shouldn't be afraid to say 'that's not up to us.' We need to have some trust in people's ability to rule themselves, to make the decisions that are best for them. We need to show some humility where now there is so much arrogance and paternalism. To believe in human diversity and local democracy is anything but wishy-washy."[16] This is not to say that these activists do not think about or imagine the possibilities, discuss options and engage in conversations about the shape of "another world," but rather that such utopian imaginings are also productively accompanied by a belief that these visions can (and should) be changed in the process of creation.

This postmodern process-oriented utopianism is, according to Rebecca Solnit, much more sustainable than the older destination-oriented model. She writes, "When activists mistake heaven for some goal at which they must arrive, rather than an idea to navigate by, they burn themselves out or they set up a totalitarian utopia in which others are burned in the flames."[17] Treating utopian ideals as touchstones for inspiring and guiding one's political projects acknowledges the complexity and unpredictability of social change. In this way, it is a utopianism that is satisfied with not having arrived, one that continues to strive toward that elsewhere and otherwise. Hope, then, is especially vital to a utopianism that accepts the open-ended quality of history and social change, but believes in the positive possibilities. In this kind of vision, a better world is not inevitable or guaranteed, but it is worth imagining, hoping for, talking about, and acting to create.

Creating Another World

Girls' utopianism is not just found in their expression of bold visions of a better world but also involves their participation in the ongoing process of building that world. In order to fully understand girls' politics of hope, we need to look at how they strategically act on hope in their day-to-day political activity and organizing. Reflecting the current interest in prefigurative and autonomous political action in the Americas, girl activists demonstrate an affinity for creative (in the sense of building alternative institutions and spaces) modes of political activism. They are largely trying to, in Holloway's words, "change the world without taking power." Changing the world through the construction of alternatives and the building of democratic spaces can take many forms. Girls' political education practices and their work to increase the democratic participation of their peers are examples of this mode of doing politics. These types of politics both create something new and prefigure the kind of world that girl activists want and imagine—a world of open-minded and open-hearted oppositional learning and of horizontal democratic participation. Girls' prefigurative practices are not, however, limited to these two kinds of objects. Through their organizing and activism, they build a wide range of communities and institutions that reflect their ideals of democracy, equality, diversity, justice, freedom, and solidarity.

Many of these institutions and communities have been introduced and described in previous chapters, but here I wish to highlight their narratives about the construction of alternatives as a hopeful and utopian mode of activism. Diana is a peer health educator at a community-run clinic that uses what she called "an empowerment model" to provide health care and information to the Latino community in Oakland, California. Describing how the organization works, she said, "It is not that we give you some money and tell you how to use it, but that the people in the community really get to come together and brainstorm, okay, what are the main problems we are facing, what are things we want to address and how do we want to address them and how can we make a change." Unlike health clinics that tell people what they need or what they should do, this clinic is part of a community conversation about health. Diana loves her work with the clinic and says it is by far "the most effective thing that I have done." Being part of this space and "being able to see that change [in the other teens who are participating] is something that is really rewarding, and something that makes you keep, want to keep working." Diana's work with the clinic prefigures the kind of world she wants, one where "people really do have access to live healthily and to address problems in their personal lives and in their communities" and is therefore a concrete manifestation of her hopes. Furthermore, the positive changes that she sees there also help her to maintain her political energy and inspiration. Being part of this alternative sustains her hope.

Isabela, a girl who lives on the streets in Buenos Aires, is an active participant in one of the many cooperative and community-run *comedores*, or soup kitchens, which emerged from the *piquetero* movement. Unlike soup kitchens that just give out food, the *comedores* are a collective experience: "You learn how to be a *compañero*." In this *comedor*, Isabela says, "Everyone is a big family, and we try to take care of this place and make sure that they don't make us close it." The *comedor* is not somewhere she goes only for food or charity but is a place she feels ownership over.

Pitu is part of the youth group that exists within another *comedor*, and she too speaks of the value of the place for more than just food. This particular *comedor* is not only a kitchen that receives food and then divides it among the families who participate; it also has a bakery and several other cooperative economic enterprises. And it is also a space for political discussion and creating a new kind of community. There are regular meetings, decisions are made democratically, and, as Pitu says, "We all help each other." For her, being part of the *comedor* is the best way to create political change. She says, "If you work with the government, they always promise things, but you are never going to really move forward like this. It doesn't have a future. . . . We can do so much work, we can do so many things here, we can have our bakery, we can do so many things . . . it is like you can see the future." Here, in the *comedor*, the future is visible. For Pitu, through collectively building an alternative, the future becomes possible to imagine.

These alternative community institutions provide social support but are distinct from "service" organizations or charity groups. Their explicit goal is not merely to ameliorate a particular social ill (such as hunger, lack of health care, and the like) but, through their example, to change the social order in such a way that the problem no longer exists. Instead of being run by service professionals or distant and large NGOs, they are democratic, cooperative, and directed by the community members themselves. Based on the values of solidarity, local control, and cooperation, they are a politicized, change-oriented alternative to charity or service. As a social movement strategy, alternative institution building emerges from girls' desire to "do something positive," to not merely critique social problems but to enact social solutions. In this way, they are a manifestation of girls' tendency to "focus on the positive." As Pitu's words indicate, however, alternative institution building is also guided by hopes for the future, particularly the hope that these model institutions will spread beyond their local iterations. As examples of the utopian in the present, such spaces are opportunities to work out one's vision for how the world could be organized. They are concrete manifestations of girls' hopes for the future.

As a political strategy, though, alternative institution building is somewhat controversial. Contrasted with the "disruptive power" of protest and direct action,[18] the reformist power of trying to influence powerful institutions and legal bodies, and the "revolutionary power" of attempting to take over the state, alternative institution building is decidedly micro, or small scale, in its approach to social change. The numerous and interminable debates between anarchists, socialists, and liberals are full of commentary about the strengths and weaknesses of each of these methods for changing the world. Rather than reiterate these here, I want to illuminate girls' narratives about these strategies—particularly their reasons for distancing themselves from state-based politics and focusing instead on the practices of alternative institution building. I indicate how their structural positions and their location within the political and ideological context of today's alter-globalization movements converge to lead them in this particular strategic direction. However, while most girls deprioritize state-based political action as a strategy for change, the Venezuelan girls have a very different relationship to the state and state politics than the girls in the other four countries. I'll discuss this relationship and how it complicates the more generalized anti-state attitude of girl activists later in this chapter.

Girl activists, as minors, are structurally excluded from formal political participation. They can neither vote nor run for office. Legislative politics, then, hold little appeal for them. Dealing with government actors, elections, and the institutionalized processes of party-building are, for the most part, marginal to their activism. Unlike adults, they have few debates about whether to put their energy into reform-based legislative politics and/or revolutionary party-building aimed at taking state power. Instead they do neither, focusing their energy on political education, building participation, and creating alternative spaces, institutions, and communities. Erica, an environmental activist in Vancouver, suggested that "mostly youth, we have a lot less power at first, which is hard sometimes. . . . So we're starting without, from the bottom. . . . [We] approach it in, I guess, sort of a more . . . direct way in some ways . . . probably a more action-oriented way than adults in general. Because . . . we're not on committees that can make decisions in the cities, so that leads us to more direct actions, I guess." Without institutional authority, young people are more likely to look to outsider tactics and to alternative mechanisms for creating social change. This is partly the result of their complete exclusion from formal political power.

In my previous research with teenage girls in the United States (only some of whom were activists), I found that they tended to explicitly distance themselves from formal, institutionalized politics, frequently claiming that they are "not politics people." This distancing, however, was rooted in their critical consciousness about the problems with (U.S.) governmental politics and their diagnoses of the inabilities of such politics to produce social justice.[19] Although for the most part the girl activists in this study do not equate the term politics only with formal politics in the way that these other, primarily non-activist, girls did, they do express a similar skepticism about the formal political sphere. Hayley, a Vancouver teen, was among the most dismissive of this kind of politics: "I don't follow politics a lot because . . . I don't really see that it often gets a lot done." Most other girls were not so quick to find the actions of the state irrelevant, and many continue to at least follow developments and debates in formal politics, but Hayley's view that it doesn't get much done was a common one. While not exactly pointless, formal politics is seen by many girls as an ineffective way to create progressive social change.

This is the lesson that Emily learned in eighth grade, the year the United States declared its latest war on Iraq, despite much public resistance to such an action. Emily spent much of that year going to anti-war protests on the weekends, and she was truly disappointed when the bombing of Baghdad began: she went home and cried about the movement's failure to stop the war. She told me, "I just really thought that it would make a difference. I was so naïve. I really, really thought that if I went, someone would notice and Bush might read in the newspaper and think 'wow, maybe this isn't what I should be doing.' I really did think I was going to make some difference in the world." But now, since deciding that the government doesn't really listen, she sees the goal of her activism differently and that is "to empower a community." She continued, "I know that Bush isn't gonna pull out of the war because I did a peace rally, but maybe I'll go to a peace rally and someone might be visiting from out of town and see the rally and think, 'wow, that's really cool.' And then maybe go home to their town [and talk about it.]" The government, according to Emily, doesn't have to be accountable to people, so it is hard to feel as if pressuring politicians is the best way to make a difference. Politics, namely formal politics, is seen by many girls as a corrupted domain, one with little potential for adequate reform. This claim is certainly not limited to girls, but is in fact quite common within the broader political culture of alter-globalization activism in the Americas. As Naomi Klein writes of these movements in general, "modern activists are not so naïve as to believe change will come from electoral politics."[20]

For some activists, the problem with trying to make change through the state is that the individuals who currently wield state power are corrupt or irresponsible. For these activists, it is not the state itself that is the problem but rather the people who currently operate it. Kayla stated that she doesn't think you can make much change through trying to pressure politicians because "people in politics generally got there because they are greedy, you know, they wanted money of their own, so a lot of politics are corrupted because they are run by greedy people, not people who are willing to change things." For Kayla, the challenge of trying to create change through the government is that the people in charge aren't the right people. In her view, then, state-driven change could someday be possible, if the politicians were a different group of individuals. But Kayla doesn't really focus on this possibility. Instead, she chooses to accept that government politics isn't working (right now), and so works on educating her peers. This position was especially common in North America where a sizable percentage of girls thought that it might (someday) be possible to have functioning, democratic governments, but in the meanwhile, their time was better spent in other arenas.

In Latin America, girls who were part of Socialist and Communist political parties expressed a similar position in that they, too, argued that the problem with working with and through the government is not state-based politics itself but the current historical situation. Like their North American counterparts, they spend almost no time canvassing or campaigning for candidates, lobbying, or otherwise trying to influence politicians. They do, as party members, devote *some* of their energy to the project of party-building, in the hopes that their party will, in the "revolutionary moment" be able to lead the workers and take up and wield state power. However, despite their membership in these parties, their actual activist practices are much more oriented toward creating alternatives than organizing people into the party. Girls like Azul, Lolita, Daniela, and many others appreciate the parties for the political education and connections that they provide, but they tend not to spend much of their time organizing for or with their parties. Instead, particularly for girls in Argentina and Mexico, the parties serve more as potential resources (in terms of both new participants and new ideas) for their other projects, which include everything from the cooperative, student-run copy center to organizing recreation activities for children in the poorest neighborhoods of their cities. These projects are done with other young activists, many of whom are not affiliated with the parties, and, in the view of most girls, do not need to be. Although the party is oriented toward state power in the long run, girl activists within these parties are focused on creating new spaces, practices, and institutions within their schools and communities, something that feels more relevant in the present.

In contrast to those girls who see the choice to emphasize the building of alternatives at the expense of a state-based strategy as a temporary situation (until there are better politicians, or until the revolution), a large number of girls suggest that the world that they want could never be instituted by the state, no matter who is running it. For these young women, the alternatives *must* be built from below, rather than imposed from above, even by a "well-meaning" revolutionary government or Left political party. Ana articulated this position clearly:

> ANA: I'm oriented more toward constructing an alternative and speaking with the people with whom I'm constructing it. . . . We have [President Néstor] Kirchner now, and later it'll be someone else, and after that someone else, and the system is the same.
>
> JKT: What do you think of Kirchner?
>
> ANA: That he is just one more . . . the same as always. He may be a little more intelligent and express things in a different way, but I don't think change will come from there. Change will come from another place, from talking with people, from seeking out a different alternative, organizing ourselves.

Ana makes clear that the changes she wants will not come through the government or from political leaders, but from the people who are taking up the more long-term project of self-organization and community-building. In addition to believing that real change must come from below, Liliana suggested several other reasons why she remains skeptical about political parties and those who want to change the world through the state. She said: "They are children of power. They are completely hierarchical, completely authoritarian, super elitist, and I truly don't want to participate in that. I don't want to be part of that kind of power, part of the power of just a few." In her view, states and parties institute and act on power and authority. They never create the radical possibility that she imagines: they do not allow a world where, as she described it, people stand side by side, looking out to a collective future, rather than up a hierarchical chain.

The complicating exception to girl activists' predominately skeptical view of governmental politics and aversion to state-based activism is in Venezuela. Unlike Mexico and Argentina where the Zapatistas and the autonomous movements provide the inspiration and contextual background for girls' anti-state tendencies, or the United States and Canada where progressive girls were unsurprisingly highly critical of their far more conservative state leaders, the most visible "revolutionary" and Left-leaning forces in Venezuela are *part* of the state. Hugo Chavez's government and the ongoing implementation of innovative social programs through the Bolivarian process make it a very different political context for activist teens. In addition, Venezuela is also held up by many on the Left as evidence that "taking power" continues to be an effective method for achieving radical social change.[21] Instead of seeing national government as either irrelevant or "the enemy," Venezuelan girl activists tend to view their government as a resource and potential collaborator for their activism. Although they are often working with the state, rather than outside and/or against it, the Venezuelan girls, like many of the other young women in this study, still focus a great deal of their energy on the prefigurative politics of creating new spaces, institutions, and models for how they want the world to be. They too demonstrate an affinity for the hopeful and utopian project of building a new, democratic, and egalitarian social fabric rather than relying on the strategies of lobbying, party-building, or running for office.

By pointing out this affinity within their actions (as opposed to their ideas about the state) my argument is not meant to erase or negate the very significant impact of having a state collaborator and believing, often quite adamantly, in the possibility of change through state power. Groups can practice prefigurative politics both with and without the state, but the world that they are foreseeing is, of course, quite different. Girls like Liliana imagine and try to construct a world without hierarchy, building spaces of what Holloway calls "anti-power," while Venezuelan youth are constructing participatory spaces that have influence partly because of the power and authority of government. The difference between these can be seen in a quick comparison of two different sets of student organizations. In Mexico City, the activists in the *cubiculos* needed to organize an occupation of the administration offices in order to implement changes to school security. In Venezuela, student activists were working with the Ministry of Education and Sports and also with the National Coordinator of the Bolivarian Schools to create democratically elected councils of students who would have a voice in school and educational policies. The *cubiculos*, as prefigurative and alternative spaces, are entirely student-run, open to all students, exist without formal leaders, and have an oppositional relation to authority (especially adult authority). The Venezuelan *vocero* organizations, on the other hand, are not entirely in the control of the students and involve only the elected individuals, but they do have substantial power in the schools, constructing a world where student power is perhaps less autonomous and egalitarian, but is more fully integrated into educational structures. Although both groups create spaces for student voice within schools, their different relationships to the state and its formal power have a profound impact on their approach.

Alternative institution building and working "outside the state" have different meanings in different national and local contexts. Despite these significant differences of meaning and the concomitant organizational and structural manifestations of these differences, girl activists tend to spend most of their political energy using this specific strategy. It appears to be a pervasive part of their activism partly because of their formal exclusion from state power, and partly because of their historical and generational context, surrounded by the numerous conversations about autonomism and the state within alter-globalization movements in the Americas. But this is not the only reason for such a focus—alternative institution building also converges with girls' narratives of the self, particularly their visions of themselves as idealistic and as people who "focus on the positive."

Being Positive

Hope, when contrasted with either apathy or cynicism, is clearly politically useful. Without some form of hope, people are far less likely to struggle for change.[22] But hope is not just a background emotion that motivates girl activists—it also shapes their political practices. Their willingness to describe and imagine another world, and their emphasis on creating that world through the construction of alternatives are forms of political practice that draw extensively on feelings of hope. Both of these tendencies are also intensely positive, rooted in optimism rather than negativity or critique. Although they are critical of many things, girl activists emphasize the positive possibilities and say that they try to "see the good things" whenever they can. This final section on girls' politics of hope explores the uses and dangers of "being positive," while also examining how different groups of girl activists develop and maintain their political optimism in the face of very real and powerful social injustices, problems, and crises.

Returning to Rae, the young Wsanec woman, I contrast her version of a politics of hope with that of some of the other girl activists in the Vancouver area in order to highlight two very different methods for maintaining hope. Rae's hope is not an innocent one that denies the troubling realities of dispossession, loss, or collective despair. The intensity of her awareness of these realities is rooted in her particular and immediate experiences as a young Wsanec woman. She knows and feels the problems of her community. Her hope does not deny the negatives, but she maintains it none the less. Just across the Strait of Georgia, less than fifty miles away in the Vancouver suburbs, girl activists' hope looks and feels very different. There, among groups of middle- and upper-middle-class girls, the shared tendency to focus on the positive and to be optimistic enables these young women to avoid discussing or engaging with controversial, difficult, or painful political topics. They maintain hope, in part, through the denial of the more troubling and complicated elements of an often inhumane world.

Girl activists involved in some of the many Vancouver global issues clubs suggest that it is better for them to focus on "positive" and humanitarian activism rather than "political" problems. For example, war and U.S. foreign policy are, according to some, "too political" for them to get involved in. This is Kayla's position: "I don't like getting involved in politics very much . . . I try to stay away from things that have to do with war and things, because I just don't know about political things." Instead, she says, she wants to work on "humanitarian issues," where it is easier to see what is right and wrong. By saying she does her activism only outside of politics and the government, and wants to do things that are "clearly positive," some of the hallmarks of a politics of hope, Kayla also shows a complete lack of interest in some of the key political issues of the day. This "humanitarian" rather than political activism is insufficient, in the view of some other Vancouver girls. Emma, for example, said, "obviously . . . no one is against helping starving people in Africa," but she thinks that the activists in these groups could also be doing much more with their time and energy if only they would engage in things that are "also political," like local poverty due to gentrification and economic development agendas, indigenous rights in the area, and the violence of imperialism and globalization. Humanitarian activism focuses on "doing good" in the world without acknowledging or engaging with the complexity of power relations and politics. Kayla and other "humanitarian" girl activists seem to believe that if more people would try to act charitably and help others, all would be well. Such a perspective, while certainly very optimistic, fails to recognize the more systemic, complex, and deeply rooted problems of social injustice.

This particular version of girl activists' commitment to hope and positivity also allows some of them to avoid a deep engagement with legitimate concerns about their own activist practices. Talking about the way they handle people who question their work to fund and build a community center in Calcutta, Megan said, "people'll be like, 'but what if you guys are providing this to these people, then what's gonna happen in that neighborhood economically?' and all this stuff. And we don't really know, and we want to stay away from what's controversial . . . and just do stuff that is really grounded in what everyone wants to see." Megan dismisses criticisms or concerns as disruptive "controversy." She claims that they are just trying to help and to do something "positive," so there can't really be anything wrong with it, and that those who have doubts are just being cynical or have a lack of faith in what could be created. Similarly, Beth says that when people question whether she can accomplish the changes she wants, she thinks of "one of my favorite quotes [which] is that people who say you can't make change shouldn't bother the people who already are." Questions about strategy, how change can and should happen, or the particulars of a given struggle can be set aside as evidence of negativity or as a distraction from hopefulness. Emphasizing only the positives and clinging to a hope that is separated from the scream of horror and negativity, in Holloway's words, can be a way for some girl activists to ignore upsetting social problems and to avoid engaging with some of the messier challenges of social movements and activism.

Looking away from the pain of the world in order to focus completely on positive possibilities is an action that emerges from privilege. It is only from a position of comfort, stability, and safety that people can ignore the deep and enduring "bitterness of history" and say that "things are really getting better everywhere," as Dara did. For girls with less economic and/or racial privilege, ignoring the brutality of the current historical moment is nearly impossible. More privileged girls like Dara acknowledge the suffering in the world and aver that it is the reason for their activism but they can easily forget about such suffering when they want to feel encouraged about how they are making a difference and "focus on the positives" in order to inspire themselves and their peers to contribute to social change. Thus they are able to detach from the negativity. This is not to say that these girls do not feel deeply about the problems of the world or that they are disingenuous in their activist motivations, but rather that they can (and do) compartmentalize their political emotions, focusing entirely on hopefulness and positivity most of the time, acknowledging horror, anger, pain, and negativity only occasionally. This does not suggest that these more privileged teens live perfect lives without any of their own personal experiences of social problems. Indeed, many North American middle-class teens frequently speak about isolation, lack of community, and loneliness. They are not immune to problems, and they do want a better world not just for the well-being and happiness of others but also for themselves, but their positions of relative privilege allow them to produce and articulate a version of hopefulness that can slide into an occasionally careless humanitarian, rather than political, optimism.

Sustaining hope does not have to rely upon denials of political complexity nor on regularly detaching from and forgetting about the worst horrors of the world. Rae is not the only girl activist who is both troubled and hopeful. In contrast to the insistent but sometimes one-sided hopefulness of more privileged teens, girls who live with the daily brutalities of poverty, racism, and homophobia cannot split their hopes from the pain and trauma of an unjust world. Lisette's younger brothers have major health problems because of the local toxic waste facility that she is trying to shut down, and Carmen migrated to Caracas alone in order to work and send money home because the rural farming economy had been destroyed. These girls and many others maintain their hope without being able to hide from the evidence of systemic violence and a world gone horribly wrong. Their hopefulness, then, is perhaps especially astounding. Given what they know, how can they be so optimistic? How do they continue to feel and express so much hope?

Azul offers one insight into this process. She argues that the problems are so great that deep and revolutionary change is absolutely necessary and therefore entirely possible. "I have my faith, that I've constructed myself. I don't adhere to any dogma in particular. I believe in humanity, but at the same time I'm disillusioned constantly. So I believe that the revolution is necessary. . . . We all believe that things have to change." As Azul sees it, there needs to be change, so she must continue to believe in it. This is, she admits, a leap of faith. It is not definite, but is a belief that exists alongside her disillusionment, her disappointment, and her frustration. Azul's hopefulness emerges out of her sense that the future is not yet settled. She believes in humanity but is regularly disappointed. In short, things could go either way—it could get better, it could get worse. And so, given the uncertainty of it all, she chooses to hope. And this hope is an act of faith, not of reason. This is Rebecca Solnit's argument as well: "Activism is not a journey to the corner store, it is a plunge into the unknown. The future is always dark."[23] Hope, then, is a choice about what to believe. As Azul suggests, because she feels that change must happen, she will believe in and work toward it.

Having this kind of faith in the possibility of a better world is, of course, easier in communities of others with similar beliefs. Many girl activists say that their hope is buoyed by their interactions with other young activists and by their sense that they are not alone in their struggles. Describing a conference with other youth activists, Haile said, "It just made me feel like there is, if there's that many people who care, then I felt more optimistic." Connecting with other youth activists from around Vancouver, Haile said she realized that there was a lot more going on than she had previously imagined, and this gave her more reasons to hope. Zitzitlini made a similar statement about the growing anarchist movement in Mexico City: "Sometimes you close yourself off and feel like it isn't possible, that there are only a few of us. But [when you look around] there are actually a lot of us." Seeing other activists, hearing about other movement successes, and connecting with a larger social movement community helps any activist to feel as if there are more reasons to be hopeful about the potential for positive change.

One of the interesting and exciting side benefits of conducting research with teenage girl activists in five different countries was the opportunity to let these girls know about the activism of their peers across the Americas. Hearing what young women were doing in other countries, was, according to several girls, a reason for them to feel even more optimistic. Delivering girls' messages of solidarity to each other was one of the most pleasurable aspects of my transnational research. These messages often focused on encouraging each other to be hopeful. Camila asked me to tell other girls, "Don't give up. Keep going, keep fighting for what you want, and know that in other parts of the world there are people who are also doing what you are doing." Her message is meant as a reminder that they can all be inspired and sustained by the knowledge of each other's work. Being part of something larger, and the certainty that her own small activist community is not alone in its struggles but is part of a global network of movements and alternatives, reminds Camila that "In this one sense, globalization is not bad." Hope, she and the other message-senders suggest, can be generated and sustained by spreading the word that there are more movements, more struggles, and more activists than any of them had previously known.

Girl activists tend to see hopefulness as a vital part of their political identities. They associate hope with their youthfulness and, at times, with their girlhood. This self-identification can then be a discursive resource that they draw upon to reaffirm and shore up their hope when they are feeling disenchanted or frustrated. Youth, they remind themselves, are *supposed* to be hopeful and idealistic. It is their social role, perhaps even their responsibility. As Erica stated, "We haven't become tired of fighting . . . we're not already thinking about, well, that will never work and we shouldn't try and

what's the point." Describing young people's obstinate belief in the possibilities, Marguerite said, "What often I find is that teenagers, because we haven't,
because we don't have as much experience, we're un-jaded. Because we don't
think that it's not possible, yeah, we don't see the obstacles, everything is just
like . . . come on and do it. And if you can't do it, you find a way to do it."
These identity narratives about themselves and their peers as hopeful, optimistic dreamers are a substantial discursive resource that girls draw upon,
encouraging themselves and each other to be both innovative and determined. Because they are young and new to activism, they are, in the social
imagination, expected to be upbeat, idealistic, and full of energy. This sense
of themselves can help girls generate and maintain their hope. Although the
association of hope with youthful innocence and enthusiasm encourages girl
activists' optimism, it also implies that such a perspective on the world is one
that will (or even should?) be lost with maturity and adulthood.

According to Avery Gordon, hopeful enthusiasm is a political attitude
that is regularly denied. She writes that we can hear the dismissal of utopian
politics in, among other things, "the longtime activist's weary and controlling response to less experienced enthusiasms."[24] The question for radical
movements is how to create political cultures in which hope is not only the
province of the young or the neophyte activist—cultures where hope is not
something activists are expected to outgrow and leave behind. Can social
movements sustain productive and action-generating hopefulness? Would
adults, if they spent more time with teenage activists, feel more hopeful?

My own experiences with these girls suggest that this is, in fact, a very
legitimate possibility. Although admittedly something of a political optimist
to begin with, I found myself feeling even more and more inclined to choose
hope as I listened to and learned from girl activists about their own political practices and struggles. When I share these girls' stories, insights, and
perspectives at academic conferences and in numerous informal conversations, there are at least a few adults in the audience whose faces light up with
a renewed sense of possibility. Girl activists' utopian imaginings can not only
shape their own politics, but also inspire and motivate adults to carry on with
the daily task of organizing to create a better world.

As scholars of oppositional consciousness have noted, a minimum
amount of hopefulness may be a precondition for political action. But girls'
hopefulness is not just minimal: the intensity of their optimism was noticeable across the Americas. It is this intensity that informs their imaginative
utopian dreaming and their creative experiments in building new spaces and
communities. Such optimism, however, is not universal. Political idealism is,

in many cases, something that has to be explained, justified, and defended. Activist girls tend to explain their hopefulness as the result of their identities: young people, girls, neophyte activists are all the bearers of idealism within social movements. But although girls' deep commitment to hope is distinctive for this reason, their hopeful political practices are also part of a much more extensive and widespread set of contemporary movement tendencies: specifically, the growth of process-based utopian thought and the autonomist-inspired commitment to alternative institution building. By exploring girls' politics of hope my analysis also exposes some of the dynamics of these tendencies within the current social movement terrain.

Girls' engagement with utopian discourse illuminates the political value of being willing to "think big," and to "be idealistic." Because they are unafraid of sounding like dreamers, these girls enjoy the process of trying to articulate what they imagine. Despite the pleasure they get out of thinking about these alternatives, and despite their willingness to articulate their dreams, building a language for describing the ideal future is still very difficult. The challenges of saying what you want for the world can be quite daunting. Neither overly specific technical details nor vague moral principles are particularly satisfying, as the first feels too emotionless and the second too abstract. In spite of these challenges, girls continue to try to voice their hopes and, in doing so, indicate that the utopian imagination is far from dead. Utopianism is not a thing of the past, as some theorists have suggested, but a discursive practice that continues to thrive within contemporary social movements.

As a concrete manifestation of utopian ideals in the present, alternative institution building is also a hopeful political practice. This is a political strategy that helps activist teens feel like they are "really making a difference." It produces visible, tangible effects, unlike some forms of strategic action where results may not be felt for many years. As a strategy, creating alternatives in the present probably feels more rewarding than agitating for institutional, legal, and macrolevel changes. The sluggish pace of legislative and governmental change may, in fact, be part of the reason for teens' reluctance to engage in such strategies. While there are many positive outcomes due to girls' use of this strategy, "focusing on the positive" and only trying to "build something new" also allows some girls to avoid engaging with some of the most significant political issues of the day. Thus, an emphasis on creating alternatives without sufficient attention to the larger macroconditions and structures can lead to a very narrow and circumscribed social change agenda. Girls' politics of hope thus highlights both the potential rewards and limitations of contemporary social movement strategies based entirely on optimistic and utopian creativity.

8

Conclusion

Still Rising

Today, a few years after my first interviews, many of the girls in this study are still doing activism. Valentina was one of several girls who recently wrote me in response to a request for updates on their political lives.[1] Shortly after our initial interview, Valentina's student center organized a major student occupation and six-day shut-down of their school. During this time, the students were living in the school, maintaining it, and, in her words, "showing that even though we are young, we are not less responsible than adults." The group's specific demands were met, but the occupation also led to something much more important in Valentina's eyes. She wrote, "The solidarity and the ties that we formed in those six marvelous days, where more than eight hundred students were in charge of the most important high school in Buenos Aires, they continue to inspire me." She went on: "We talked day and night, we cooked for ourselves, we laughed, we cried, we sang, we rested, and we took care of each other in a way that I doubt any of us had ever dreamed was possible. The love that we were able to construct inside those giant walls is not something you see everyday." This amazing experience, Valentina wrote, continues to be a powerful touchstone in her political life. She was deeply changed by the experience, and her political life today remains animated by what she saw, felt, and learned as a teenage girl activist. Several years after our initial conversation, Valentina has now gone on to university, but she has not stopped dreaming or believing in the possibility of radical change. She wrote that "things aren't going well in the world, especially here in my Latin America. Everything is collapsing in a shocking manner, but I trust in the youth, I trust in the women . . . I trust in our revolutionary instinct." Valentina continues to believe in the power of youth activism.

The responses I received from the many girls who wrote were heartening; they suggest that at least some of these girls continue to hold many of the same political ideals and to make the same strategic choices, prioritizing learning, participation, and hope. They are part of groups focused on environmental racism, forest defense, independent media, abortion and reproductive rights, housing, indigenous rights, body image, students' rights, and workers' rights. Many continue in the same groups or parties, others have found new spaces that reflect the practices they developed in their previous organizations. Marina, for example, has started a new student center because her university didn't have one, and she wanted a space there for democratic student participation, like there was in her high school. She continues to do work in the *villas* and avoids political parties because "in this environment, there is a lot of control in the parties, and we want to help the community in the form that we believe is better for expressing our personal political opinions." Marina still tries to practice politics in a horizontal fashion, and she focuses her energy on creating alternatives.

No longer girls, the young women who were part of this study have grown and changed, yet many of them continue to engage in radical political thought and action. Rereading some of their updates, I wonder about how the experiences of being a teenage girl activist have impacted the rest of their lives and the lives of those around them. What do they carry with them from their girlhood politics? What do they leave behind? If their strategies are so closely tied to their identities as youth and as girls, will they take up new strategies as their identities change? Does tying these strategic choices so closely to a transitory identity make them temporary strategies? Will girls "age out" of their open-ended, community-focused, and optimistic approach to activism? And, perhaps more importantly, should they? What would it look like if adult movements encouraged girls to maintain their youthful strategies? Which of girls' strategic practices should be replicated by adults and can they be? What might adults learn from greater collaboration with girl activists, and what might girls learn from collaboration with adults? Much of this final chapter is devoted to speculations on these questions and an assessment of the potential value of adult/girl coalitions within social movements. What can girl activists teach us about contemporary girlhood and youth culture? And what can this tell us about the relationship between identity, culture and strategy?

Empowered Girlhoods and Youth Culture

Anita Harris has described a powerful ideal version of girlhood that today's girls are expected to model themselves after. This idealized girl citizen, "the can-do girl," is privatized, individualized, and fully responsible for her own well-being.[2] She is an avid consumer, a diligent worker, and an active participant in managed forms of civic life. Self-made and self-constructing, "can-do girls" come in many forms. Whether it is the hard-working teen who is earning her own money in the world's export processing zones, the village girl who stands up to "tradition" and resists an arranged marriage, the spunky middle-class teenager whose fierce independence and technological savvy are admired by dazed adults, or the dedicated girl leader who is volunteering in her community or raising money for a good cause, these young women are held up as celebrated examples of empowered girlhood. The contemporary version of the Horatio Alger myth, the image of the can-do girl suggests that any girl with enough spirit and determination can truly "be anything."

Can-do girls, however, represent only one type of empowered girlhood. On the one hand, these girls represent a version of empowerment focused on incorporating girls into the social order as it stands, rather than empowering them to make meaningful changes to it. The girls in this book, on the other hand, are not that kind of empowered girl citizen. Their vision of empowered girlhood is not based on individual success in a flawed system of inequalities and injustices, but in the belief that they have something to contribute to making the world a better, more just, and more sustainable place. The can-do girl is an individual achiever, but the girl activist is an agent of collectively imagined radical social change. Girl activists show us some of the limitations of a can-do girlhood, modeling an alternative approach to girls' empowerment that goes well beyond that offered in shopping malls, popular culture discourses, and even many well-intentioned organizations for girls.

However, despite these important differences, both can-do girls and girl activists share a common preoccupation: the perpetual making and remaking of the self. Fashioning the self is one of the key tasks of contemporary social life, but such a task has even greater import for teenagers. Identity work is a central feature of today's adolescence. As Amy Best argues, "Youth are called upon to fashion their own identities, to think of the self as a willful project of inventing, reinventing, refining." She adds that this requires young women to navigate the "slippery slope of contemporary femininity—the new girlhoods, where young women are supposed to have power, and be self-determining and in control of their lives and destinies."[3] Asserting that they can resist the negative media stereotypes, challenge tradition, and become leaders in their communities, girl activists don't always sound very different from the can-do girls. On the treacherous neoliberal terrain of the new girlhoods, activists' claim that young women can do anything, become anything, and face any challenge can easily become a meritocratic view of free-floating individuals who are not bound by the constraints of social structures, persistent inequalities, and history.

Hinging on this belief in girls' ability to become and be anything in today's world, contemporary discourses of girlhood encourage girls to try out a variety of identities, to practice making and remaking themselves in different ways. Numerous studies of youth culture have indicated that consumption and the display of different consumer styles are key domains in which this identity work is accomplished.[4] My research suggests that the work of making the teenage self, of finding and demonstrating some kind of authentic youthful identity, is not always tied to consumption and style. Girl activists are constantly narrating their identities, telling stories about who they are and who they are trying to become. They also demonstrate their identities through their political practice, through the public actions they take together within their schools and communities. Their identity talk and their political strategies suggest two additional methods by which youth create themselves. This is not to say that these activists don't also perform their identities through their consumption patterns. The Che Guevara T-shirts, the blouses made by indigenous women, the handwoven bags, and the politicized music on their MP3 players all suggest that a teenage activist identity can be made visible through participation in consumer cultures as well. But a teenage activist identity can not be entirely defined or created in the marketplace. Girl activists are very critical of those youth who "look like activists" but don't actually participate in social movements (i.e., the kids in the Che T-shirts who don't come to meetings, plan events, or engage in collective political action). Girls' activist identities are remade, reinvented, and performed not through participation in consumption or particular youth subcultural styles, but through their stories of the self, through their political talk, and through their collective strategic actions.

In their narratives of the self and in their movement strategies, girl activists are doing important identity work. This identity work simultaneously reinforces *and* challenges popular and widespread ideas about what it means to be a girl and to be a teenager. They actively embrace certain characteristics of youthful and girlish identities, reinterpreting these popular images for their own purposes. Rebellion, creativity, enthusiasm, optimism, and playfulness are all incorporated into their definitions of themselves, but are also given particular political meaning. These girls also consistently demonstrate that girls and youth are not merely passive victims of social problems nor are they entirely apathetic, self-interested, and self-absorbed. They play with adult expectations of them, creatively using and refusing various tropes about who they are. Girl activists, like other teens, are engaged in some identity play, as well as identity work. Like other teens, they are fashioning their identities in conversation with one another and with their broader cultural contexts, but they have chosen to do so in a way that challenges many adults' assumptions about the behaviors, lives, and practices of teenage girls.

Identity, Culture, and Strategy

Teenage girl activists tell many stories about themselves, making numerous claims about what it means to be a girl, a young woman, a youth, and an activist. As marginalized political subjects, girl activists' political identities are not readily evident to them. Taking up and rejecting various identity categories as needed, they strategically lay claim to a set of characteristics and traits that they associate with both girlhood and youth, and infuse these traits with political importance, using them to claim social movement standing and authority in the public sphere. They say that they are open-minded, still learning and becoming, emotional, good listeners, caring, socially oriented, and optimistic dreamers. These identity claims combine with both transnational and local political cultures to bolster the development of political strategies that reflect these proclaimed characteristics, skills, and abilities. Girls' narration of themselves as subjects in process, as students, and as people who are still "becoming," dovetails with the pedagogical theories of Zapatismo to produce a shared strategic emphasis on ongoing political education. Their stories of themselves as relational, socially oriented, and egalitarian unite with the organizational models of horizontalism to encourage the development of participatory and democratic political communities. Their claims to optimism, idealism, and positivity intersect with the conversations of contemporary radical utopians to provide discursive support for a political strategy oriented toward the construction of hopeful alternatives.

Girls' political subjectivities and practices are also formulated and worked out in relationship to the transnational and local political cultures that surround them. The conversations around participatory democracy, horizontalism, Zapatismo, prefigurative social movements, and transnational resistance to neoliberal globalization, while uneven, are increasingly part of the context of social movements across the Americas. Although their activist identities and practices have some shared features, they also vary a great deal. Whether it is the Venezuelan girls' support for state-based strategies, the Spanish-speakers' linguistic freedoms around naming and identifying the space between girlhood and womanhood, the Canadians' myth of egalitarian activist groups, the Argentine memory of the disappearances, or the Latin American girls' extensive opportunities to develop vocabularies of resistance, location clearly matters to the shape and quality of girls' identities and activism. Girl activists are not a homogenous group; by looking at some of the differences between girls in different locations, the importance of being able to use and draw upon political vocabularies, memories, and traditions becomes clear. Latin American girls, in general, are much more thoroughly connected to the histories of social struggle in their countries, while North American girls tend to be unaware of previous youth activism. In part because of their ability to draw upon these traditions, Latin American girls' activist communities are also more theoretical but not *necessarily* more ideological. They have a wider set of political concepts, words, and intellectual tools that they can use as they develop, critique, and improve their activism. Clearly, local and transnational political cultures provide girl activists with toolkits of ideas, meanings, and repertoires of contention from which they develop their own strategic political practices. These toolkits are actively interpreted by people, in this case, by teenage girls. As they draw on these cultural formations, they make their own interventions, connecting the broader symbolic forms to their own identity narratives, their stories about who they are.

Girl activists' political identities and strategic practices are interrelated. How they choose to construct, claim, and narrate their identities as young people, as girls, and as activists all influence the ways that they do politics in their organizations and communities. As girl activists define their political identities, they also claim traits associated with particular kinds of political action. In defining themselves in particular ways, girl activists also define some of how they will do their activism. This is, at least in part, due to the fact that "activist" is not just an identity claim but also implies an ongoing set of actions. In Argentina, girls' frequent use of the verb *militar* illuminates this dynamic. *Militar*, "doing activism," has no equivalent in English. Girl activists in Argentina are not just *"militantes,"* but they *militan* with their friends and comrades. Activist identity requires doing; it has to be performed through the ongoing practice of activism. How someone defines and constructs their activist identity will then, of course, shape how they do their activism. An activist does activism; an idealistic, fun-loving activist does idealistic and fun activism.

My primary theoretical intervention here is to elaborate on one of the ways that identity shapes strategy: through the mechanism of identity claims. This is, first and foremost, an anti-essentialist move. Identity does not shape strategy due to anything inherent in a group's identity. Rather, it shapes strategy through a group's negotiated and active assertion of the political meaning of that identity. I do not argue that identity determines strategy, but I do suggest that there is a relationship between the two, and that this relationship is best understood through looking at the mechanism of identity narratives and identity claims. Identity's influence on strategy is not direct. Instead, identity shapes strategy in a much more tenuous process of asserting the meaning of one's identity and then, once a group understands themselves in that way, using those identity claims to guide, support, or reaffirm strategic choices. If a group sees itself as being made up of people who are "good listeners," as these girls do, we should not be surprised that they choose to use a listening-oriented pedagogical style when planning workshops. The story of themselves as "good listeners," encourages them to continue to make political choices that build on this particular supposed skill. Identity narratives that identify these kinds of traits will encourage groups to take particular kinds of actions that allow them to play to their strengths. Identity narratives and identity claims can also be mobilized internally when political strategies are being debated and contested. For example, the shared understanding of a group as being "open-minded" can be used to convince group members to forego producing materials with messages that are seen as too dogmatic. As these examples both indicate, it is through the process of narration, or through discourse, that activists' identities come to influence their strategies.

Doing Activism with Girls

If girl activists associate their strategic practices so closely with their identities as girls or as young people, what happens when they grow up and no longer claim this particular identity configuration? Answering this question would require additional, longitudinal research. Without such research, all we can do is speculate. It is my belief that increasing adult-youth collaborations and coalitions could enable the diffusion of these strategies into adult organizations and spaces, thereby encouraging girls to hold on to and maintain effective modes of strategic political practice. Adults could learn from and take up many of these practices, showing girls that these methods are not exclusively the domain of teens, and thus supporting the maintenance of these practices over time. Optimism, participatory communities, and the idea that everyone is still learning do not have to discursively belong only to young or neophyte activists. And if they do not, it is far more likely that these girls will continue such practices throughout their activist lives. Pushing against and refusing the anti-utopian tendencies of the "weary dismissal"[5] of young activists' enthusiasm, I encourage readers to imagine multigenerational social movement communities where girls' insights, identities, and political practices are supported, developed, and treated as potential models for contemporary activism. Becoming an adult activist should not necessarily mean that girls must give up their ideas about how social movements can and should be. This would not be the only benefit or value of adult-youth collaboration, for there is much that each group can learn from each other.

Girl activists reflect the growing contemporary interest in what has been variously named and described as a practical, concrete, realist, militant, posthegemonic or contested utopianism.[6] More specifically, girls' political talk and action illuminates the value of three interlocking utopian commitments, namely commitments to process, democracy, and enthusiasm, each of which I'll discuss briefly below. Guided by these three utopian and prefigurative ideals, girls' political practices are generally effective at building political communities, mobilizing other teens, and sustaining participation in their organizations. Their attempts to build political organizations that are pleasurable and supportive have, largely, paid off. While always wishing they had more members, they've generally been pleased with how many other teens they've educated, inspired, and gotten to become involved in social movements. Their organizations, while not without flaws, continue to grow and thrive. Girls' open-minded and open-hearted approach to learning, their fun-filled political events, and their optimistic, hopeful attitudes are all very effective mechanisms for mobilization. Much of what they have to teach adults, then, can be found in their powerful capacity for creating vibrant political communities.

Girl activists' commitment to an open-ended process of learning and becoming activist makes their organizations and communities far more approachable than many adult groups. Girls speak frequently about their own unfinished trajectories of becoming, rather than being, activists. They are still learning, still growing, still developing, still changing, still trying to figure out how the world works and how they want to contribute to it. Such humility and the accompanying process-based pedagogical approach, encourages other youth to explore activism with them. Dialogue, conversation, and the development of vocabularies of resistance, rather than fixed ideologies and dogma, is an effective strategy for engaging the curious, not just the committed or knowledgeable. Girl activists also indicate some of the ways that a commitment to radical democracy is beneficial to the construction of social movement communities. They emphasize the central importance of involving people, including youth, in an ongoing, iterative process of collective political discussion and engagement, rather than merely recruiting them to a social movement with an already set agenda and direction. This explicit commitment to a participatory democratic and open-ended process, as Francesca Polletta argues, has substantial innovatory, developmental, and solidary benefits for social movement organizations.[7] Finally, girls' enthusiasm and energy also adds a great deal to the vibrancy of their political communities.

Enthusiasm, as enacted and articulated by girl activists, is a way of approaching politics with smiling, rather than grim, determination. It is a way of doing politics that is serious and focused without being gloomy or boring. Enthusiasm colors everything girl activists do, making it all more lively, joyful, creative, and optimistic. Enthusiasm is found in girls' commitment to not giving up and to trying things out, and in their belief that they can make a difference. It is the sparkling, improvisational, and energetic heart of their politics, and it motivates and sustains their political communities.

Girl activists have much to teach adults about building strong, vibrant, and enjoyable political communities. Their utopian commitments are inspiring and could reinvigorate weary adult activists and adult movements. But there is also much that girl activists could gain from increasing collaboration with adults. There seems to be a real benefit to knowing more about the history of youth activism and youth movements in one's community. Historical memory helps Buenos Aires and Mexico City teens to feel connected to larger social struggles, giving them a sense of the importance of their contemporary work. In places where teens' organizations don't have this kind of institutional memory, adult activists can be a powerful link to historical knowledge. Adults can give teen activists more information about the many historic contributions of youth, helping them to see the connections between their contemporary struggles and previous social movements. But, even more significantly, girl activists could learn a great deal from adult movements' strategic actions and campaign planning. Girl activists tend to focus on movement building rather than on campaign-planning and ongoing action to achieve particular political goals. This is not to say that their community-building work is not strategic action, nor is it an affirmation of a rigid conceptual divide between prefigurative and strategic movements. Girls focus much of their energy on building youth political community and only somewhat on developing political power and influence. Building political community and effective youth leadership is a strategic action, but it is largely an internally oriented one. Adult movements, on the other hand, as girls' regularly noted, often pay less attention to the internal but have much to offer girls in the way of externally focused action planning. Adult movements could learn from girls' careful attention to internal movement dynamics, but girls could learn from adults' practices of clarifying their external political goals and making strategic choices that further those goals.

Unfortunately, there are currently some substantial barriers to effective, meaningful cross-age collaboration within social movements in the Americas. Girl activists discursively construct adults as straw-men against which they compare their own activism, assuming that adults' activism is very different (and, in some cases, normatively worse) than their own. Adults dismiss girls' insights and knowledge, assuming that their inexperience and age means that they have little to offer. These two sets of presuppositions about the activist inabilities and failures of the other group reduce each age cohort's interest in working across age and generational lines. Both of these sets of assumptions about the other group also operate in the context of an unequal power relationship and social hierarchy which consistently places adults above youth and children. Barry Checkoway writes that "Adultism refers to all of the behaviors and attitudes that flow from the assumption that adults are better than young people, and are entitled to act upon young people in many ways without their agreement."[8] It is one specific form of ageism and plays a major role in young people's interactions with adults. Jenny Sazama, a staff member at Youth On Board has outlined some of the following manifestations of adultism:

The basis of young people's oppression is disrespect. Manifestations of the oppression include: systematic invalidation, denial of voice or respectful attention ("Not right now dear, I don't have time"), physical abuse, lack of information ("don't worry about it, you wouldn't understand anyway"), misinformation, denial of any power, economic dependency, lack of rights (parents can take money from young people's bank accounts without their consent), lack of high expectations, and any combination of the above.[9]

Adultism is therefore part of the background and social context of all adult/youth relationships, including social movement relationships.

Given both their ideas about the failures and limitations of adult activists *and* their concerns about adult power, it is not surprising that many of the girls I interviewed conduct all of their activism without any contact or interaction with adults. School-based groups are likely to be made up entirely of teenagers, particularly in those cities where there is a history of teenage self-organization in the schools. While U.S. and Canadian teens may need faculty sponsors to organize clubs, this is not the case for Buenos Aires' student centers or Mexico City's political *cubiculos*. Even in some of these North American groups, faculty sponsors are never actually present or involved. This separation from adults is sometimes an explicit choice made by teenage groups who are anxious about the possibility of adults controlling their actions. Lucy, for example, is glad that her group is teen-only because "adults want to decide a lot for us." Many young people are skeptical about the ability of adults to work with them on equal footing. As one Vancouver group found, even well-meaning adults can dominate and over-manage young people's political action. Despite saying that the teens are in charge, this group had an advisor who regularly intervened and halted the group's plans for reasons that were never entirely clear to the girl participants. Working alone, without the interference of adults, allows young activists to be fully in-charge of their politics and to develop their own way of approaching activism.

Girls whose organizations do have some adult involvement also had very strong positions about the need for adults to step back and let teenagers lead their own organizations. Some of these organizations, like Yelitza's children's rights group in Colombia, in the view of the young people, do a good job allowing youth to truly be in charge: "Adults are just there to advise us. The kids are the ones who make the decisions. They advise us, just advise us so that everything is well organized." Similarly, in Violet's Bay Area Jewish youth group, "one thing that does work very well for the most part is that youth leadership is taken seriously and really honored. There is a youth planning committee that I was on for a couple of years that plans all of the stuff, plans all the meetings and the retreats." Letting youth make the decisions and do the majority of the planning was seen by girl activists as a crucial requirement for positive adult-youth relationships within these organizations.

Girls' position on the utility of these youth-led or youth-only spaces is reflected in the larger literature on identity and activism. One of the primary lessons of identity politics is that particular self-identified groups "need to have a 'room' of their own," which can be used as starting points for building coalitions across differences.[10] The past thirty-five years of writings of feminists of color also indicate the value of strategic essentialisms that allow for organizing in distinct groups before forming broader alliances and argue for ongoing attention to the dynamics of power within both types of spaces.[11] Unfortunately, there are few true adult-youth coalitions being formed in the five cities that formed my research. Instead, youth and adults largely continue to do their activism in their age-segregated spaces, or, at the most, there may be one or two adult staff members who do logistical and support work for a group of youth activists. As Ramona stated, "it's bad, but we are really separated. Within the university, for example, now with the strike, a lot of students from the CCHs [Colegios de Ciencias y Humanidades], from the other high schools have come to support us, but when we see a workers' movement or peasants' movement, we don't go, or only a few of us do. There is not a lot of relationship. I think that we see ourselves as very separate." In her view, the generation gap between adult and youth activists was partly about misunderstanding and a lack of communication and connection. Several other girls argued that adults, as those with more political power, have a greater responsibility for building these relationships. They need to do more to reach out to teenagers. Adults, they contend, don't pay attention to teenage politics and don't express much interest in supporting them or acting in solidarity with their movements. Chela said "In a lot of organizing spaces the language is not youth friendly. It is not a space for youth, for them. It is not really open." According to Diana, "I don't think that adult activists are very supportive of us, in terms of . . . giving us information, like, how we can do things and how we can better our tactics or how we can improve our plans. And . . . there's no . . . animosity, but there is no real connections either." Without explicit connections to youth and an effort to involve them as full participants, young people are not likely to be involved in adult-dominated organizations and movements. Marginalized communities are not likely to be a part of movements or organizations that do not speak to their needs and issues, particularly if the other participants come from a more socially dominant group.[12]

If adults and youth can indeed benefit from more interaction, one of the more important concrete contributions this study can make is to share messages from girls about what they want from adult activists and how they would like adults to treat them. Listening to girls about the ideal role of adults in youth organizing is an important step in building positive and equitable cross-generational relationships with teenage activists. I find that there are three ways that adults can support youth-led and youth-only groups. First, both political community and political education thrive in youth groups where the teens have a physical space in which to gather together. The case of the Mexico City *cubiculos* shows the value of these rooms for the development of deeper political knowledge and analysis, and for encouraging participation. Adults, and particularly adults who work in schools, could do much to support teenage activism by helping these groups to find a permanent physical home within their high schools. This might be a classroom where everyone knows that the members of this group regularly hang out and spend their lunch break. Or, in some cases, there may even be the opportunity to create hallways similar to those found in Mexico City, where each club or group has a room of its own.

Second, adults have access to financial resources that teens often do not. According to Erica, adults could "provide us with some resources to start out with. And then we can sort of build on that and get more resources, but just something to start with." This interest in tapping into adults' financial resources in particular was primarily a concern of North American girls and is in fact something that is beginning to be addressed by the many North American funding collaboratives and foundations. Opportunities for grants for "youth organizing" and "youth-led social change" have increased dramatically in the past several years.[13] As with most grants, however, accessing these resources requires groups to have certain formal characteristics, such as a board of directors and organizational bylaws. Therefore, they are much more likely to go to organizations with higher levels of adult involvement.[14] Interested adults can play a key role in helping teens find and access grant money for their activist projects.

Third, girl activists admit that they would really like to hear more positive feedback from the adults in their lives. Instead of ignoring youth politics or telling teens that what they want to do is impossible, girls want adults to provide "reassurance. . . . So if we don't see immediate change, we don't see progress in a way that we sometimes want to see it reflected—an adult saying, you know what, you are making an impact, keep on fighting, keep on doing what you do, I think that is really important. To reassure us that we are doing something that is worth doing" (Diana). According to Greta, a Mexico City seventeen-year-old, "adults should support youth because when you feel the support of an adult you feel much, much stronger." Hearing from adults sentiments such as, "I'm glad you are doing this, and I don't look down on you, and I don't think it's all for nothing," in Haile's words, can help teenagers to feel more confident in their own activist identities.

Adults who are excited about and encouraging of young people's activism sometimes go too far, crossing over into the discourse of exceptionality described in chapter 2. This "wowing," as one girl called it, tells teens that the work they do is interesting *only* because they are teenagers, not because it actually matters. Patricia says when she has experienced this it is "uncomfortable." I asked her what she does in those situations and she responded, "I laugh. Really, I can't do much. There are people that, like, how to explain it, I don't know, that see you like, 'oh, look at the girl that is there, how sweet that she came to the World Social Forum.' As if I am a novelty, right? A lot of people think like this." Chantal also said this happens to her a lot, "They treat me like I'm stupid or something like this. Yes, I've met people that say, 'oh, how wonderful that you are here doing something. It is so admirable.'" Lisette says that this patronizing way of talking about youth means that they "don't really take us seriously." Instead of being over-awed by youth activists, girls say that adults should treat them as they treat other activists: with honest respect for the work that they are doing.

This principle of honest respect is vital to the creation of just and equitable collaborative relationships between adult and youth activists. Girl activists want adults to treat them as equal partners, rather than future leaders, ignorant children, or exceptional icons. Despite their skepticism about adults and the tendency to view adult activists in a negative light, many girls told me that they wished they had better and stronger relationships with adults because they think there is a great deal that adults could offer them, specifically in terms of information and knowledge. Daniela said that learning is the most important aspect of her relationships with adults. "I am in touch with one adult, Juan, who already has more knowledge about these themes and who talks with me a lot. It is a great conversation." Rae also noted that "young people don't have all that experience of all the things have gone on. We don't have all the experiences of the outcomes that the older people know, so a lot of questions need to be asked. I have to go ask my uncles and my aunts and my parents and my grannies what they think because they've lived their lives, and they know all the negatives that might happen and they know what could occur. . . . Yeah, I think we need to be in communication." These teens were very interested in learning from the experiences, insights, and collectively developed knowledge of adult activists. But, as much as they want to learn from adults' experiences, girls emphasize that they also need to be allowed to make mistakes and learn from their own process of trial and error as well. They want adult input, but not adult authority. They may disagree with their adult collaborators and, in their opinion, they should be allowed to go their own way.

Teenagers' willingness to listen to adults also needs to be complemented by adults' understanding that they can learn from teenagers. According to Celia, "It is important that youth and adults work together because each one can learn from the other." And, in Camila's view, "It's good when we have the possibility to get together. The two groups can meet . . . the older can learn from the younger and the younger can learn from the older." Adults' voices of experience should be heard, but with a clear acknowledgement that youth have knowledge to offer as well. Discussing the difference between some adults and the current mentor for her group, Tamara said that other adults wanted to tell the teens what to do and did not acknowledge how much the teenagers actually knew. In contrast to these adults who kept directing the teens to get involved in counterrecruitment because that would be "best," their new mentor listens to their ideas and offers her own opinions, but doesn't try to force the group in any particular direction. She helps them think about their choices, makes suggestions based on her experiences, but also acknowledges that the teens have another kind of knowledge and does not disregard their political authority and legitimacy.

In order to construct effective cross-generational political coalitions, there are significant issues of age-based power and authority that have to be navigated. Many teens want to build stronger and more meaningful relationships with adult activists, but they feel that most adults do not fully respect them. Listening to youth as equals, as legitimate social and political actors with their own standing and authority, is not easy for adults who are unaware of the very impressive reality of many young people's capabilities and activist skills. Many adults are not cognizant of the dynamics of age as an axis of inequality, and therefore they fail to interrogate their own age-based privilege or think critically about their treatment and perceptions of teenagers. Learning about youth politics and about adultism are crucial steps for adults who want to develop supportive, equitable relationships with teenage activists.[15] On the other hand, although teenage girl activists are critical of adults' assumptions about their age group, they also make many of their own assumptions about the failings of adult activists and sometimes dismiss the possibilities of adult contributions to their political communities. For adults and youth to build strong cross-age relationships, both sides of this dynamic need to be addressed.

By paying attention to the perspectives and practices of teenage girl activists in the Americas, this book has outlined many of the strengths of girls' political ideals and commitments. In doing so, I hope it has shown adults that they do, in fact, have things to learn from teenage girls. Girls' utopian and prefigurative approach to politics is well supported by their identity claims, but it is also not uniquely "girl." Adult activists and scholars across the Americas are discussing and experimenting with many similarly utopian tendencies. Including girl activists in this vibrant and vital political conversation can only strengthen and enrich it, providing all of us, no matter what our age or gender, with more ideas and inspiration for changing the world.

Methodological Appendix

This book is based on interviews and participant observation with seventy-five girl activists in five different cities in the Americas, approximately fifteen girls per location. The research was conducted between September 2005 and September 2006 in the San Francisco Bay Area, Mexico City, Caracas, Vancouver, and Buenos Aires, in chronological order. Given both a lack of research on girls' activism and my interests in girl activists' subjective experiences and perspectives, an in-depth, qualitative approach was most appropriate for this project. This method of research has several major benefits. It enables flexibility, allowing the researcher to follow out different ideas with different individuals; it provides me with more detailed, textured, and complicated data that is lively and engaging; it incorporates the voices of a group whose words and ideas are not quite what most readers expect, giving space for their own understandings and interpretations; and it includes data on what people say about their lives, but also notes and observations on some of what they do in their various contexts.

Site Selection

Each of the five selected cities has a well-known and well-documented social movement history, each continues to be a site of heightened political activism, and each has a particularly strong youth movement sector. They are, in short, "hotspots" for activism in general and youth activism in particular. Each city also has symbolic and material importance within social movement communities in the Americas. Given this importance, an academic literature on the movements in each of these cities already exists and provides a set of ideas that this book responds to. By focusing on major urban areas, I was able to limit my study to issues faced by urban girls and their movements. Limiting my study to the Americas enables me to pay particular attention to some of the distinctive dynamics of the social movements and politics of this region. But, each site is also a vastly different political context and presented me with a diverse array of windows into teenage girls' activism.

Finding Girl Activists

Girl activists are a very difficult group to access. They are largely invisible within social movement spaces, so attending adult movement events and seeking out girls rarely yields much contact. Within their schools, the place where they most often gather, they are heavily protected from outsiders by institutional gatekeepers. Because they are such a small percentage of teens and often do not participate in the same social spaces as their peers, seeking them out at "typical" teen hangouts and locations is also nearly impossible. Their organizations, furthermore, receive less media coverage and have less online presence than many adult groups of similar size. Finally, there is no complete (or even partial) list of youth activists from which one could draw a statistically random sample. In short, the girls in this study are not necessarily a representative or generalizable sample of activist girlhood. They are, however, an interesting and diverse group of teenage girls with a wide range of political experiences and opinions.

In order to find girl activists, I had to be more than a little persistent and more than a little creative. For each location, I conducted preliminary research before arrival, gathering information about local social movement organizations and youth activist groups. I contacted as many of these adult and youth groups as possible, asking for their assistance in locating teenage girl activists. Then I would follow the suggestions and leads of these local movement participants, seeking out girl activists by visiting the recommended locations, organizations, and events. When choosing which leads to follow and which groups or organizations to contact, I focused only on those that could roughly be considered part of Left and/or progressive social movements. I did not include organizations and events that primarily emphasized individual growth and personal development, government-centered political participation, or community service. Instead I looked to spaces and groups engaged in collective, nongovernmental, and change-oriented political activities.

When I encountered teenage girls in these social movement contexts and spaces, I would ask them not only if they were interested in participating in the study, but also if they would self-identify as activists. Only those girls who acknowledged and claimed an activist identity or who said that they were somewhere on the route to becoming activists were then interviewed.

Girls who said that they were not really active, who were just stopping by this single event to see a friend, or who were not regular or frequent participants in any kind of collective political project were not interviewed. Thus, ongoing involvement in social movement activities, spaces, and/or organizations and an activist self-identification were necessary conditions in my own determination of who was or was not a girl activist.

Introducing myself to potential participants, I regularly identified myself as a North American (U.S.) activist and researcher, writing a book about teenage girls' activism. In emails and phone conversations, I also frequently mentioned my age (twenty-seven/twenty-eight at the time). By highlighting my own connections with social movements, I was intentionally trying to build girls' trust. I wanted them to know that I was sympathetic to their struggles. Frequently girls would ask me more about my own activist background, probing to find out a little more about me and my credibility. I would answer honestly, talking about my experiences with movements and organizing, and often saw them relax a little knowing that they were talking to someone who was part of the same "movement of movements." Furthermore, by referring to my project as a book, I wanted girls to realize the real-world relevance of the research and to understand that the project was not just for my own degree or my own personal benefit.

Most of the girl activists I encountered were excited about the research and willing to participate in the study. Interestingly, it was in San Francisco that I encountered the most girls who declined participation. These girls frequently cited security concerns (I don't know you, why should I trust you to write about my group) or the fact that such studies were not particularly new or interesting (I've already talked to researchers or reporters about youth activism). Youth activism in the Bay Area isn't seen as particularly exciting or special. Because it is so institutionalized, it is heavily discussed. On the other hand, in locations where I had traveled, many girls expressed excitement that I had come all this way to talk to them and their peers. They appeared to be genuinely glad to talk with me. This does not mean that all intended interviews actually happened: several girls expressed interest in the project, set up appointments with me, and then failed to show up. I would then try to track them down through cell phones, text messages, and their friends, but there were many interviews that never happened for reasons that are not entirely self-evident. It may have been that these girls changed their mind about participating, that their parents would not give permission, or that they just forgot. I have no way of knowing the difference between those girl activists who I then interviewed and those who I did not.

Once I had made contact with some girl activists in each city, I used a snowball sampling approach, asking the girls themselves for their help finding other activist teens. This means that for each city there are a few tendencies and groupings of girls, each branching out from an original set of contacts. In many cases, I interviewed several girls who were part of the same organization or collective. Most significantly, however, snowballing means that my interviews and observation in a given city was generally focused on a particular segment, or set of segments, within the youth movement in that location. I persisted in trying to make initial contacts in any other segment I heard about from either adults or girls, but in some cases I was never able to actually connect with girls from a particular branch of the local youth activist scene. For example, in Vancouver, my contact with Native youth movements was substantially less than I had hoped, while my interviews, because of the snowballing, focused more on girls involved in "global issues" clubs and organizations than is necessarily representative. These were the primary groups and organizations that other activists knew about and connected me to. I found little evidence of girls in other social movements in the area. Snowballing, then, while necessary and useful for accessing this very difficult-to-reach group, leads to a certain amount of potential over-emphasis on a few particular spaces, movements, or organizations within each urban context.

Interviews

I conducted, recorded, and transcribed in-depth qualitative interviews with the seventy-five girl activists. Most of these interviews were conducted individually, but a few were done in pairs, at the request of the girls involved. The interviews were generally between thirty minutes and two hours in length, with most being substantially over one hour. These interviews took place in both English (in the U.S. and Canada), and Spanish (in Mexico, Venezuela, and Argentina), and were all transcribed in the language in which they were conducted. I did the transcription for English interviews myself and hired several native Spanish speakers to transcribe those interviews.

The interviews were semi-structured, involving questions about girls' activist experiences and practices, their personal social contexts, their analyses of social problems, their opinions on the movements in their communities, their ideas about democracy, and their thoughts on girlhood, girl culture, and girl activism. Some girls had a lot to say about one or two of these themes with only a few comments on another, while others provided extensive commentary in response to every subject raised. Their different experiences and interests meant that no interview was exactly the same. The interviews were also generally fairly informal, often conducted over coffee or tea in cafes and coffeehouses. This more casual setting and the social dynamics of chatting over a cup of coffee usually produced a very relaxed and free-flowing conversation.

Interviews are, of course, a particular and distinctive kind of social interaction. The narratives that people construct in these interviews should not be seen as fully transparent. Rather, they are inevitably shaped by how they see the social setting of the interview and its purpose. Interviewees are cognizant of the implications of their words and engage in a great deal of image management. The stories girl activists chose to share or to omit are tied to how they wanted to present themselves, their peers, and their movements to outsiders. In addition to wanting to give a good impression of their work to the researcher, they were also trying to indicate the value of their organizing to adults in general and to U.S. readers. For example, in the case of Venezuela, girl activists paid substantial attention to communicating to a U.S. audience, which they felt was likely to have misperceptions about the Bolivarian revolution, the message that Chavez is not a dictator. They were doing political work throughout the interview, making choices about how they wanted U.S. audiences to understand their organizing and their activism.

In addition to the ongoing issues of political image management present throughout the interviews, complex dynamics of race, nation, gender, and age also emerge in interviewing interactions. I have written elsewhere about some of the challenges of a young woman doing research with girls,[1] challenges that are even messier when considered in relationship to transnational research. How girls interact with me and how they respond to my questions vary, based on their own perceptions of our similarities and differences. In some cases, they might feel that there are things I already know and understand and which therefore do not need explanation, while in others there are aspects of their lives that they might feel I could never possibly understand. Some girls, particularly in North America, would end the interview by asking me questions, seeking my advice on problems they were having in their groups, and using me as a resource. The interview was also occasionally a space for political education. Canadian and U.S. girls would ask me how I understand and define neoliberalism and globalization, two topics that I raised and that they felt as if they wanted or needed to know more about. On the other hand, I was rarely seen as a source of political advice or analysis in Latin America, but was instead called upon to explain the failures and decisions of the U.S. electorate.

Participant Observation and Movement Documents

In addition to conducting interviews where girls talk about their political identities and practices, I intentionally included ethnographic observation in order to address what girl activists do and how they do it, in the contexts of their political communities and groups. I sat in on many meetings and social gatherings, and attended numerous workshops, rallies, and other public political events. I was certainly not a full participant in most of these activities. For example, I did not have a vote in group decisions, but I would march with teens or sing along during their street theater performances. I was always there, at least in part, as a researcher and never tried to hide this role from the girls with whom I was close or from any of their peers. I took extensive field notes after each of these activities and kept an ongoing electronic journal of both the notes and my reflections on them. Unfortunately, because of the extent to which girls' activism happens within the confines of their schools, there were also many activities that I was not able to access. Therefore, my ethnographic observation was not as extensive as I had initially hoped and intended it to be.

A third methodological approach used in this study was the collection and analysis of various organizational documents, propaganda, or other printed materials produced by the groups in which girl activists participate. These materials were used primarily to describe the overall agendas and ideas of a given organization, or to provide background and context for girls' political practices.

Coding and Data Analysis

These three methodological practices created a large amount of text to work with and analyze. I entered interview transcripts, field notes, and a few summaries of particularly interesting organizational documents into a qualitative research software program, ATLAS.ti. This program assisted me in the process of organizing and coding the high volume of materials. I began with an open and inductive coding process, coding a few interviews from each location, labeling the various themes and topics as they emerged in these texts. Then, I went back to my code list, refining, reorganizing, and labeling the codes to more accurately reflect the theoretical issues that were emerging from the texts. This reworking of codes happened several times as I experimented with different coding structures and approaches until I found a system that emerged from the data itself and fit with the themes I was interested in exploring from that data. I used this more focused code list to code the remaining interviews, only occasionally adding new codes. The coding system that I ended up working with had a few code families, each with many subcodes and several independent codes, which did not connect to any family. A few of the major families included a set of codes that covered the "how" of girls' politics (e.g., fun, passion, hopeful, independent, determined, welcoming), a set on the various political issues they talk about and organize around (e.g., racism, globalization, environmentalism, poverty), a set for the various identities or social groups that they would reference (e.g., adults, youth, girls, boys, activists), a set for their political tactics (e.g., self-education, educating others, protest, creating alternatives), a set of codes on their ideas, visions and values (e.g. helping others, knowledge, democracy), and several other codes that identified some of the experiences that they were going through and talking about but did not fit into any of these sets (e.g., becoming an activist, leaving girlhood, and feeling different). Many statements were coded with multiple codes, allowing me to note the frequency with which girlhood, as an identity, was associated with hopefulness, as a "how," for example. ATLAS.ti also enables the researcher to write memos and notes on the codes, code families, and selected quotations. My analysis emerged from the data and my various ways of organizing and reflecting upon it as I identified and began to write about particular themes, moving back and forth between the codes, the quotations, and my memos.

Reflexive Research and Partial Perspectives

Taking seriously the insights of critical ethnographers, feminist researchers, and anti-racist scholars, I am aware of the ways that research is not a neutral or transparent process.[2] Instead, it produces texts that are always partial perspectives on a deeply complicated and never fully understood social world. This does not mean, however, that the arguments offered here are irrelevant. Despite being an always partial perspective, my research interventions offer some important insights into girls' activist identities and practices. Avoiding what Donna Haraway calls "the god trick,"[3] or the spatial metaphor that places the researcher outside the social world, looking down on the complete whole from above, I have been drawn to the metaphor of windows as a way to think about this project and my own relationship to it. Seeing girls' lives through these windows, I know that I am not getting a full picture but only what passes in front of me. And too, the smudges on the window glass can distort, color, or smear even that. The windows into girls' activism that

I write about here may not be perfect or crystal clear, and they can't capture the entirety of girl activists' lives and ideas, but they do give us several views.

My location in the social world and my perspectives influenced the research process and the text that it produces. Furthermore, the multiple and complex ways that my identity mattered to the research are almost certainly not all apparent to me. But I believe that it is our responsibility as reflexive researchers to at least consider some of these dynamics. I have written elsewhere about some of the issues around age-based authority, adult surveillance, memory, and studying teens and many of the topics I covered in that piece are also relevant here.[4] But as I suggested in my discussion of the interviews, there are also some particular dynamics relating to being a U.S. citizen and scholar conducting transnational research with young people who are deeply critical of the policies and actions of the U.S. government. As an example, any given young activist may have censored her anti-U.S. sentiments or emphasized them, depending on her own political intent for our discussion. Furthermore, my ability to ask appropriate follow-up questions in a given location was, of course, impacted by my own knowledge (or lack of knowledge) about a given movement, issue, or topic. Thus, our differences certainly impacted both my own and girls' actions and words in our interviews.

Diane Wolf explores the complicated issue of constant power differentials in the research process as a significant feminist dilemma. She writes, "Naming the exploitation inherent in research relationships meant having to explicitly acknowledge that serious power differentials exist between the researcher and her subjects."[5] One of the issues here is that the researcher is always "despite good intentions, using (and exploiting) others for their own ends."[6] The acknowledgment that research is inherently power-charged does not mean that all research is equally exploitative. There are clearly more and less egalitarian and equitable research practices, and I have tried, through a few mechanisms, to engage the girls as much as possible as active participants with a voice in the direction of this project. Although I engaged some of the girls in the research process and discussed what I was writing with them, this does not remove my authority and power in representing them. I can only hope that they find this story to be interesting, honest (if partial), and not just one of the many scholarly texts written by adults that is about them—but not for them. Indeed, it is my hope that this research does something for them, whether directly or indirectly. Its significance and relevance should be evident not only to those readers who are unfamiliar with girls' activism but also to the girls themselves.

Demographic Tables

TABLE 1. *Age.*
Numbers in each cell are actual counts, not percentages

Area	Younger than fifteen	Fifteen-year-olds	Sixteen-year-olds	Seventeen-year-olds	Eighteen-year-olds	Over eighteen
SF Bay Area	0	2	1	8	5	0
Vancouver	0	1	1	6	4	1
Mexico City	0	0	7	10	1	1
Caracas	1	4	2	3	1	0
Buenos Aires	1	0	3	7	2	0
Other	1	0	0	1	0	0
Totals:	3 (4%)	7 (9%)	14 (19%)	35 (47%)	13 (18%)	2 (3%)

Note: For all of the demographic information included in this appendix, I asked girls to self-identify and use their own words to describe themselves. This, inevitably, led to much more complicated sets of identifications than can be fully encapsulated in these tables. In the case of race and ethnicity, this complexity is further complicated by the fact that girls use very different words to talk about these identities in different locations. For many of the Latin American girls, race and ethnicity were not salient categories. Instead, they defined themselves in and through their national identities, and, when I asked if they identified with a particular racial group or ethnicity, said that they did not.

TABLE 2. *Class Background.*
Numbers in each cell are actual counts, not percentages

Area	Poor or working	Lower-middle	Middle	Upper or upper-middle
SF Bay Area	5	3	3	5
Vancouver	2	0	9	2
Mexico City	2	7	9	1
Caracas	2	2	7	0
Buenos Aires	1	2	9	1
Other	1	0	0	1
Totals:	13 (18%)	14 (19%)	37 (50%)	10 (13%)

TABLE 3. *Sexual Identity.*
Numbers in each cell are actual counts, not percentages

Area	Heterosexual	Lesbian, bisexual, or questioning
SF Bay Area	13	3
Vancouver	12	1
Mexico City	14	5
Caracas	11	0
Buenos Aires	12	1
Other	2	0
Totals:	64 (86%)	10 (14%)

TABLE 4. *Racial and Ethnic Identities (North America)*
Numbers in each cell are actual counts, not percentages

Area	White/European-Descent	Asian-Descent	African-Descent	Latina	Indigenous	Multi-Racial
SF Bay Area	7	0	3	4	0	2
Vancouver	8	4	0	0	1	0
Totals:	15 (52%)	4 (14%)	3 (10%)	4 (14%)	1 (3%)	2 (7%)

TABLE 5. *Racial and Ethnic Identities (Latin America)*
Numbers in each cell are actual counts, not percentages

Area	National Identity	White/European-Descent	African-Descent	Indigenous	Mixed or Mestiza	None
Mexico City	6	0	0	0	6	7
Caracas	5	2	0	0	1	3
Buenos Aires	8	1	0	0	0	4
Other	1	0	1	0	0	0
Totals	20 (44%)	3 (7%)	1 (2%)	0	7 (16%)	14 (31%)

Notes

NOTES TO CHAPTER 1

1. Erika Hayasaki, "2-4-6-8, This Is How We Demonstrate," *Los Angeles Times*, Feb. 22, 2004.

2. Brenda Norrell, "Denver Police Arrest 245 for Blocking Columbus Day Parade," *Indian Country Today*, Oct. 14, 2004, http://www.indiancountrytoday.com/archive/28174374.html.

3. João Pedro Stedile, "Brazil's Landless Battalions," in *A Movement of Movements: Is Another World Really Possible?*, ed. Tom Mertes (New York: Verso, 2004).

4. Mattie Weiss, "Youth Rising," (Oakland, CA: Applied Research Center, 2003).

5. "Over 100,000 Students Walk out and Protest War around the Nation and the Globe," *Democracy Now*, Mar. 6, 2003, http://www.democracynow.org/2003/3/6/over_100_000_students_walk_out.

6. The choice to study only progressive and Left-leaning girl activists was made for several reasons. First, I was particularly interested in the transnational youth culture connected to the diverse articulations and formations of the alter-globalization movement. Many of the girls I interviewed, then, are loosely connected to this broad movement formation and culture. By focusing on movements with at least some commonalities in their political ideologies, I am able to explore girls' interventions and strategies in greater detail. I might have found a much wider range of strategic actions had I included girls involved in right-wing and conservative activism. While this would have been interesting, it would have sacrificed depth for breadth. This leads to a second rationale for the more narrow focus: including right-wing girls would have added an additional level of comparisons to the already complex project of discussing five different national contexts and, in doing so, would have made analysis of any patterns and divergences exceedingly difficult. Future research on girls in these movements would, of course, offer many new and valuable insights.

7. On girls' self-esteem and psychology, see Lyn Mikel Brown and Carol Gilligan, *Meeting at the Crossroads* (New York: Ballantine Books, 1992); Peggy Orenstein, *Schoolgirls: Young Women, Self-Esteem, and the Confidence Gap* (New York: Doubleday, 1994); Mary Pipher, *Reviving Ophelia: Saving the Selves of Adolescent Girls* (New York: G. P. Putnam's Sons, 1994). On sexuality, see Sharon Thompson, *Going All the Way: Teenage Girls' Tales of Sex, Romance, and Pregnancy* (New York: Hill and Wang, 1995); Sue Lees, *Sugar and Spice: Sexuality and Adolescent Girls* (London: Penguin Press, 1993). On friendship, peer relationships and school, see Valerie Hey, *The Company She Keeps: An Ethnography of Girls' Friendships* (Buckingham: Open University Press, 1997); Pamela J. Bettis and Natalie G. Adams,

eds., *Geographies of Girlhood: Identities In-Between* (Mahwah, NJ: Lawrence Erlbaum Associates, 2005). On identity construction. see Lorraine Delia Kenny, *Daughters of Suburbia: Growing up White, Middle Class and Female* (New Brunswick, NJ: Rutgers University Press, 2000); Joyce A. Ladner, *Tomorrow's Tomorrow: The Black Woman* (Lincoln: University of Nebraska Press, 1971); Julie Bettie, *Women without Class: Girls, Race and Identity* (Berkeley, CA: University of California Press, 2003); Jill Denner and Bianca L. Guzman, eds. *Latina Girls: Voices of Adolescent Strength in the United States* (New York: New York University Press, 2006); Yasmin Jiwani, Candis Steenbergen, and Claudia Mitchell, eds., *Girlhood: Redefining the Limits* (Montreal: Black Rose Books, 2006). On media consumption and cultural practices, see Dawn Currie, *Girl Talk: Adolescent Magazines and Their Readers* (Toronto: University of Toronto Press, 1995); Sherrie A. Inness, ed., *Delinquents and Debutantes: Twentieth-Century American Girls' Cultures* (New York: New York University Press, 1998); Mary Celeste Kearney, *Girls Make Media* (New York: Routledge, 2006).

8. Key texts on girls' resistances include Dawn H. Currie, Deirdre M. Kelly, and Shauna Pomerantz, "'The Geeks Shall Inherit the Earth': Girls' Agency, Subjectivity and Empowerment," *Journal of Youth Studies* 9, no. 4 (2006); Catherine Driscoll, *Girls: Feminine Adolescence in Popular Culture and Cultural Theory* (New York: Columbia University Press, 2002); Deirdre M. Kelly, Shauna Pomerantz, and Dawn Currie, "Skater Girlhood and Emphasized Femininity: 'You Can't Land an Ollie Properly in Heels,'" *Gender and Education* 17, no. 3 (2005); Lauraine LeBlanc, *Pretty in Punk: Girls' Gender Resistance in a Boys' Subculture* (New Brunswick, NJ: Rutgers University Press, 1999); Angela McRobbie, *Feminism and Youth Culture*, 2nd ed. (New York: Routledge, 2000). The few texts which have addressed girls' political identities include Kum-Kum Bhavnani, *Talking Politics: A Psychological Framing for Views from Youth in Britain* (Cambridge: Cambridge University Press, 1991); Anita Harris, "Revisiting Bedroom Culture: New Spaces for Young Women's Politics," *Hecate* 27, no. 1 (2001); Anita Harris, "Dodging and Weaving: Young Women Countering the Stories of Youth Citizenship," *International Journal of Critical Psychology* 4, no. 2 (2001). Harris's work is primarily a theoretical discussion of girls' political spaces and narratives, while Bhavnani's presents a qualitative study of youth political consciousness around employment and unemployment in Britain. Both call for further research in this area, and neither focuses specifically on girl activists.

9. Work on third-wave feminism and young women's relation to feminism is, despite the frequent use of the word "girl," dominated by an emphasis on the experiences and perspectives of those over the age of eighteen. This includes Jennifer Baumgardner and Amy Richards, *Manifesta: Young Women, Feminism and the Future* (New York: Farrar, Straus and Giroux, 2000); Ophira Edut, ed., *Adios Barbie: Young Women Write About Body Image and Identity* (Seattle: Seal Press, 1998); Barbara Findlen, ed., *Listen Up: Voices from the Next Feminist Generation* (Seattle: Seal Press, 1995); Rebecca Walker, ed., *To Be Real: Telling the Truth and Changing the Face of Feminism* (New York: Anchor Books, 1995).

10. Examples of this can be found in Angela McRobbie, "Pecs and Penises: The Meaning of Girlie Culture," *Soundings* 5 (Spring 1997); Imelda Whelehan, *Overloaded: Popular Culture and the Future of Feminism* (London: The Women's Press, 2000).

11. See, for example, Philip G. Altbach, ed., *Student Political Activism: An International Reference Handbook* (New York: Greenwood Press, 1989); Richard G. Braungart, "Historical and Generational Patterns of Youth Movements: A Global Perspective," *Comparative Social Research* 7 (1984); Rebecca Klatch, *A Generation Divided: The New Left, the New*

Right, and the 1960s (Berkeley: University of California Press, 1999); Nella Van Dyke, "Hotbeds of Activism: Locations of Student Protest," *Social Problems* 45, no. 2 (1998).

12. Carlos Muñoz, *Youth, Identity, Power: The Chicano Movement* (New York: Verso, 1989); Taylor Branch, *Parting the Waters: America in the King Years, 1954–63* (New York: Simon and Schuster, 1988); John A. Kirk, *Redefining the Color Line: Black Activism in Little Rock, Arkansas, 1940–1970* (Miami: University Press of Florida, 2002).

13. Bernice McNair Barnett, "Invisible Southern Black Women Leaders in the Civil Rights Movement: The Triple Constraints of Gender, Race and Class," *Gender and Society* 7, no. 2 (1993); Joshua Gamson, "Messages of Exclusion: Gender, Movements and Symbolic Boundaries," *Gender and Society* 11, no. 2 (1997); Jenny Irons, "The Shaping of Activist Recruitment and Participation: A Study of Women in the Mississippi Civil Rights Movement," *Gender and Society* 12, no. 6 (1998); Doug McAdam, "Gender as a Mediator of the Activist Experience: The Case of Freedom Summer," *American Journal of Sociology* 97, no. 5 (1992); Belinda Robnett, *How Long? How Long? African American Women in the Struggle for Civil Rights* (Oxford: Oxford University Press, 1997); Beth Schneider, "Political Generations and the Contemporary Women's Movement," *Sociological Inquiry* 58, no. 1 (1988); Verta Taylor and Nancy Whittier, "Collective Identity in Social Movement Communities: Lesbian Feminist Mobilization," in *Frontiers in Social Movement Theory*, ed. Carol Mueller (New Haven: Yale University Press, 1992); Nancy Whittier, *Feminist Generations: The Persistence of the Radical Women's Movement* (Philadelphia: Temple University Press, 1995).

14. The most significant and notable exception to this invisibility is a very recent addition: Hava Rachel Gordon, *We Fight to Win: Inequality and the Politics of Youth Activism* (New Brunswick, NJ: Rutgers University Press, 2009).

15. Saskia Sassen, *Globalization and Its Discontents* (New York: The New Press, 1998)

16. Altha J. Cravey, *Women and Work in Mexico's Maquiladoras* (Lanham, MD: Rowman and Littlefield, 1998).

17. Deborah Barndt, *Tangled Routes: Women, Work and Globalization on the Tomato Trail* (Lanham, MD: Rowman and Littlefield, 2002); Carla Freeman, *High Tech High Heels in the Global Economy* (Durham, NC: Duke University Press, 2000); Barbara Kaoru Ige, "For Sale: A Girl's Life in the Global Economy," in *Millennium Girls: Today's Girls around the World*, ed. Sherrie A. Inness (Lanham, MD: Rowman and Littlefield, 1998).

18. AFL-CIO, *Women in the Global Economy*, http://www.aflcio.org/issues/jobseconomy/globaleconomy/women/.

19. International Labor Organization, "Shackled Dreams, Lost Learning: The Costs of Child Domestic Labour," July 2004, http://www.ilo.org/public/english/bureau/inf/features/04/domestic.htm [accessed Dec. 16, 2004].

20. Ariana-Sophia Kartsonis, "A Tightrope Made of Sari Silk: The Delicate, Perilous World of Girlhood in India," in *Running for Their Lives: Girls, Cultural Identity and Stories of Survival*, ed. Sherrie A. Inness (Lanham, MD: Rowman and Littlefield, 2000).

21. The UN World Youth Report estimates that 2 million girls between the ages of five and fifteen are introduced into sex work each year. *2003 World Youth Report* (United Nations, 2003).

22. "Girl Power," *Chain Store Age*, Sept. 1, 1999; Nina Munk, "Girl Power," *Fortune*, Dec. 8, 1997; Jennifer Purvis, "Teen Fashions Keep Japanese Garment Industry Active," *TDC Trade*, Feb. 25, 2003, http://www.tdctrade.com/mne/garment/clothing082.htm.

23. Lynnea Mallalieu and Kay M. Palan, "How Good a Shopper Am I? Conceptualizing Teenage Girls' Perceived Shopping Competence," *Academy of Marketing Science Review* 10 (2006).

24. Michael Brenner. "Girl Power: Teen Girls Spend More Than Boys," International Communications Research, Aug. 15, 2005, http://www.icrsurvey.com/Study.aspx?f=Teen_Survey_0805.html.

25. Anita Harris, "Jamming Girl Culture: Young Women and Consumer Citizenship," in *All About the Girl: Culture, Power, and Identity*, ed. Anita Harris (New York: Routledge, 2004), 163.

26. See also Driscoll, *Girls*; Jessica K. Taft, "Girl Power Politics: Pop-Culture Barriers and Organizational Resistance," in Harris, *All About the Girl*.

27. Anita Harris, *Future Girl: Young Women in the Twenty-First Century* (New York: Routledge, 2004), 2.

28. Chandra Talpade Mohanty, "Under Western Eyes Revisited: Feminist Solidarity through Anticapitalist Struggles," in *Feminism without Borders: Decolonizing Theory, Practicing Solidarity* (Durham, NC: Duke University Press, 2003), 239.

29. James M. Jasper, "A Strategic Approach to Collective Action: Looking for Agency in Social-Movement Choices," *Mobilization: An International Quarterly* 9, no. 1 (2004).

30. Ibid., 10.

31. Ann Swidler, "Culture in Action: Symbols and Strategies," *American Sociological Review* 51, no. 2 (1986): 273.

32. Mary Bernstein, *"The Analytic Dimensions of Identity: A Political Identity Framework,"* in *Identity Work in Social Movements*, ed. Jo Reger, Daniel J. Myers, and Rachel L. Einwohner (Minneapolis: University of Minnesota Press, 2008), 290.

33. Ibid.

34. Sunaina Maira and Elisabeth Soep, introduction to *Youthscapes: The Popular, the National, the Global*, ed. Sunaina Maira and Elisabeth Soep (Philadelphia: University of Pennsylvania Press, 2005).

35. There are numerous theoretical works, personal accounts, and collections of essays by scholars and movement participants that describe this diverse movement field. For some examples, see Richard J. F. Day, *Gramsci Is Dead: Anarchist Currents in the Newest Social Movements* (Ann Arbor, MI: Pluto Press, 2005); Michael Hardt and Antonio Negri, *Multitude: War and Democracy in the Age of Empire* (New York: Penguin Press, 2004); John Holloway, *Change the World without Taking Power: The Meaning of Revolution Today*, rev. ed. (Ann Arbor, MI: Pluto Press, 2005); Tom Mertes, ed., *A Movement of Movements: Is Another World Really Possible?* (New York: Verso, 2004); Notes From Nowhere, *We Are Everywhere: The Irresistible Rise of Global Anti-Capitalism* (New York: Verso, 2003); Donatella della Porta et al., eds., *Globalization from Below: Transnational Activists and Protest Networks* (Minneapolis: University of Minnesota Press, 2006); David Solnit, ed., *Globalize Liberation: How to Uproot the System and Build a Better World* (San Francisco: City Lights Books, 2004); Amory Starr, *Naming the Enemy: Anti-Corporate Movements Confront Globalization* (New York: Zed Books, 2000); Amory Starr, *Global Revolt: A Guide to the Movements against Globalization* (New York: Zed Books, 2005); Eddie Yuen, Daniel Burton-Rose, and George Katsiaficas, eds., *Confronting Capitalism: Dispatches from a Global Movement* (Brooklyn, NY: Soft Skull Press, 2004).

36. For more extensive discussions on some of these dynamics, see Sonia E. Alvarez, Evelina Dagnino, and Arturo Escobar, eds., *Cultures of Politics, Politics of Cultures: Re-Visioning Latin American Social Movements* (Boulder, CO: Westview Press, 1998); Hank Johnston and Paul Almeida, eds., *Latin American Social Movements: Globalization, Democratization, and Transnational Networks* (Lanham, MD: Rowman and Littlefield, 2006).

37. Elizabeth A. Armstrong, *Forging Gay Identities: Organizing Sexuality in San Francisco, 1950–1994* (Chicago: University of Chicago Press, 2002); Gary Delgado, *Beyond the Politics of Place: New Directions in Community Organizing in the 1990s* (Berkeley: Chardon Press, 1997); Troy Johnson, Joane Nagel, and Duane Champagne, eds., *American Indian Activism: Alcatraz to the Longest Walk* (Urbana: University of Illinois Press, 1997); Chris Rhomberg, *No There There: Race, Class, and Political Community in Oakland* (Berkeley: University of California Press, 2004).

38. Robert Cohen and Reginald E. Zelnik, eds. *The Free Speech Movement: Reflections on Berkeley in the 1960s* (Berkeley: University of California Press, 2002).

39. Helene Whitson, "The San Francisco State College Strike Collection: Introductory Essay," San Francisco State University Library, 1999, http://www.library.sfsu.edu/about/collections/ strike/essay.html.

40. Ryan Pintado-Vertner, "The West Coast Story: The Emergence of Youth Organizing in California" (New York: The Funders Collaborative on Youth Organizing, 2004), 7.

41. Gordon, *We Fight to Win.*

42. Andreana Clay, "'All I Need Is One Mic': Mobilizing Youth for Social Change in the Post-Civil Rights Era," *Social Justice* 33, no. 2 (2006).

43. For a discussion of the state of SF Bay Area anti-war and anti-racist politics during this time see Nadine C. Naber, "So Our History Doesn't Become Your Future: The Local and Global Politics of Coalition Building Post September 11th," *Journal of Asian American Studies* 5, no. 3 (2002).

44. Arthur Leibman, "Student Activism in Mexico," *Annals of the American Academy of Political and Social Science* 395 (1971); Michael Soldatenko, "Mexico '68: Power to the Imagination!" *Latin American Perspectives* 32, no. 4 (2005).

45. Bruce Lindsay, "Students Strike in Mexico," *Arena Magazine*, Oct. 1999; Gilda Waldman, "Los Movimientos Estudiantiles De 1968 Y 1999: Contextos Historicos Y Reflexiones Criticas," *Revista Mexicana de Ciencias Políticas y Sociales* 44, no. 178 (1999).

46. Subcomandante Insurgente Marcos, *The Other Campaign/La Otra Campaña* (San Francisco: City Lights, 2006).

47. See Steve Ellner and Daniel Hellinger, eds., *Venezuelan Politics in the Chavez Era: Class, Polarization, and Conflict* (London: Lynne Rienner Publishers, 2003); Richard Gott, *Hugo Chavez and the Bolivarian Revolution* (New York: Verso, 2005); Gregory Wilpert, *Changing Venezuela by Taking Power: The History and Policies of the Chavez Government* (New York: Verso, 2006).

48. Mark Weisbrot, "Americans Need to Look Beyond the Media on Venezuela," *Huffington Post*, Jan. 15, 2008, http://www.huffingtonpost.com/mark-weisbrot/americans-need-to-look-be_b_81644.html.

49. Eva Golinger, *The Chavez Code: Cracking U.S. Intervention in Venezuela* (Northampton, MA: Olive Branch Press, 2006).

50. Nicholas Blomley, "Landscapes of Property," *Law and Society Review* 32, no. 3 (1998); Stefan Christoff and Sawsan Kalache, "The Poorest Postal Code: Vancouver's Downtown Eastside in Photos," *Dominion: News From the Grassroots*, Jan. 12 2007, http://www.dominionpaper.ca/articles/909.

51. Given the history of colonialism and white researchers' casual use and misuse of information about indigenous communities, the mistrust I encountered is entirely understandable and probably should have been expected on my part.

52. For contextual information on the political activity of the Argentine poor before 2001, see Javier Auyero, *Poor People's Politics: Peronist Networks and the Legacy of Evita* (Durham, NC: Duke University Press, 2001). For discussions of the movements of the 2001 crisis, and the context of these movements, see Elizabeth Borland and Barbara Sutton, "Quotidian Disruption and Women's Activism in Times of Crisis, Argentina 2002–2003," *Gender and Society* 21, no. 5 (2007); Colectivo Situaciones, *19 Y 20: Apuntes Para El Nuevo Protagonismo Social* (Buenos Aires: Colectivo Situaciones, 2002); Patricio McCabe, "Argentina's New Forms of Resistance," in D. Solnit, *Globalize Liberation*; Jennifer Whitney and John Jordan, "Que Se Vayan Todos: Argentina's Popular Rebellion," in D. Solnit, *Globalize Liberation*; Raúl Zibechi, *Genealogia De La Revuelta : Argentina, La Sociedad En Movimiento* (Buenos Aires: Nordan Comunidad, 2003).

53. I also sent interview transcripts and encouraged the interviewees to read and make changes to these, if they desired. Only a few girls responded with changes, but several others wrote to say hello, acknowledging receipt of the transcript but no changes. Those who did want to make changes tended to have requests about removing some of the filler words in their transcripts in order to make them sound more polished, or changed their pseudonym at this point. In particular, I had a few Mexican girls switch from more European-sounding names to those with a slightly more indigenous quality, indicating something of their own shifting identifications and affiliations.

54. Kenny, *Daughters of Suburbia*.

55. For a discussion of translation issues as they relate to the development of new political languages, see Marina Sitrin, *Horizontalism: Voices of Popular Power in Argentina* (Oakland, CA: AK Press, 2006), v–viii.

56. Inderpal Grewal and Caren Kaplan, "Introduction: Transnational Feminist Practices and Questions of Postmodernity," in *Scattered Hegemonies: Postmodernity and Transnational Feminist Practices*, ed. Inderpal Grewal and Caren Kaplan (Minneapolis: University of Minnesota Press, 1994), 18.

57. A few of the many texts on these movements with which girls' activism particularly resonates include Rebecca Solnit, *Hope in the Dark: Untold Histories, Wild Possibilities* (New York: Nation Books, 2004); Holloway, *Change the World*; Sitrin, *Horizontalism*; Day, *Gramsci Is Dead*. Further resonance can be found with many of the ideas and practices of Zapatismo: Manuel Callahan, "Why Not Share a Dream? Zapatismo as Political and Cultural Practice," *Humboldt Journal of Social Relations* 29, no. 1 (2005); Ziga Vodovnik, ed., *Ya Basta! Ten Years of the Zapatista Uprising: Writings of Subcomandante Insurgente Marcos* (Oakland, CA: AK Press, 2004).

NOTES TO CHAPTER 2

1. Kofi Annan, "No Development Tool More Effective Than Education of Girls," United Nations Information Service, 2004, http://www.unis.unvienna.org/unis/pressrels/2004/sgsm9118.html.

2. Nike Foundation, "Who We Are," http://www.nike.com/nikebiz/nikefoundation/who.jhtml, accessed Mar. 20, 2007.

3. Chris Bobel, "'I'm not an activist, though I've done a lot of it': Doing Activism, Being Activist and the 'Perfect Standard' in a Contemporary Movement," *Social Movement Studies* 6, no. 2 (2007).

4. For a discussion of the various scholarly definitions of social movements and how movements differ from other forms of political action and collective behavior, see David A. Snow, Sarah A. Soule, and Hanspeter Kriesi, "Mapping the Terrain," in *The Blackwell Companion to Social Movements*, ed. David A. Snow, Sarah A. Soule, and Hanspeter Kriesi (Malden, MA: Blackwell Publishing, 2004).

5. David S. Meyer, "Opportunities and Identities: Bridge-Building in the Study of Social Movements," in *Social Movements: Identity, Culture and the State*, ed. David S. Meyer, Nancy Whittier, and Belinda Robnett (New York: Oxford University Press, 2002), 11.

6. For a discussion of some of the scholarly debates over the meaning of an activist identity and a proposed measure of such, see Alexandra F. Corning and Daniel J. Meyers, "Individual Orientation toward Engagement in Social Action," *Political Psychology* 23, no. 4 (2002).

7. This is not surprising given that "fostering or halting change is the raison d'être for all social movements." Snow, Soule, and Kriesi, "Mapping the Terrain," 8.

8. Paul Lichterman, *The Search for Political Community: American Activists Re-Inventing Commitment* (New York: Cambridge University Press, 1996), 21.

9. Sinikka Aapola, Marnina Gonick, and Anita Harris, *Young Femininity: Girlhood, Power and Social Change* (New York: Palgrave Macmillan, 2005), 54.

10. Harris, *Future Girl*. In some cases, this power over the self is literally power over one's own physical body: Jacobs Brumberg argues that North American girls today center on their bodies as projects in a way that was not the case at the turn of the century. Their bodies are something to work on, to develop power over and to construct. Joan Jacobs Brumberg, *The Body Project: An Intimate History of American Girls* (New York: Random House, 1997).

11. These quotes are drawn directly from the public Web sites of these three organizations.

12. Aapola, Gonick, and Harris, *Young Femininity*.

13. Harris, *Future Girl*, 25.

14. Chandra Talpade Mohanty, "Under Western Eyes: Feminist Scholarship and Colonial Discourses," in *Third World Women and the Politics of Feminism*, ed. Chandra Talpade Mohanty, Ann Russo, and Lourdes Torres (Bloomington: Indiana University Press, 1991).

15. Nicholas Kristof and Sheryl WuDunn, "The Women's Crusade," *New York Times Magazine*, Aug. 17, 2009.

16. Nike Foundation, "Who We Are."

17. Nathan Teske, in his study of political activists in North America also finds that these individuals' activist identities are "built on a high valuation of doing something about what they see as the problems of our society and world" (98). Teske, *Political Activists in America: The Identity Construction Model of Political Participation* (Cambridge: Cambridge University Press, 1997).

18. Unlike Verta Taylor and Nella Van Dyke who use "protest" as the catch-all word for many of the tactics and strategies of social movements saying that it is "the collective use of unconventional methods of political participation to try to persuade or coerce authorities to support a challenging group's aims," girl activists have a much more narrow

understanding of the term, using it primarily to refer to marches, rallies, and other similar large-scale, public demonstrations of a political position. Taylor and Van Dyke, "Get up, Stand Up: Tactical Repertoires of Social Movements," in Snow, Soule and Kriesi, *Blackwell Companion to Social Movements*, 263.

19. Mary Fainsod Katzenstein, *Faithful and Fearless: Moving Feminist Protest inside the Church and Military* (Princeton, NJ: Princeton University Press, 1998); Andrea Densham, "The Marginalized Uses of Power and Identity: Lesbians' Participation in Breast Cancer and Aids Activism," in *Women Transforming Politics: An Alternative Reader*, ed. Cathy J. Cohen, Kathleen B. Jones, and Joan C. Tronto (New York: New York University Press, 1997); Taylor and Whittier, "Collective Identity in Social Movement Communities"; Gamson, "Messages of Exclusion"; Sharon Kurtz, *Workplace Justice: Organizing Multi-Identity Movements* (Minneapolis: University of Minnesota Press, 2002); Brett Stockdill, "Forging a Multi-Dimensional Oppositional Consciousness: Lessons from Community-Based Aids Activism," in *Oppositional Consciousness: The Subjective Roots of Social Protest*, ed. Jane Mansbridge and Aldon Morris (Chicago: University of Chicago Press, 2001).

20. Katzenstein, *Faithful and Fearless*; Verta Taylor and Marieke Van Willigen, "Women's Self-Help and the Reconstruction of Gender: The Postpartum Support and Breast Cancer Movements," *Mobilization: An International Journal* 1, no. 2 (1996); Paula Stewart Brush, "The Influence of Social Movements on Articulations of Race and Gender in Black Women's Autobiographies," *Gender and Society* 13, no. 1 (1999).

21. Taylor and Van Dyke, "Get Up, Stand Up," 270.

22. Notes From Nowhere, *We Are Everywhere*, 174.

23. Sitrin, *Horizontalism*, 4.

24. Ejército Zapatista de Liberación Nacional, "Sixth Declaration of the Selva Lacandona," 2005, http://www.ezln.org/documentos/2005/sexta3.en.htm.

25. Sarah Wagner, "The Legal and Practical Basis of Citizen Power in Venezuela," *Venezuela Analysis*, Dec. 2, 2004, http://www.venezuelanalysis.com/articles.php?artno=1328.

26. Amory Starr notes that "participants in the revolt against globalization increasing conclude that elites can not be trusted and that institutionalized politics aimed at state power have failed to break free of the neoliberal agenda." Therefore, she continues, "the most widely recognized and celebrations of the movement [against globalization] are direct." Starr, *Global Revolt*, 174. Girls' use of direct action thus links up with the direct action practices of the movements around them.

27. Wini Breines, *Community and Organization in the New Left, 1962–1968: The Great Refusal* (New Brunswick, NJ: Rutgers University Press, 1989); Sitrin, *Horizontalism*; Uri Gordon, "Anarchism Reloaded," *Journal of Political Ideologies* 12, no. 1 (2007).

28. The framing of mobilization primarily as a recruitment process is common across a range of theoretical tendencies in social movement research. Some of the many examples of this include John D. McCarthy and Mayer N. Zald, "Resource Mobilization and Social Movements: A Partial Theory," *American Journal of Sociology* 82, no. 6 (1977); Doug McAdam and Ronnelle Paulsen, "Specifying the Relationship between Social Ties and Activism," *American Journal of Sociology* 99, no. 3 (1993); James M. Jasper and Jane D. Poulsen, "Recruiting Strangers and Friends: Moral Shocks and Social Networks in Animal Rights and Anti-Nuclear Protests," *Social Problems* 42, no. 4 (1995).

29. Descriptions and scholarly analysis of these programs is extensive. See, for example, Peter Levine and Cynthia Gibson, *The Civic Mission of Schools* (New York: Carnegie Cor-

poration of New York and CIRCLE: The Center for Information and Research on Civic Learning and Engagement, 2003); Barry N. Checkoway and Lorraine N. Gutierrez, eds., *Youth Participation and Community Change* (New York: Haworth Press, 2006).

30. Shelley Billig, Sue Root, and Dan Jesse, "The Impact of Participation in Service-Learning on High School Students' Civic Engagement," (College Park, MD: CIRCLE: The Center for Information and Research on Civic Learning and Engagement, 2005); Edward Metz, Susan Stroud, and Brett Alessi, "An Exploratory Study of National Youth Service Policy in 19 Countries in Latin America and the Caribbean," (Washington, DC: Innovations in Civic Participation, 2006).

31. Mary Teresa Bitti, "Is Forced Volunteering Helping Anyone?" *World Volunteer Web*, Apr. 30, 2007, http://www.worldvolunteerweb.org/news-views/viewpoints/doc/is-forced-volunteering-helping.html.

32. Metz, Stroud, and Alessi, "National Youth Service Policy," 8.

33. Girl Scouts USA, "Take the Lead: Girl Scout Service," 2002, http://jfg.girlscouts.org/How/Leadership/Service/index.htm.

34. Girl Scouts USA, Government Relations and Advocacy, 2002, http://www.girlscouts.org/advocacy/index.html.

35. Molly W. Andolina, Krista Jenkins, Cliff Zukin, and Scott Keeter, "Habits from Home, Lessons from School: Influences on Youth Civic Engagement," *PS: Political Science and Politics* 36, no. 2 (2003); Billig, Root, and Jesse, "The Impact of Participation in Service-Learning"; Edward Metz, Jeffrey A. McLellan, and James Youniss, "Types of Voluntary Service and Adolescents' Civic Development," *Journal of Adolescent Research* 18, no. 2 (2003).

36. For descriptions and discussions of some of these programs see Judith Bessant, "Mixed Messages: Youth Participation and Democratic Practice," *Australian Journal of Political Science* 39, no. 2 (2004); Eliana Guerra, "Citizenship Knows No Age: Children's Participation in the Governance and Municipal Budget of Barra Mansa, Brazil," *Environment and Urbanization* 14, no. 2 (2002); Goretti Horgan and Paula Rodgers, "Young People's Participation in a New Northern Ireland Society," *Youth and Society* 32, no. 1 (2000); Caspar Merkle, "Youth Participation in El Alto, Bolivia," *Environment and Urbanization* 15, no. 1 (2003).

37. Howard Williamson, "Supporting Young People in Europe: Principles, Policy and Practice," (Strasbourg, France: Council of Europe, 2002), 89.

38. Guerra, "Citizenship Knows No Age."

39. Yael Ohana, "Participation and Citizenship: Training for Minority Youth Projects in Europe" (Strasbourg, France: Council of Europe, 1998).

40. Bessant, "Mixed Messages"; David Maunders, "Head of a Movement or Arms of the State? Youth Councils and Youth Policy in Australia, 1941–1991," *International Journal of Adolescence and Youth* 6, no. 2 (1996).

41. Jessica K. Taft, "I'm Not a Politics Person: Teenage Girls, Oppositional Consciousness and the Meaning of Politics," *Politics and Gender* 2 (2006).

42. Harris, *Future Girl*, 138.

43. James Youniss, Susan Bales, Verona Christmas-Best, Marcelo Diversi, Milbrey McLaughlin, and Rainer Silbereisen, "Youth Civic Engagement in the Twenty-First Century" *Journal of Research on Adolescence* 12, no. 1 (2002); Ohana, "Participation and Citizenship."

44. Daniel Hart et al., "Youth Bulges in Communities: The Effects of Age Structure on Adolescent Civic Knowledge and Civic Participation," *Psychological Science* 15, no. 9 (2004).

45. Many scholars have emphasized the centrality of collectivity and political communities to social movements, highlighting the importance of activists' collective identities. See, for example, William A. Gamson, "Commitment and Agency in Social Movements," *Sociological Forum* 6, no. 1 (1991); Taylor and Whittier, "Collective Identity in Social Movement Communities"; Alberto Melucci, "The Process of Collective Identity," in *Social Movements and Culture*, ed. Hank Johnston and Bert Klandermans (Minneapolis: University of Minnesota Press, 1995); Francesca Polletta and James M. Jasper, "Collective Identity and Social Movements," *Annual Review of Sociology* 27 (2001); Mary Bernstein, "Identity Politics," *Annual Review of Sociology* 31 (2005).

46. James M. Jasper, *The Art of Moral Protest: Culture, Biography and Creativity in Social Movements* (Chicago: University of Chicago Press, 1997), 87.

47. Levine and Gibson, *Civic Mission of Schools*, 5.

48. United Nations, *World Youth Report 2007: Young People's Transition to Adulthood: Progress and Challenges* (New York: United Nations, 2007), 67.

49. Michael X. Delli Carpini, "Gen.Com: Youth, Civic Engagement, and the New Information Environment," *Political Communication* 17, no. 4 (2000); Matt Henn, Mark Weinstein, and Dominic Wring, "A Generation Apart? Youth and Political Participation in Britain," *British Journal of Politics and International Relations* 4, no. 2 (2002); Youniss et al., "Youth Civic Engagement in the Twenty-First Century."

50. The 2005 United Nations *World Youth Report* notes that, as of yet, there are no studies that provide statistical information on the numbers of youth who participate in social movements. United Nations, *World Youth Report 2005: Young People Today and in 2015* (New York: United Nations, 2005), 110–30. Without such information, it is difficult to draw conclusions on the actual prevalence of teen activists. My own anecdotal evidence suggests, however, that adults are more likely to underestimate youth activism, falling back on the powerful discourse of youth apathy, than to overestimate it.

NOTES TO CHAPTER 3

1. Richard Flacks, *Making History: The American Left and the American Mind* (New York: Columbia University Press, 1988).

2. Doug McAdam, Sidney Tarrow, and Charles Tilly, *Dynamics of Contention* (New York: Cambridge University Press, 2001), 8.

3. See, for example, Polletta and Jasper "Collective Identity and Social Movements"; Mary Bernstein, "Identity Politics"; Alberto Melucci, "The Process of Collective Identity."

4. This three-part framework for understanding the processes of collective identity formation is proposed in Taylor and Whittier, "Collective Identity in Social Movement Communities."

5. Karen Beckwith, "Lancashire Women against Pit Closures: Women's Standing in a Men's Movement," *Signs* 21, no. 4 (1996): 1063.

6. Ibid., 1040.

7. Ibid.

8. Women activists' construction of their political agency at least partially as women is common across many social movements. See, for example, Lorraine Bayard de Volo, *Mothers of Heroes and Martyrs: Gender Identity Politics in Nicaragua, 1979–1999* (Baltimore, MD: Johns Hopkins University Press, 2001); Elizabeth Borland, "The Mature Resistance of Argentina's Madres De Plaza De Maya," in *Latin American Social Movements: Globalization, Democratization, and Transnational Networks,* ed. Hank Johnston and Paul Almeida (Lanham, MD: Rowman and Littlefield, 2006); Nancy Naples, ed., *Community Activism and Feminist Politics: Organizing across Race, Class, and Gender* (New York: Routledge, 1998).

9. Kristin Luker, *Dubious Conceptions: The Politics of Teenage Pregnancy* (Cambridge, MA: Harvard University Press, 1996).

10. A handful of the teens I spoke with are over eighteen and therefore above the age of majority and of voting age.

11. Bessant, "Mixed Messages"; Sarane Spence Boocock and Kimberly Ann Scott, *Kids in Context: The Sociological Study of Children and Childhoods* (Lanham, MD: Rowman and Littlefield, 2005); Checkoway and Gutierrez, eds. *Youth Participation and Community Change.*

12. David F. Burg, *Encyclopedia of Student and Youth Movements* (New York: Facts on File, Inc, 1998).

13. Gordon, *We Fight to Win,* 9.

14. Bessant, "Mixed Messages."

15. Alan Prout and Allison James, "A New Paradigm for the Sociology of Childhood? Provenance, Promise and Problems," in *Constructing and Reconstructing Childhoods,* ed. Alan Prout and Allison James (London: Falmer Press, 1990).

16. Gordon, *We Fight to Win.*

17. The National Youth Rights Association "defends the civil and human rights of young people in the United States through educating people about youth rights, working with public officials and empowering young people to work on their own behalf. We believe certain basic rights are intrinsic parts of American citizenship and transcend age or status limits." National Youth Rights Association, "About Us," Jan. 18, 2007, http://www.youthrights.org.

18. Chela Sandoval presents this as "the equal rights form of consciousness-in opposition" in Sandoval, *Methodology of the Oppressed* (Minneapolis: University of Minnesota Press, 2000). Jane Mansbridge also emphasizes the centrality of the perception that existing inequalities are unjust to the formation of oppositional consciousness in Jane Mansbridge, "Complicating Oppositional Consciousness," in Mansbridge and Morris, *Oppositional Consciousness.*

19. Mary Bernstein, "Celebration and Suppression: The Strategic Uses of Identity by the Lesbian and Gay Movement," *American Journal of Sociology* 103, no. 3 (1997).

20. Patricia Hill Collins, *Black Feminist Thought: Knowledge, Consciousness and the Politics of Empowerment* (New York: Routledge, 1990); Nancy C. M. Hartsock, "The Feminist Standpoint: Developing the Ground for a Specifically Feminist Historical Materialism," in *The Second Wave: A Reader in Feminist Theory,* ed. Linda Nicholson (New York: Routledge, 1997 [1983]).

21. Karl Mannheim, "The Problem of Generations" in *Essays on the Sociology of Knowledge* (New York: Routledge and Paul, 1952).

22. Richard G. Braungart and Margaret M. Braungart, "Life-Course and Generational Politics," *Annual Review of Sociology* 12 (1986), 215.

23. Defining a generational identity is a very fuzzy prospect and is often region-specific. But, many demographers generally agree on the rough outlines of this generation as being those born between approximately 1980 and 2000. The girls in this study are right in the middle of this generational construct, which is perhaps most relevant in the United States and Canada, but not without salience in Latin America.

24. Jean M. Twenge, *Generation Me: Why Today's Young Americans Are More Confident, Assertive, Entitled—and More Miserable Than Ever Before* (New York: Free Press, 2006); Neil Howe and William Strauss, *Millennials Rising: The Next Great Generation* (New York: Vintage Books, 2000); Don Tapscott, *Growing up Digital: The Rise of the Net Generation* (New York: McGraw-Hill, 1998); Mike Males, *Framing Youth: Ten Myths About the Next Generation* (Monroe, ME: Common Courage Press, 1999).

25. Much of what is "new" about the political struggles that make up the social movement context for many of the girl activists is well captured in Day, *Gramsci Is Dead*.

26. For a review of this literature, see Braungart and Braungart, "Life-Course and Generational Politics."

27. Mike A. Males, *The Scapegoat Generation: America's War on Adolescents* (Monroe, ME: Common Courage Press, 1996); Males, *Framing Youth*.

28. For a discussion of the idea of "trickle-up political socialization," in which young people's political engagement inspires more engagement from their parents, see Amy Linimon and Mark R. Joslyn, "Trickle up Political Socialization: The Impact of Kids Voting USA on Voter Turnout in Kansas," *State Politics and Policy Quarterly* 2, no. 1 (2002).

29. For brief summaries of some of these youth-led struggles, see Timothy Hatfield, "Chile's Student Protests and the Democratization of a Semi-Democratic Society," Council on Hemispheric Affairs, 2006, http://www.coha.org/2006/07/06/chile%e2%80%99s-student-protests-and-the-democratization-of-a-semi-democratic-society/; Aisha Labi, "Greek Students Protest Proposals to Reform Universities," *Chronicle of Higher Education*, June 23, 2006; Elaine Sciolino, "French Protests over Youth Labor Law Spread to 150 Cities and Towns," *New York Times*, Mar. 19, 2006.

30. Braungart and Braungart, "Life-Course and Generational Politics," 210.

NOTES TO CHAPTER 4

1. Yasmin Jiwani, Candis Steenbergen, and Claudia Mitchell, "Girlhood: Surveying the Terrain," in *Girlhood: Redefining the Limits*, ed. Yasmin Jiwani, Candis Steenbergen, and Claudia Mitchell (Montreal: Black Rose Books, 2006); Aapola, Gonick, and Harris, *Young Femininity*; Driscoll, *Girls*.

2. The dominance of girls within high school activism is confirmed by both Mattie Weiss and Daniel Hosang in their studies of youth-organizing groups within the United States. Daniel Hosang, "Youth and Community Organizing Today," (New York: The Funders Collaborative on Youth Organizing, 2003); Weiss, "Youth Rising."

3. Nicholas O. Alozie, James Simon, and Bruce D. Merrill, "Gender and Political Orientation in Childhood," *Social Science Journal* 40 (2003); Oren Pizmony-Levy, "Youth Support for Social-Movements in 28 Countries" (paper presented at the American Sociological Association Annual Meeting, New York, 2007); Debi Roker, "Young Women and Social

Action in the United Kingdom," in *Next Wave Cultures: Feminism, Subcultures, Activism*, ed. Anita Harris (New York: Routledge, 2008); Ariadne Vromen, "Traversing Time and Gender: Australian Young People's Participation," *Journal of Youth Studies* 6 (2003).

4. Angela McRobbie and Jenny Garber, "Girls and Subcultures," in *Resistance through Rituals: Youth Subcultures in Post-War Britain*, ed. Stuart Hall and Tony Jefferson (New York: Routledge, 1976); Angela McRobbie and Mica Nava, eds. *Gender and Generation* (London: Macmillan, 1984); Christine Griffin, *Representations of Youth* (Cambridge: Polity, 1993); Mary Celeste Kearney, "Producing Girls: Rethinking the Study of Female Youth Culture," in Inness, *Delinquents and Debutantes*; LeBlanc, *Pretty in Punk*; McRobbie, *Feminism and Youth Culture*.

5. Carol Hardy-Fanta, *Latina Politics, Latino Politics: Gender, Culture, and Political Participation in Boston* (Philadelphia: Temple University Press, 1993); Nancy Naples, *Grassroots Warriors: Activist Mothering, Community Work and the War on Poverty* (New York: Routledge, 1998).

6. Aapola, Gonick, and Harris, *Young Femininity*, 91 and 176.

7. Boocock and Scott, *Kids in Context*, 176.

8. Currie, Kelly, and Pomerantz, "Geeks Shall Inherit the Earth," 422.

9. Kelly, Pomerantz, and Currie, "Skater Girlhood and Emphasized Femininity"; LeBlanc, *Pretty in Punk*.

10. Maira and Soep, introduction to *Youthscapes*, xxvi.

11. American Psychological Association Task Force on the Sexualization of Girls, *Report of the A.P.A. Task Force on the Sexualization of Girls* (Washington, DC: American Psychological Association, 2007); Sharon Lamb and Lyn Mikel Brown, *Packaging Girlhood: Rescuing Our Daughters from Marketers' Schemes* (New York: St. Martin's Press, 2006).

12. Girls' self-regard and self-esteem are shaped not only by gender but by race, class, and other contexts for their lives. Images of dominant (white, middle class) girlhood do not have the same impact on all girls. Sumru Erkut et al., "Diversity in Girls' Experiences: Feeling Good About Who You Are," in *Urban Girls: Resisting Stereotypes, Creating Identities*, ed. Bonnie J. Ross Leadbeater and Niobe Way (New York: New York University Press, 1996).

13. A significant amount of research in girls' studies has addressed girls' responses to and resistant readings of media discourses of girlhood. Meenakshi Gigi Durham, "Articulating Adolescent Girls' Resistance to Patriarchal Discourse in Popular Media," *Women's Studies in Communication* 22, no. 2 (1999); Currie, *Girl Talk*; Lyn Mikel Brown, *Raising Their Voices: The Politics of Girls' Anger* (Cambridge, MA: Harvard University Press, 1998).

14. Mary Celeste Kearney offers an extensive analysis of how media literacy programs have a protectionist approach to girlhood and thereby unintentionally disempower girls. She contrasts such programs with projects aimed at encouraging girls' media production as a tool for critical and empowered relationships to media. Kearney, *Girls Make Media*.

15. Kelly, Pomerantz, and Currie, "Skater Girlhood and Emphasized Femininity," 238.

16. Lyn Mikel Brown, *Girlfighting: Betrayal and Rejection among Girls* (New York: New York University Press, 2003); Meda Chesney-Lind and Katherine Irwin, "From Badness to Meanness: Popular Constructions of Contemporary Girlhood," in Harris, *All About the Girl*.

17. Some examples of this concern include Brown and Gilligan, *Meeting at the Crossroads*; Orenstein, *Schoolgirls*; Pipher, *Reviving Ophelia*. For a critique of the "Ophelia industry" that has emerged from this discourse, see Aapola, Gonick, and Harris, *Young Femininity*.

18. Brown, *Girlfighting*, 33.

19. Karen Wells notes the "iconic status in Western imagery of the child as the embodiment of innocence and playfulness and hope for the future." Karen Wells, "Narratives of Liberation and Narratives of Innocent Suffering: The Rhetorical Uses of Images of Iraqi Children in the British Press," *Visual Communication* 6, no. 1 (2007): 55. But this imagery often obscures many children's experiences of and knowledge about inequality, oppression, and exploitation.

20. Ann Bookman and Sandra Morgen, "Rethinking Women and Politics: An Introductory Essay," in *Women and the Politics of Empowerment*, ed. Sandra Bookman and Ann Morgen (Philadelphia: Temple University Press, 1988); Cathy J. Cohen, Kathleen B. Jones, and Joan C. Tronto, "Introduction: Women Transforming U.S. Politics: Sites of Power/Resistance," in *Women Transforming Politics: An Alternative Reader*, ed. Cathy J. Cohen, Kathleen B. Jones, and Joan C. Tronto (New York: New York University Press, 1997).

21. Jean Bethke Elshtain, *Public Man Private Woman: Women in Social and Political Thought* (Princeton: Princeton University Press, 1981); Carol Pateman, "Feminist Critiques of the Public/Private Dichotomy," in *Public and Private in Social Life*, ed. S. I. Benn and G. F. Gaus (London: Croom Helm, 1985); Anne Phillips, introduction to *Feminism and Politics*, ed. Anne Phillips (Oxford: Oxford University Press, 1998).

22. For a discussion of this dynamic, see chap. 7 of Driscoll, *Girls*.

NOTES TO CHAPTER 5

1. Rhoda E. Howard-Hassmann, *Compassionate Canadians: Civic Leaders Discuss Human Rights* (Toronto: University of Toronto Press, 2003); Eva Mackey, *The House of Difference: Cultural Politics and National Identity in Canada* (New York: Routledge, 1999).

2. Hosang, "Youth and Community Organizing Today."

3. Weiss, "Youth Rising," 93.

4. For a discussion of the paucity of spaces for "public-spirited" conversation and political talk in the United States, see Nina Eliasoph, *Avoiding Politics: How Americans Produce Apathy in Everyday Life* (New York: Cambridge University Press, 1998).

5. Hosang, "Youth and Community Organizing Today."

6. Saul D. Alinsky, *Rules for Radicals: A Practical Primer for Realistic Radicals* (New York: Vintage Books, 1989 [1971]); Delgado, *Beyond the Politics of Place*; Rinku Sen, *Stir It Up: Lessons in Community Organizing and Advocacy* (San Francisco: Jossey-Bass, 2003).

7. Sen, *Stir It Up*, lxiii.

8. Ibid., 165.

9. Social science and historical research on the Latin American Left is extensive. A few of the many discussions of this extensive political culture include Donald C. Hodges, *Mexican Anarchism after the Revolution* (Austin: University of Texas Press, 1995); Evelina Dagnino, "Culture, Citizenship and Democracy: Changing Discourses and Practices of the Latin American Left," in *Cultures of Politics, Politics of Cultures: Re-Visioning Latin American Social Movements*, ed. Sonia E. Alvarez, Evelina Dagnino, and Arturo Escobar (Boulder, CO: Westview Press, 1998); Jorge G. Castañeda, *Utopia Unarmed: The Latin American Left after the Cold War* (New York: Vintage Books, 1994); James Petras, *The Left Strikes Back: Class Conflict in Latin America in the Age of Neoliberalism* (Boulder, CO: Westview Press, 1999).

10. Whether reading collectively or individually, girl activists usually said that they chose to read books and articles that had been recommended to them by someone else from their political community. Thus, one girl's interaction with Kropotkin based on the recommendation of an older youth activist might then lead to other girls in her collective reading the same material at a later date. They share ideas about what to read (and actual books) with each other, which encourages them to build a shared political vocabulary.

11. Herbert Marcuse, *An Essay on Liberation* (Boston: Beacon Press, 1969), 17.

12. Ibid., 4–5.

13. Ibid., 31.

14. Ibid., 79.

15. Jeff Goodwin and James M. Jasper, eds., *Rethinking Social Movements: Structure, Meaning, and Emotion* (Lanham, MD: Rowman and Littlefield, 2003); Jeff Goodwin, James M. Jasper, and Francesca Polletta, eds., *Passionate Politics: Emotions and Social Movements* (Chicago: University Of Chicago Press, 2001); Jasper, *Art of Moral Protest*; Jeff Goodwin, "The Libidinal Constitution of a High-Risk Social Movement: Affectual Ties and Solidarity in the Huk Rebellion, 1946–1954," *American Sociological Review* 62, no. 1 (1997); Cheryl Hercus, "Identity, Emotion, and Feminist Collective Action," *Gender and Society* 13, no. 1 (1999); Verta Taylor, "Watching for Vibes: Bringing Emotions into the Study of Feminist Organizations," in *Feminist Organizations: Harvest of the New Women's Movement*, ed. Myra Marx Ferree and Patricia Yancey Martin (Philadelphia: Temple University Press, 1995).

16. Jasper, *Art of Moral Protest*; Verta Taylor and Leila J. Rupp, "Loving Internationalism: The Emotion Culture of Transnational Women's Organizations, 1888–1945," *Mobilization: An International Journal* 7, no. 2 (2002).

17. Jasper and Poulsen, "Recruiting Strangers and Friends"; Jasper, *Art of Moral Protest*.

18. Audre Lorde, *Sister Outsider* (Trumansburg, NY: The Crossing Press, 1984); Verta Taylor and Nancy Whittier, "Analytical Approaches to Social Movement Culture: The Culture of the Women's Movement," in *Social Movements and Culture*, ed. Hank Johnston and Bert Klandermans (Minneapolis: University of Minnesota Press, 1995); William A. Gamson, "Constructing Social Protest," in Johnson and Klandermans, *Social Movements and Culture*.

19. See, for example, Hercus, "Identity, Emotion, and Feminist Collective Action."

20. Brown, *Raising Their Voices*, 12.

21. This idea of a politics rooted in love is certainly not new. From Che Guevara's often quoted (including by several girl activists) statement that "the true revolutionary is guided by great feelings of love" to Chela Sandoval's analysis of love as a hermeneutics of social change, the idea of love as central to oppositional subjectivity has been a recurring theme in radical theory and activism. See Sandoval, *Methodology of the Oppressed*, 140–57.

22. Georg Lukács, *History and Class Consciousness*, trans. Rodney Livingstone (Boston: MIT Press, 1972).

23. Thomas Olesen, "The Zapatistas and Transnational Framing," in Johnson and Almeida, *Latin American Social Movements*.

24. Jordan Camp, "Zapatismo and Autonomous Social Movements: Reading the Communiqués Politically" (unpublished masters thesis, University of California at Santa Barbara, 2006), 14.

25. Callahan, "Why Not Share a Dream," 13.

26. Honor Ford-Smith, "Ring Ding in a Tight Corner: Sistren, Collective Democracy, and the Organization of Cultural Production," in *Feminist Genealogies, Colonial Legacies, Democratic Futures*, ed. M. Jacqui Alexander and Chandra Talpade Mohanty (New York: Routledge, 1997); Michelle Rosenthal, "Danger Talk: Race and Feminist Empowerment in the New South Africa," in *Feminism and Anti-Racism: International Struggles for Justice*, ed. France Winddance Twine and Kathleen M. Blee (New York: New York University Press); Amrita Basu, ed., *The Challenge of Local Feminisms: Women's Movements in Global Perspective* (Boulder, CO: Westview Press, 1995).

27. Susan Stall and Randy Stoecker, "Community Organizing or Organizing Community: Gender and the Crafts of Empowerment," *Gender and Society* 12, no. 6 (1998): 746.

28. Sitrin, *Horizontalism*, viii.

29. John Holloway, "Zapatismo Urbano," *Humboldt Journal of Social Relations* 29, no. 1 (2005): 171.

30. Mansbridge and Morris, *Oppositional Consciousness*.

NOTES TO CHAPTER 6

1. For more on the development and meaning of horizontalism in Argentina, see Sitrin, *Horizontalism*. Sitrin frequently maintains the use of the Spanish word, *horizontalidad*, in her work, arguing that it can not be fully captured by the translation to horizontalism, because it is "a new way of relating, based on affective politics, and against all the of the implications of isms" (vi). This is a compelling argument, but I choose to use horizontalism in this book because, for the girl activists I studied, it is a practice and approach that is not entirely rooted in its specific meanings and locations within Argentina. While my participant Marina is explicitly referring to the Argentine *horizontalidad*, many of the other girls in this study demonstrate an affinity for a less specific horizontalism.

2. For discussions on the distinctions between power as coercion (or power-over) and power as capacity (or power-to), particularly as these relate to political organization and engagement, see Martha Acklesberg, "Rethinking Anarchism/Rethinking Power: A Contemporary Feminist Perspective," in *Reconstructing Political Theory: Feminist Perspectives*, ed. Mary Lyndon Shanley and Uma Narayan (University Park, PA: Pennsylvania State University Press, 1997); Holloway, *Change the World*; Anna Yeatman, "Feminism and Power," in Shanley and Narayan, *Reconstructing Political Theory*.

3. This divide between the traditional parties and the autonomous movements in Argentina is not just found in student organizing, but exists across the board. For more on the autonomous movements, including (but not limited to) the *piquetero* movements, the neighborhood assemblies, and the well-recognized reclaimed factory movement, see Sitrin, *Horizontalism*; Cooperativa de Trabajo Lavaca, *Sin Patrón: Stories from Argentina's Worker-Run Factories*, trans. Katherine Kohlstedt (Chicago: Haymarket Books, 2007).

4. Massimo De Angelis, "PR Like Process! Strategy from the Bottom-Up," *Ephemera: Theory and Politics in Organization* 5, no. 2 (2005).

5. Ibid., 196.

6. Ibid., 204.

7. Sitrin, *Horizontalism*, vi.

8. Ibid., 3.

9. Jasper refers to some of the choices (and challenges) that girl activists face around participation as "the extension dilemma," indicating some of the reasons that some movements take a different approach. James M. Jasper "A Strategic Approach to Collective Action: Looking for Agency in Social Movement Choices," *Mobilization: An International Journal* 9, no. 1 (2004).

10. Robert D. Putnam, *Bowling Alone: The Collapse and Revival of American Community* (New York: Simon and Schuster, 2000).

11. For a discussion of some images of self-centered and isolated teens, see Susannah R. Stern, "Self-Absorbed, Dangerous, and Disengaged: What Popular Films Tell Us About Teenagers," *Mass Communication and Society* 8, no. 1 (2005).

12. Ken J. Rotenberg and Shelley Hymel, eds., *Loneliness in Childhood and Adolescence* (New York: Cambridge University Press, 1999).

13. Stuart Hall and Tony Jefferson, eds., *Resistance through Rituals: Youth Subcultures in Post-War Britain* (New York: Routledge, 1975); LeBlanc, *Pretty in Punk*.

14. On the pleasures of protest and solidarity and their role in sustaining activist identities, see Barbara Epstein, *Political Protest and Cultural Revolution: Nonviolent Direct Action in the 1970s and 1980s* (Berkeley: University of California Press, 1993); Jasper, *Art of Moral Protest*; Temma Kaplan, *Taking Back the Streets: Women, Youth and Direct Democracy* (Berkeley: University of California Press, 2004).

15. Ben Shepard, "The Use of Joyfulness as a Community Organizing Strategy," *Peace and Change* 30, no. 4 (2005). See also Starr, *Global Revolt*, 239–45; Holloway, "Zapatismo Urbano."

16. Subcomandante Marcos, "Urgent Telegram to Civil Society," in *Ya Basta! Ten Years of the Zapatista Uprising*, ed. Ziga Vodovnik (Oakland: AK Press, 2004), 240.

17. Jasper, *Art of Moral Protest*, 183–209.

18. For a review of the research on the importance of peer group relationships to adolescents, see Barbara M. Newman, Brenda J. Lohman, and Philip R. Newman, "Peer Group Membership and a Sense of Belonging: Their Relationship to Adolescent Behavior Problems," *Adolescence* 42, no. 166 (2007).

19. Some of the many texts on the importance of relationships to girls include Brown and Gilligan, *Meeting at the Crossroads*; Jill McLean Taylor, Carol Gilligan, and Amy Sullivan, *Between Voice and Silence: Women and Girls, Race and Relationship* (Cambridge, MA: Harvard University Press, 1995).

20. Sitrin, *Horizontalism*, vii.

21. For analyses of girls' social aggression and "meanness" see Brown, *Girlfighting*; Chesney-Lind and Irwin, "From Badness to Meanness."

22. Research on the stratification of adolescent peer groups within high schools is extensive. A few examples include Bettie, *Women without Class*; Pamela J. Bettis, Debra Jordan, and Diane Montgomery, "Girls in Groups: The Preps and the Sex Mob Try out for Womanhood," in *Geographies of Girlhood: Identities in-Between*, ed. Pamela J. Bettis and Natalie G. Adams (Mahwah, NJ: Lawrence Erlbaum Associates, 2005); Penelope Eckert, *Jocks and Burnouts: Social Categories and Identity in the High School* (New York: Teachers College Press, 1989); Donna Eder, *School Talk: Gender and Adolescent Culture* (New Brunswick: Rutgers University Press, 1995).

23. Valerie Hey argues that it is primarily "between and amongst girls as friends that identities are variously practiced, appropriated, resisted, and negotiated." Hey, *The Company She Keeps*, 30. For a review of the literature on the role of friendships in girls' identity formation, see Aapola, Gonick, and Harris, *Young Femininity*.

24. This is not to say that all adult organizations are less friendly and supportive than youth organizations, but rather to point out how noticeably harmonious, warm, and loving these communities appeared.

25. Francesca Polletta, *Freedom Is an Endless Meeting: Democracy in American Social Movements* (Chicago: University of Chicago Press, 2002).

26. Ibid.

27. Chittaroopa Palit, "Monsoon Risings: Mega-Dam Resistance in the Narmada Valley," in Mertes, *Movement of Movements*; David Graeber, "The New Anarchists," in Mertes, *Movement of Movements*; M. P. Parameswaran, "Participatory Democracy," in *Another World Is Possible: Popular Alternatives to Globalization at the World Social Forum*, ed. Thomas Ponniah (New York: Zed Books, 2003).

28. De Angelis, "PR Like Process! Strategy from the Bottom Up," 197.

29. Randy Schutt, "Consensus Is Not Unanimity: Making Decisions Cooperatively," Vernal Project, http://www.vernalproject.org/papers/process/ConsensusNotUnanimity.html.

30. Polletta, *Freedom Is an Endless Meeting*, 7.

31. Jo Freeman, "The Tyranny of Structurelessness," *Berkeley Journal of Sociology* 17 (1972). For a more recent discussion, Dylan Rodriguez and Nancy Stoller, "Reflections on Critical Resistance," *Social Justice* 27, no. 3 (2000).

32. Jean Lau Chin et al., eds., *Women and Leadership: Transforming Visions and Diverse Voices* (Malden, MA: Blackwell, 2007); Robnett, *How Long? How Long?*

33. Judy Schoenberg and Kimberlee Salmond, "Exploring Girls' Leadership," (New York: Girl Scouts of the USA, 2007), 15. See also Dawn M. Shinew and Deborah Thomas Jones, "Girl Talk: Adolescent Girls' Perceptions of Leadership," in *Geographies of Girlhood: Identities In-Between*, ed. Pamela J. Bettis and Natalie G. Adams (Mahwah, NJ: Lawrence Erlbaum Associates, 2005).

34. "The New Girls' Movement: Charting the Path" (New York: Ms. Foundation for Women, 2000), 6.

35. Some girls who work outside of this more collaborative model feel it is important that they show how girls can be assertive and in charge. Valentina, for example, argued that it is important to have girls in official leadership positions because it shows "that we are equal to men, and that we can do the same things." Girls, she suggested, should be able to take on non-feminized leadership roles. They should not be constrained to the cooperative model. She also noted she felt like other students hated her because she was acting against gendered norms of behavior by being too assertive, too "in charge," and too dominant.

36. Only a few girl activists had an approach to leadership that did not place substantial emphasis on sharing power and moving toward more egalitarian relationships. This included a group of Vancouver girls who felt that they had "too many" formal leaders in their organization and a couple of Buenos Aires teens who were the elected leaders of their student centers.

37. For just a few of the many discussions of inequalities within social movement organizations and spaces, see Elizabeth (Betita) Martinez, "Does Anti-War Have to Be Anti-Racist Too?" *RaceWire*, Aug. 2003, http://www.arc.org/racewire/030812e_martinez_a.html.; Bernice Johnson Reagon, "Coalition Politics: Turning the Century," in *Home Girls: A Black Feminist Anthology*, ed. Barbara Smith (New York: Kitchen Table Press, 1983); Stockdill, "Forging a Multi-Dimensional Oppositional Consciousness"; Kristine Wong, "Shutting Us Out: Race, Class and the Framing of a Movement," in *Confronting Capitalism: Dispatches from a Global Movement*, ed. Eddie Yuen, Daniel Burton-Rose, and George Katsiaficas (New York: Soft Skull Press, 2004).

38. The feminist literature discussing the various tensions around race, class, gender, and sexuality within this previous wave of movements includes: The Combahee River Collective, "The Combahee River Collective Statement," in *Home Girls: A Black Feminist Anthology*, ed. Barbara Smith (New York: Kitchen Table Press, 1983); Winifred Breines, *The Trouble between Us: An Uneasy History of White and Black Women in the Feminist Movement* (New York: Oxford University Press, 2006); Audre Lorde, *Sister Outsider* (Trumansburg, NY: The Crossing Press, 1984); Cherrie Moraga and Gloria Anzaldua, eds., *This Bridge Called My Back: Writings by Radical Women of Color* (New York: Kitchen Table Press, 1983); Benita Roth, *Separate Roads to Feminism: Black, Chicana, and White Feminist Movements in America's Second Wave* (New York: Cambridge University Press, 2004).

39. Weiss, "Youth Rising," 94.

40. Tamara and Niamh were girls I met at an activist event in San Diego. Although San Diego is not exactly the same political context as the San Francisco Bay Area, some of the dynamics around the history of race, class, and gender issues splitting social movements are very similar. These girls were also quite similar to the Bay Area teens in terms of the level of reflection about the issues of power and difference within movements. Therefore, I include Tamara and Niamh's comments here.

41. Dionne Brand, *Bread out of Stone: Recollections on Sex, Recognitions, Race, Dreaming and Politics* (Toronto: Coach House Press, 1994).

42. Ibid.

43. Obviously, each of these countries has its own unique racial and ethnic history and distinctive, complex contemporary racial formations. Several recent books, articles, and edited collections in English address issues of racial formation and racialization in Latin America from a comparative perspective, including George Reid Andrews, *Afro-Latin America, 1800–2000* (New York: Oxford University Press, 2004); Nancy P. Appelbaum, Anne S. Macpherson, and Karin Alejandra Rosemblatt, eds., *Race and Nation in Modern Latin America* (Chapel Hill: University of North Carolina Press, 2003); Jean Rahier, "The Study of Latin American Racial Formations: Different Approaches and Different Contexts," *Latin American Research Review* 39, no. 3 (2004).

44. The main exception to this is Yelitza, an Afro-Colombian girl I met at the World Social Forum.

45. This also may be, at least in part, a result of my more thoroughly outsider status. These girls may have chosen not to share things that would make their groups look less functional. Given my brief time in each location, I was not necessarily able to observe enough of each organization to sufficiently see the internal racial dynamics, nor to have known exactly the right questions to ask to elicit their comments on these topics.

46. Jean Muteba Rahier, "Mestizaje, Mulataje, Mestifagem in Latin American Ideologies of National Identities," *Journal of Latin American Anthropology* 8, no. 1 (2003): 42.

47. Marina Sitrin describes this moment of convergence between the two different movements based in two different classes. Sitrin, *Horizontalism*. Other scholars, and several of the adult activists I spoke with in Buenos Aires, however, have noted that the relationships between these two forces were not (and are not now) necessarily smooth. Elizabeth Borland has discussed some of the differences in framing and tensions between women's groups from different classes: Elizabeth Borland, "Feminist and Non-Feminist Framing in Argentina" (paper presented at the Collective Behavior and Social Movements Workshop, Hofstra University, 2007).

48. See, for example, Mohanty, "Under Western Eyes."

49. Alma Garcia, in her discussion of Chicana feminisms, notes that Anglos often present machismo, as a cultural force, as a rational for the problems faced by Chicanos, rather than looking to the structural dynamics of inequality. Alma M. Garcia, "The Development of Chicana Feminist Discourse, 1970–1980," *Gender and Society* 3, no. 2 (1989). The Western (feminist) assumptions of the patriarchal nature of third-world cultures have also been extensively analyzed in Uma Narayan, *Dislocating Cultures: Identities, Traditions, and Third-World Feminism* (New York: Routledge, 1997).

50. Lorde, *Sister Outsider*; Maria Lugones, "Playfulness, 'World'-Travelling, and Loving Perception," in *Feminist Social Thought: A Reader*, ed. Diana Tietjens Meyers (New York: Routledge, 1997); Sandoval, *Methodology of the Oppressed*.

51. Francesca Polletta outlines the hopes and failures of a feminist participatory democratic process within the U.S. women's movement in *Freedom Is an Endless Meeting*. Other discussions of the feminist commitments to democracy and communal politics both inside and outside of their movements include M. Jacqui Alexander and Chandra Talpade Mohanty, "Introduction: Genealogies, Legacies, Movements," in *Feminist Genealogies, Colonial Legacies, Democratic Futures*, ed. M. Jacqui Alexander and Chandra Talpade Mohanty (New York: Routledge, 1997); Jill M. Bystydzienski and Joti Sekhon, eds., *Democratization and Women's Grassroots Movements* (Bloomington: Indiana University Press, 1999); Catherine Eschle, *Global Democracy, Social Movements, and Feminism* (Boulder, CO: Westview Press, 2001).

52. Epstein, *Political Protest and Cultural Revolution*.

NOTES TO CHAPTER 7

1. Holloway, *Change the World Without Taking Power*, 6.

2. Ibid., 8.

3. R. Solnit, *Hope in the Dark*, 16.

4. See Avery Gordon's "Some Thoughts on the Utopian" for a discussion of the power of the dismissal in the "merely utopian," and Holloway for commentary on how the (youthful, initial) scream of horror-and-hope is silenced as "foolish." Avery F. Gordon, *Keeping Good Time: Reflections on Knowledge, Power, and People* (Boulder, CO: Paradigm Publishers, 2004); Holloway, *Change the World without Taking Power*.

5. Sarah S. Amsler, "Pedagogy against Disutopia: From Conscientization to the Education of Desire" (paper presented at the American Sociological Association Annual Meeting, New York, 2007).

6. Mark Coté, Richard J. F. Day, and Greig De Peuter, "Introduction: What Is Utopian Pedagogy," in *Utopian Pedagogy: Radical Experiments against Neoliberal Globalization*, ed. Mark Coté, Richard J. F. Day, and Greig De Peuter (Toronto: University of Toronto Press, 2007), 13.

7. Gordon, *Keeping Good Time*, 126.

8. R. Solnit, *Hope in the Dark*, 15–17.

9. Robin D. G. Kelley, *Freedom Dreams: The Black Radical Imagination* (Boston: Beacon Press, 2002), 10.

10. Gordon, *Keeping Good Time*, 117.

11. Gregory Wilpert analyzes the policies and institutions that the Chavez government has been enacting in order to delineate one set of meanings for this concept. This version of socialism imagined and enacted by the state is not, however, the only version that circulates. Wilpert, *Changing Venezuela by Taking Power*.

12. Starting with Engels's "Socialism: Utopian and Scientific," some groups have used "utopian" as a pejorative term for forms of socialist thought and action that they disagree with. The scientific/utopian divide has been a powerful discursive tool in sectarian debates and Leftist infighting.

13. The critiques of liberal multiculturalism are quite extensive and not limited to its failures to address racism, inequality, and power. They also include criticisms of the tendencies toward cultural essentialism and bureaucratic, top-down management of difference. See, for example, David Theo Goldberg, ed., *Multiculturalism: A Critical Reader* (Cambridge, MA: Blackwell, 1994); Avery F. Gordon and Christopher Newfield, eds., *Mapping Multiculturalism* (Minneapolis: University of Minnesota Press, 1996); Vijay Prashad, *Everybody Was Kung Fu Fighting: Afro-Asian Connections and the Myth of Cultural Purity* (Boston: Beacon Press, 2001).

14. Kelley, *Freedom Dreams*, xi.

15. In English, see Eduardo Galeano, *Walking Words*, trans. Mark Fried (New York: W. W. Norton and Company, 1997). In Spanish, Eduardo Galeano, *Las Palabras Andantes* (Mexico D.F.: Siglo 21, 1993).

16. Naomi Klein, "Reclaiming the Commons," in Mertes, *Movement of Movements*, 228.

17. R. Solnit, *Hope in the Dark*, 84.

18. Frances Fox Piven, *Challenging Authority: How Ordinary People Change America* (Lanham, MD: Rowman and Littlefield, 2006).

19. J. K. Taft, "'I'm Not a Politics Person,' Teenage Girls, Oppositional Consciousness, and the Meaning of Politics," *Politics and Gender* 2: 329–52.

20. Klein, "Reclaiming the Commons."

21. Gregory Wilpert's book *Changing Venezuela By Taking Power* is both a discussion of Venezuelan politics and, as he stated in an interview on the book, "an indirect polemic with John Holloway's notion. . . . I try to show that it is possible to change the world for the better by taking (state) power and that the Venezuelan experience even shows that such state power might be necessary if we want to achieve social justice now, rather than in a century or so." "Znet Book Interview with Gregory Wilpert," *ZNet*, Sept. 21 2007, http://www.zmag.org/content/showarticle.cfm?ItemID=13835.

22. Mansbridge and Morris, eds., *Oppositional Consciousness.*

23. R. Solnit, *Hope in the Dark*, 58.

24. Gordon, *Keeping Good Time*, 123.

1. Given the changes in girls' lives over the past few years and their varying levels of access to the Internet, I do not have functioning email addresses for all of the participants. The recent request for updates was sent to (and not bounced back from) only fifty-four of the seventy-five girls. Of those, seventeen responded within a few weeks.

2. Harris, *Future Girl*.

3. Amy L. Best, *Fast Cars, Cool Rides: The Accelerating World of Youth and Their Cars* (New York: New York University Press, 2006), 164.

4. Dick Hebdige, *Subculture: The Meaning of Style* (London: Metheun and Co., 1979); LeBlanc, *Pretty in Punk*; Sunaina Maira, *Desis in the House: Indian American Youth Culture in New York City* (Philadelphia: Temple University Press, 2002); David Muggleton, *Inside Subculture: The Postmodern Meaning of Style* (Oxford: Berg, 2000).

5. Gordon, *Keeping Good Time*, 123.

6. Amsler, "Pedagogy against Disutopia"; Coté, Day, and De Peuter, "Introduction: What Is Utopian Pedagogy"; Henry A. Giroux, "Utopian Thinking in Dangerous Times: Critical Pedagogy and the Project of Educated Hope," in Coté, Day, and De Peuter, *Utopian Pedagogy*; Gordon, *Keeping Good Time*; R. Solnit, *Hope in the Dark*.

7. Polletta, *Freedom Is an Endless Meeting*.

8. Barry N. Checkoway, "Adults as Allies," (Battle Creek, MI: W. K. Kellogg Foundation, 1996), 13.

9. Jenny Sazama, "Get the Word Out!" (Somerville, MA: Youth On Board, 2001), 3.

10. Jill M. Bystydzienski and Steven P. Schacht, eds., *Forging Radical Alliances across Difference: Coalition Politics for the New Millennium* (New York: Rowman and Littlefield, 2001), 7.

11. Maria Lugones, "Purity, Impurity and Separation," *Signs* 19, no. 2 (1994); Lorde, *Sister Outsider*; Reagon, "Coalition Politics"; Bonnie Thornton Dill, "Race, Class and Gender: Prospects for an All-Inclusive Sisterhood," *Feminist Studies* 9, no.1 (1983).

12. Stockdill, "Forging a Multi-Dimensional Oppositional Consciousness"; Wong, "Shutting Us Out"; in *Confronting Capitalism: Dispatches from a Global Movement*, ed. Eddie Yuen, Daniel Burton-Rose, and George Katsiaficas (New York: Soft Skull Press, 2004); Elizabeth (Betita) Martinez, "Does Anti-War Have to Be Anti-Racist Too."

13. Evidence of this increased foundational interest in youth leadership, "engagement," and organizing can be seen in the shifts within funding for youth issues around the world. According to the International Youth Foundation's 1998 annual report, only about 3 percent of their grants went to youth leadership and engagement, while their 2006 annual report says that nearly a third of grants went to programs in this area. These reports can be found at www.iyfnet.org. Information on the funding dynamics of youth organizing in the United States can also be found from the Funders' Collaborative on Youth Organizing: www.fcyo.org.

14. For an extensive discussion on the problems of nonprofit status, the formal requirements that nonprofits must meet, and the ways that this places substantial limits on social movement organizations, including but not limited to youth organizations, see Incite! Women of Color Against Violence, ed., *The Revolution Will Not Be Funded: Beyond the Non-Profit Industrial Complex* (Cambridge, MA: South End Press, 2007).

15. Several youth activist organizations in the United States have begun working on educating adults on these issues and on becoming better allies for youth. The Freechild Project offers an extensive bibliography for adults on this topic. "Reading List for Adult Allies of Young People," Freechild Project, 2007, http://www.freechild.org/ReadingList/adultallies.htm.

NOTES TO METHODOLOGICAL APPENDIX

1. Jessica K. Taft, "Racing Age: Reflections on Anti-Racist Research with Teenage Girls," in *Representing Youth: Methodological Dilemmas in Critical Youth Studies*, ed. Amy L. Best (New York: New York University Press, 2007).

2. Some of the texts that have been particularly important to my own thinking about research include Amy L. Best, ed., *Representing Youth*; Bettie, *Women without Class*; Patricia Clough, *The End(S)of Ethnography: From Realism to Social Criticism* (New York: Peter Lang, 1998); France Winddance Twine and Jonathon W. Warren, eds., *Racing Research, Researching Race: Methodological Dilemmas in Critical Race Studies* (New York: New York University Press, 2000); Diane L. Wolf, ed., *Feminist Dilemmas in Fieldwork* (Boulder, CO: Westview Press, 1996).

3. Donna Haraway, "Situated Knowledges: The Science Question in Feminism and the Privilege of Partial Perspective," *Feminist Studies* 14, no. 3 (1988).

4. Taft, "Racing Age."

5. Diane L. Wolf, "Situating Feminist Dilemmas in Fieldwork," in Wolf, *Feminist Dilemmas*, 19.

6. Ibid., 21.

Index

Ableism, 28

Accountability, corporate, 27

Action, 3, 45, 182; activism and, 31–33; adult inaction and, 64–65, 68, 69; direct, 35, 36, 164; internally focused, planning, 185–86; planning, 63; socially responsible, 35; state-based political, 164; theory and, 31

Activism, 7; action and, 31–33; anti-war, 1, 15, 27, 165; civic engagement and, 31–39; defining identity of, 45; definition of, 26, 33; empowerment and, 24–31; girl-dominated, 75–79, 91, 114, 216n291; girlhood and, 91–92; high school, 42, 43, 47; humanitarian *vs.* political, 170–72; identity and, 24, 25, 26, 31, 39, 41, 88, 90, 187, 194, 211n6, 211n17; ideology and, 39–40; media, 1; reinvention of, 33–34; style, 182–83. *See also* Movement(s); *specific activisms*

ACT UP. *See* AIDS Coalition to Unleash Power

Adult(s), 99, 106; authority, 190, 191; behavior, 59–60, 64–65; failure, 64–65, 68; hope and, 174; inaction, 64–65, 68, 69; input, 190–91; inspiration, 65–66; negligence, 47, 48; power, 9, 186–87, 191; radicalism, 19; role of, 52, 53; surveillance, 200

Adult activism, 43, 44; difference between youth activism and, 56–59, 60, 61–64, 138; equality of youth activism and, 53–55, 69, 186, 187, 190, 191; girl activism and, 178, 183–91; support from, 69, 70, 188–89

Adultism, 186, 191

Affection, 130, 134, 149

AFL-CIO. *See* American Federation of Labor and Congress of Industrial Organizations

African American(s), 2, 5, 60, 62, 76; communities, 11

Age, 4, 5, 8, 10, 43, 53, 56, 58–59, 69, 96, 118, 141, 149, 197; authority and, 190, 191, 200; collaboration and, 69–70; identities, 150; location and, *201*

Ageism, 5, 28, 186

Agencies: regulating, 3; youth service, 11

Aggression, relational, 84–85, 87

Agrupaciones, 125

AIDS Coalition to Unleash Power (ACT UP), 130

Alinsky, Saul, 107

Alter-globalization movement, 27, 130, 148, 149, 164, 166, 169, 205n6

Alternative(s): building, institutions, 35, 163–64, 169, 175; building, *vs.* protesting, 153–54, 155; constructing, 35, 162, 166, 167, 178; girlhood and, 91, 92; imagining positive, 155–61; open-endedness of, 160, 161

American Federation of Labor and Congress of Industrial Organizations (AFL-CIO), 5

Amsler, Sarah, 154

Analysis, 107, 118; data, 198–99; political, 108, 109, 110

Anarchism, 40, 108, 119, 164, 173

Anger, 111, 113–14

Annan, Kofi, 23

Anti-capitalism, 3, 6, 28

Apathy, 68, 169, 180; youth, 18, 24, 41–43, 44, 45

Employment, 2

Empowerment, 6, 8, 18, 88, 104, 116, 117; activism and, 24–31; of community, 165; girls', 23–24, 28–31, 37, 45; youth culture and girls', 178–81

Enthusiasm, 8, 70, 174, 180, 184

Environment, 66; racism and, 2, 11, 54, 178

Epstein, Barbara, 149

Equality, 56, 68, 150, 155, 156, 157, 162; diversity and, 159; economic, 158; in education, 40; gender, 30, 40, 79, 146; participation and, 141–48; race, 27; of youth/adult activism, 53–55, 69, 186, 187, 190, 191

An Essay on Liberation (Marcuse), 112

Essentialism, 187

Ethics, 157

Ethnicity, 145, 148, 198; location and, *203*

European Social Forum, 125

Exceptionality, 42, 43, 44, 45, 83, 139, 189

Exclusion, 18, 54, 64, 135

Experience, 147, 170, 190

Exploitation, 157, 200

Export processing zone, 3, 4, 5, 179

Facilitation, 63

Fairness, 157, 158

Faith, *vs.* reason, 172

Fear, 59, 64, 68

Feedback, positive, 189

Feelings, 122, 156; critical, 101; political education producing, 111–15. *See also* Emotions

Femininity, 76, 78, 79, 179

Feminism, 4, 30, 87, 127, 159, 187, 206n9; horizontalism and, 148–50

Film screenings, 50, 101, 102, 111, 113

Finances, 9, 189, 226n13, 226n14

Ford Foundation, 6

Forest defense, 178

Formalization, 135, 140, 164, 165; resistance to, 135

Freedom, 112, 152, 155, 162; meaning of, 160

Freeman, Jo, 139

Frente Francisco Miranda, 43

Friendship, 130–32, 135

Future, 163, 164, 172

Galeano, Eduardo, 108, 160

Gender, 4, 5, 8, 10, 48, 91, 96, 118, 127, 132, 141, 142, 197; based violence, 28; equality, 30, 40, 79, 146; hierarchy, 3, 146, 149; identities, 150; inequality, 147–48; leadership and, 140, 146–48; roles, 75–79, 80; self-esteem and, 217n12

Generation(s), 5, 8, 9, 10, 59, 66, 129, 191; collaboration between, 69–70; gap, 188; identity and, 58

Generation Y, 58

Gentrification, 11, 27, 170

Girl activism, 3, 4, 5, 7, 12, 13, 14, 15–16, 24–25, 34, 51, 67, 126; adult activism and, 178, 183–91; collective, 44–45; dominance of, 75–79, 91, 114, 216n2; goals, 27–28, 36; issues, 92–93; physical space for, 188; political practices of, 18, 19; present time and, 52–53, 54, 55, 68; responsibility and, 65, 66, 68–70; skills/contributions of, 59–64; style, 129

Girl activists: disassociating from girlhood, 83–90, 93, 94–95, 132; finding, 194–96; identity of, 71–72, 95–96, 120, 138, 139, 180; image of, 84; supporting each other, 85

Girlhood, 18, 178, 217n13, 217n14; activism and, 91–92; alternative, 91, 92; complexity of, 95; discourses of, 29; escaping/defining, 71–74; girl activists disassociating from, 83–90, 93, 94–95, 132; meaning of, 95; multiplicity of, 74; rebellion and, 79; resisting popular, 79–80; Spanish vocabulary of, 74; womanhood and, 73–74, 88, 91–92, 95

Girls: as caretakers of community, 76–77; as consumers, 5–6, 18; economy and, 6; empowerment of, 23–24, 28–31, 37, 45; empowerment of, and youth culture, 178–81; identity and, 88; images of, 18; labor of, 5; leadership of, 222n35, 222n36; male approval and, 87; meanness of, 84–85, 87; organizations for, 28, 29; politics and, 10, 92–93; representing voice of, 16–17; rivalry between, 85; studies on, 4, 5, 18, 87, 95

Motivation, 151, 184; emotions and, 113

Movement(s): autonomous, 220n3; documents and research, 198; gay/lesbian, 11; global justice, 9, 27; indigenous, 3, 14, 144–45, 196; network of, 173; student, 5; transnational, cultures, 9, 10; women's, 54, 118, 149, 224n47, 224n51. *See also* Activism; *specific movements*

Multiculturalism, 159, 225n13

Music, 1, 128

National Institute for Women, 147

National Youth Rights Association, 53, 215n17

Native Americans, 14, 210n51; land of, 35, 144, 151–53; movements of, 3, 14, 144–45, 196; preserving culture of, 151–53; rights of, 170, 178

Native Youth Movement (Vancouver), 14

Needs, 112

Negativity, detachment from, 170–72

Negligence, adult, 47, 48

Negotiation, 48

Neoliberalism, 9, 27, 108, 181, 197

Network(s): of movements, 173; social, 10, 41, 86, 130, 133

New York, 3

New York Times Magazine, 30

Nike Foundation, 23, 30

Noche de Los Lápices, 67, 123

No Child Left Behind, 99, 100, 105

No One Is Illegal (Vancouver), 15

North America, 5, 17–18, 67, 75, 88, 134, 137, 155, 158, 166, 172, 182, 186–87, 189, 195; political education in, 107–8, 110

Oakland Tribune, 99

Oil industry, 13

Open-heartedness, 111, 122, 162, 184

Open-mindedness, 8, 34, 60, 70, 101, 118, 122, 138, 150, 162, 181, 183, 184

Open Veins of Latin America (Galeano), 108

Opportunity, 23, 30, 124

Oppression, 113, 142, 186; forms of, 28

Optimism, 8, 18, 58, 78, 153, 169, 174, 175, 180, 181, 183, 184. *See also* Hope; Positivity

Organizations: community-based, 11, 41, 107; for girls, 28, 29; in high schools, 40–41, 42, 75; identity and, 39–40, 41; localized, 40; nonprofit, 6; participatory democratic, 135–41; *piquetero*, 16, 145, 163; workers', 3; youth, 38, 40, 107. *See also* Institutions; *specific organizations*

Organizing, 45, 61; vs. recruitment, 36; self, 167; skills, 62–63

La Otra Campaña, 1, 13

Palestine, 27

Participation, 7, 18, 132–33, 134, 150, 178, 183; collective, 135–36; context and, 148; in democratic organizations, 135–41; equality and, 141–48; formal, 164; making, fun, 127–29; political, 49; politics of, 123–27; in research, 195, 198; rights to, 48; youth, 37–38, 39. *See also* Civic engagement; Participatory democracy

Participatory democracy, 15, 51–52, 54, 137, 138, 140, 148, 149, 181, 185

Passion, 77, 102, 115, 156

Patriarchy, 29

Patronizing, 190

Peace, 28, 156

Peers, 29; education, 3, 61, 62, 99, 100, 102, 162, 166; engagement of, 45, 61, 184; support of, 10

Perspective, 60, 70, 119; youth, 56, 57

Peru, 57

Petition drives, 35

Pew Charitable Trusts, 6

Philadelphia, 3

Philanthropy, 11

Pintado-Vertner, Ryan, 11

Pleasure, in politics, 126, 127–34, 135, 148, 149, 184, 185

Police, 67; brutality, 27, 56

Policy, 49; educational, 51, 56; foreign, 170; public, 35

Political education, 2, 7, 18, 34–36, 50, 100, 164; creating knowledge, 101–10; issue-specific vs. comprehensive, 107–10; in Latin America, 107–10; methods of, 113; in North America, 107–8, 110; as ongoing process, 115–22, 181, 183; producing feelings, 111–15

Political party, 50, 124–25, 167, 178; building, 35, 164, 166
Politics, 1, 6, 9, 66, 90, 100; affective, 130;
analysis of, 108, 109, 110; discussion of,
109, 110; formal, 165; girl activism and,
18, 19; girls and, 10, 92–93; of hope,
151–54, 162; humanitarianism vs., 170–72;
idealism and, 174–75; identity and, 58;
involvement in, 170; in Latin America,
108; legislative, 164; literature on, 2, 108,
116; of participation, 123–27; participation in, 49; pleasurable, 126, 127–34, 135,
148, 149, 184, 185; power and, 38, 185;
prefigurative, 35, 162, 168, 181, 184, 191;
repression and, 1, 47, 48; strategies and,
8, 19, 109, 180; vocabulary of, 105, 107,
108, 109; youth and, 41–42, 128. See also
Political education; Political party
Polletta, Francesca, 135, 138, 185
Pomerantz, Shauna, 79
Positivity, 181, 189; alternatives and,
155–61; focus on, 169–75. See also Hope;
Optimism
Poverty, 1, 2, 35, 60, 62, 170, 172; reducing, 23
Power, 3, 105, 124, 125, 126, 130, 148, 159, 164,
220n2, 223n40; adult, 9, 186–87, 191; cor-
porate, 9; differentials and research, 200;
internal, dynamics, 141–43; personal,
28–29, 211n10; political, 38, 185; sharing,
149, 222n36; of youth activism, 177
Prague, protests in, 3
Prejudice, 159
Press conferences, 2
Prisoners, 27, 28
Privatization, 27, 56
Privilege, 171, 172
Process: attention to, 160, 161; importance
of, 120; open-ended learning, 160, 161, 183,
184, 185; political education as ongoing,
115–22, 181, 183. See also Bolivarian process
Progress, 25, 69, 205n6
Protests, 32, 33, 36, 39, 117, 164, 211n18;
building alternatives vs., 153–54, 155; in
Prague, 3
Prout, Alan, 53
Psychology, 4

Public good, 26
Purpose, collective, 120
Putnam, Robert, 127

Race, 5, 10, 18, 57, 60, 74, 81, 104, 141, 142,
149, 197; dynamics of, 223n45; equality,
27; location and, 203; responsibility and,
76; self-esteem and, 217n12
Racism, 6, 27, 28, 40, 107, 113, 144, 145, 158,
172; environmental, 2, 11, 54, 178
Radicalism, 107; adult, 19
Rahier, Jean Muteba, 145
Rallies, 2, 32–33, 99–100, 116, 130, 198
Reading, 108–9, 116, 120, 219n10
Reason, 115; faith vs., 172
Rebellion, 66, 68, 75, 121, 180; girlhood and,
79; youthful, 59, 60
Recruitment, 184, 212n28; organizing vs., 36
Recycling, 35
Refugees, 15, 111
Relationships, 4, 135, 138, 141, 149, 181;
strong, 130–32
Religion, 74
Repression, 12, 13, 15, 28, 58, 67, 111; political, 1, 47, 48
Research, 4, 5, 18, 87, 95, 113, 140, 173, 180,
205n6; coding/data analysis, 198–99;
education and, 104; in-depth/qualita-
tive approach to, 193; interviews, 196–97,
210n53; movement documents and, 198;
partial perspectives of, 199–200; participant observation and, 198; participation
in, 195; power differentials and, 200;
reflexive, 199–200; site selection/time
frame, 193–94; social movement, 48;
software program (ATLAS.ti), 198; transnational, 197, 200; on youth cultures, 75
Resistance, 33, 75, 122, 181; to formalization,
135; to popular girlhood, 79–80
Resources, 9, 62, 197; financial, 189, 226n13,
226n14; intellectual, 110
Respect, 135, 138, 190; for difference, 159
Responsibility, 58, 92, 124, 159, 177; civic,
23; girl activism and, 65, 66, 68–70; race/
class and taking, 76; shared, 160; social,
35; youth, 49

Tlatelolco massacre, 12, 67
Torture, 27
Tourism, 5
Toxic waste, 2, 62, 172
Trade: fair, 35, 102; free, 27
Tradition, 1, 67, 118, 156, 182; challenging, 179
Translation, 17, 210n55
Transparency, 197
Trust, 41, 42, 135, 195

UNAM. *See* Universidad Nacional Autonoma de Mexico
Unemployment, 27
United Nations, 23, 41–42, 214n50
Universidad Nacional Autonoma de Mexico (UNAM), high schools and, 12
Utopianism, 152, 153–54, 155, 158, 160, 174, 175, 184, 185, 191, 225n12; ongoing, 162–63, 165–69; open-ended, 161; present, 164

Values, 26; moral/social, 157
Vancouver, Canada, 1, 10, 14–15, 40, 52, 53, 63, 64, 73, 78, 81, 101, 102, 103, 111–12, 117, 127, 128, 143, 164, 170, 173, 187, 196
Van Dyke, Nella, 33
Venezuela, 1–2, 10, 14, 28, 34, 40, 43, 52, 54, 55, 56–57, 65–66, 67, 71, 107, 108, 109, 119, 120, 128, 134, 137, 145, 156–58, 164, 181, 197; economy of, 13; government of, 168, 225n21. *See also* Caracas
Venezuelan Communist Youth. *See* Juventud Comunista de Venezuela (JCV)
Verticalism, 124–26, 146
Victimhood, 18, 54, 86, 180
Violence, 13, 47, 68, 113, 151, 152; domestic, 1; gender-based, 28; state-based, 27, 58, 172
Vision, 26, 65, 118; expressions of, 156–57
Vocabulary, 110, 121, 128, 175, 181, 182, 184; political, 105, 107, 108, 109; Spanish, of girlhood/womanhood, 74
Las Voces, 34, 41, 57, 128, 137, 139
Volunteerism, 35, 37, 179
Voting, 41, 49, 52, 164; methods, 135–38
War, 58, 170; anti-, activism, 1, 15, 27, 165;

Iraq, 3, 27, 116, 165
Weisbrot, Mark, 13
Weiss, Mattie, 104, 142
Williamson, Howard, 37
William T. Grant Foundation, 6
Wolf, Diane, 200
Womanhood, 23, 54, 59, 118, 147, 149, 181, 224n47, 224n51; girlhood and, 73–74, 88, 91–92, 95; Spanish vocabulary of, 74
Women, 87, 147; movements, 54, 118, 149, 224n47, 224n51; rights for, 32, 59, 87
Worker(s): organizations, 3; rights of, 27, 57, 76, 178; sex, 3, 5; youth, 41
Workshops, 101, 102, 103, 104, 107, 116, 117, 120, 198
World Bank, 27
World Social Forum, 14, 57, 71, 105, 134, 146
World Trade Organization, 27
World Youth Festival, 14
World Youth Report (United Nations), 41–42, 214n50
www.stopwar.ca, 15

Young Femininity, 76
Youniss, James, 39
Youth, 1–2, 226n13; adult *vs.*, behavior, 59–60; apathy, 18, 24, 41–43, 44, 45; in Bolivarian process, 55; civic engagement programs, 6, 37, 38–39; of color, 60, 62, 76; dissent, 39; as identity, 49, 118, 143; issues, 56; justice, 11, 27, 56; justice facilities, 3; leadership, 185, 187, 226n13; organizations, 38, 40, 107; participation, 37–38, 39; perspectives, 56, 57; politics and, 41–42; rebellion and, 59, 60; responsibility, 49; rights, 27, 41, 53, 56, 215n17; service agencies, 11; social change and, 66–67; workers, 41. *See also* Youth activism; Youth culture; *specific youth organizations*
Youth activism, 1, 3, 4, 10, 14, 180; adults supporting, 69, 70, 188–89; Bolivarian process and, 55; difference between adult activism and, 56–59, 60, 61–64,

About the Author

JESSICA K. TAFT is Assistant Professor of Sociology at Davidson College.